Discovering the Dutch

Discovering the Dutch

On Culture and Society of
the Netherlands

EDITED BY

EMMELINE BESAMUSCA

JAAP VERHEUL

Amsterdam University Press

ISBN   978 90 8964 100 7
e-ISBN 978 90 4850 827 3
NUR   688

Cover design: Kok Korpershoek
Book design and image research:
Kok Korpershoek, Jonatan van der Horst and Jorien Janssen
Index: Anne-Lieke Struijk

Table of Contents

History

Art & Culture

Contemporary Issues

The Netherlands

Legend:
- Below sea level
- Above sea level
- Provincial border
- National border
- Regional border

GRONINGEN
Groningen

Leeuwarden

Waddenzee

NORTH
FRIESLAND

Assen

DRENTHE

Den Helder

Emmen

NORTH HOLLAND
IJsselmeer
Emmeloord

North Sea

Alkmaar
Lelystad
Zwolle
OVERIJSSEL

FLEVOLAND

Haarlem
Almere
Deventer
Hengelo

Amsterdam
GELDERLAND
Enschede

Leiden
Amersfoort
Apeldoorn

Den Haag (The Hague)
WEST
Utrecht
Arnhem
IJssel
EAST

Delft
UTRECHT

Rotterdam Lek

Nijmegen
Rijn (Rhine)

SOUTH HOLLAND
Waal
Dordrecht

ZEELAND
NORTH-BRABANT
's-Hertogenbosch (Den Bosch)

SOUTHWEST
Breda
Tilburg
SOUTH
Maas (Meuse)

Middelburg

Vlissingen
Eindhoven
Venlo

LIMBURG

Heerlen

Maastricht

0   20km

© Geomedia UU 7680

GeoMedia, Faculty of Geosciences, Utrecht University

Introduction

Emmeline Besamusca & Jaap Verheul

This volume is intended as a helpful guide for anyone interested in exploring the culture and society of the Netherlands. Like any dedicated tour guide, it builds on inside knowledge and native familiarity. All chapters are written by experts in their field who bring their personal perspectives, enthusiasms and some local color to their topics. Rather than offering exhaustive, data-filled overviews, they engage in conversations with the reader about what they feel is essential to an understanding of the Netherlands. They may even politely try to persuade their readers of a few convictions and insights.

While building on inside knowledge, this volume anticipates the outside perspectives and expectations of new audiences as well. Some traditions, structures or cultural institutions that are simply taken for granted by the locals beg for explanation to newcomers and outside observers. More importantly, such a comparative perspective is essential to put the Netherlands on the global mental map. This volume, then, can best be understood as a helpful dialogue between knowledgeable connoisseurs and those on their way to becoming one.

It is tempting to start the journey with a conversation about Dutch identity. Global popular culture is full of references to articles or habits considered "typically Dutch." For some foreigners, essential "Dutchness" is expressed in the omnipresence of bicycles, either the nameless thousands that are stacked near railway stations or the elegant transport bikes urban parents have acquired to transport their offspring to day care centers. Those interested in foodways may think of the many varieties of licorice known as *drop*, the addictive *stroopwafels* and *pannekoeken,* or the nutritious *stamppotten* with mashed potatoes served in winter. To sports enthusiasts, the Netherlands may invoke the image of fans at international sports events who invariably manifest themselves in playful orange outfits, suggesting a sense of colorful and exuberant patriotism. Those with an eye for art may visualize the Netherlands as seen in the urban skating scenes painted by Hendrick Avercamp or the neatly arranged interiors of Johannes Vermeer. Others may compare the Dutch landscape to the squares and lines of Piet Mondrian and Gerrit Rietveld, constructed as it seems by the methodical Dutch engineers who are said to have carved their country out of the sea. These observers may look for the origins of unique Dutch traits in the collective struggle against the water which regulated not only geography, but society as well. Others point at the Dutch social tradition of *gezelligheid* that is expressed in the circular seating at birthday parties, the festivities around the yearly arrival of Sinterklaas or the persistent urban myth that the Dutch always keep their curtains open so that the neighbors can check the order and cleanliness of their household.

More critically minded observers may associate the particular character of Dutch social behavior with provincialism, penny-pinching materialism or even blunt rudeness, as may be apparent from the absence of a service-oriented attitude in shops and restaurants, or from candid directness in business meetings.

Yet Dutch national identity cannot be captured in such anthropological observations or examples of folklore and tradition, even if they offer a rich source for emotional identification – or differentiation. Nor can a demarcation be drawn around "Dutchness" that represents it as a sheltering haven against the modern forces of globalization, Europeanization, individualism or multiculturalism. If nothing else, the Netherlands is a highly modern, densely populated country that is interconnected with the world by a myriad of trade relationships, migratory movements, cultural exchanges, international networks, alliances and collaborations. As a result, Dutch national identity is not static, but rather the outcome of a continuous process of identification, negotiation and exploration. Yet this incessant interaction does not make Dutch culture and society indefinable and inaccessible. On the contrary, this book hopes to show some of the many routes that open up vistas of the vibrant distinctiveness – and familiarity – of Dutch society.

This volume organizes perspectives on Dutch culture and society into four different sections. The section on society explores the most characteristic institutions and arrangements of the Dutch state and body politic. As a constitutional monarchy with a long democratic tradition, the Netherlands is known for its internationally oriented economy which is organized around well-established welfare arrangements and a consensual political culture that is sometimes affectionately described and even promoted as a "polder-model." In spite of the rural images of windmills and tulips, the western *Randstad* is one of the most densely populated and cosmopolitan spots in the world. The pervasive international outlook is also expressed in a foreign policy that is informed by both self-interest and idealism.

The next section on history shows a Dutch past that is marked by a slow rise from the obscurity of a swampy river delta, a dramatic revolt against the Spanish empire, and a subsequent period of global enterprise, republican freedoms and stunning riches during the seventeenth century. Legacies of the Golden Age, such as traditions of tolerance and religious multiformity, continued to manifest themselves in the following centuries. The 1960s represented an important fault line in those legacies when the denominational segregation in society, often described as "pillarization," disintegrated, leaving marks in the political arena and beyond well into the twenty-first century. In spite of many persistent continuities, the Second World War formed another dramatic turning point in the twentieth century as Dutch society experienced the atrocities of war and genocide and faced dilemmas that influenced, and continue to influence, public culture and debates about governmental powers, discrimination and international interventions to the present day.

The section on art and culture guides the reader on a tour of cultural expressions and traditions that support the Dutch in their claim to international fame as a cultural nation. It is an intriguing question, however, to which degree the works of some of the famous Dutch painters can be regarded "typical" of Dutch art, as the examples of Rembrandt and Van Gogh illustrate. The character of Dutch architecture, which has traditionally been inspired by views on society and reflected social values, is changing now that building seems to be increasingly regarded in terms of real estate development. In the realm of literature the position and role of authors has been subject to cultural changes as well, as was experienced by Willem Frederik Hermans and Gerard Reve, two of the most influential writers in modern Dutch literature.

The Dutch approach to emancipation and integration – seen by many as a distinct contribution to the global debate – is illustrated through an analysis of three feminist cultural artifacts which reflect Dutch feminist thought in three consecutive waves. The intellectual horizon of the Netherlands – the Dutch mindset – is also very much a product of the internationally acclaimed tradition of its higher education, which in turn has been shaped by the aspirations and historical developments of the society it serves.

The last section on contemporary issues explores public debates in Dutch society at the beginning of the twenty-first century. The Netherlands are routinely described as a "Calvinist" nation – even by devout Catholics or agnostics – with roots in strong religious identification and dissension. Yet one can also argue that modern Dutch society today is better described in terms of tolerance, secularization and a religious diversity that now includes Islam. Many impassioned discussions about Dutch identity have been sparked by the related issues of immigration and assimilation, and their political and social consequences. Equally fundamental to an understanding of Dutch society have been the recurring public debates about ethical issues such as prostitution, abortion, drugs and euthanasia. Some of these vital questions have been met at times with policy compromises that have confounded government, public and foreign onlookers alike. A very real threat to Dutch existence, which consistently attracts foreign attention as well, is posed by the ubiquitous water that continuously requires protective measures and difficult choices. All these challenges and achievements have shaped a particular Dutch culture and society and also determined the foreign perspectives on the Netherlands.

As all the chapters aim to illuminate the reader on issues related to Dutch culture and society, some common themes reappear throughout the volume. Some, such as "pillarization," tolerance and the "poldermodel," go right to the heart of the Dutch social fabric. Others, such as urbanization, the Golden Age and internationalization, are connected with the specific historical traditions of the Netherlands. Inevitably, such core concepts are discussed in connection with a variety of topics in this volume, and may appear in a different light as they are discussed and interpreted by the authors, as reality sometimes escapes uniform definitions and categories. This multifocal perspective on such shared themes only underlines the central position they necessarily should have in an understanding of Dutch culture and society.

All these chapters can be read in the successive order of a textbook, or one may decide to venture out on a free-flowing tour, as all chapters are written so they can be read independently. The reader is further encouraged to browse the many vignettes on canonical Dutch personae and phenomena that are sparked throughout the book. Some topics also appear in the historical canon that has been commissioned by the Dutch government, but many other vignette topics are related to contemporary society. Although these miniature windows on Dutch culture and society are connected to the themes of the chapters, they can also be followed as a separate trail.

We would like to thank all of our colleagues who took up the challenge of sharing their insight into the culture and society of the Netherlands by connecting their academic expertise as scholars to their personal expertise as natives. We hope that, in offering their many perspectives and as many possible road plans to travel, this volume will offer the reader an enjoyable experience in discovering the Dutch.

Neither Wooden Legs nor Wooden Shoes: Elusive Encounters with Dutch Identity

Wiljan van den Akker

I'm travelling by train somewhere in the United States. It is my first trip to a country I believe I know because I have seen it on television ever since I was a child. I am completely absorbed in a new book that I've saved for what was going to be a long trip. The man sitting next to me carefully looks at the cover several times before asking me in a polite and soft voice what language I am reading. When I explain to him that my book is in Dutch, more specifically that it is a history of modern Dutch literature, he starts to smile: "Do the Dutch really have a literature of their own?"

I immediately realize that this encounter might end up being one of the amusing stories that one happily brings back home as a souvenir of the journey. A tale that fits quite well within the prejudices we share about identities: people not knowing their language or geography. That is to say: the *other* people. Not us, the Dutch, of course. The stranger on the train and I start a gentle conversation and the trip becomes so enjoyable that I don't even notice that the train has arrived. With a "Nice talking to you, nice meeting you," he vanishes into the crowd. And I realize that this ending to the story will also fit into the familiar picture later on. "They don't mean that. They are used to superficial conversation." Unlike us, in the Netherlands, where we have constant discussions with each other about Schopenhauer, Spinoza or Sartre while traveling by public transportation. Because we are never superficial. Shallowness is something for the others only.

National identities are like stories and, as with every story, always contain some truth. The only problem is how to find that part, the part that actually is true. One thing seems clear: the less we know about the others, the easier it becomes to define their identity. Perhaps we construct these myths of identities out of a fear of being alone or alienated. As long as we do not have to question our way of

life – our rules, our habits, our laws – as long as we keep on telling ourselves that our customs are normal, that they belong especially to us or even to the natural order of things, we will be safe. The rules, habits and laws of the others seem strange, or even unnatural.

What does not fit into our frame of reference will be isolated, stored and recognized as different later on. It is remarkable that when traveling we say that we yearn for difference, but cannot help looking for resemblances. The problem, however, is that most of these similarities hide themselves behind the mask of difference and can at best be recognized after a long period of very close observation. And vice versa: what seemed so different can end up being strikingly familiar.

The famous columnist and professor of Slavic literature, the late Karel van het Reve, once put it brilliantly. Suppose, he said, that you are leaving for work by bus in the morning. Someone with a wooden leg is struggling to get a seat. You look at him, feel sorry for the man and travel on. In the evening, traveling home by bus again, there is a woman with a wooden leg sitting in the back. What a coincidence, you tell your wife over dinner, two wooden legs in one day. If your marriage is good, she will smile, thinking: could there be a more interesting story to tell? Now suppose the same thing happens during a short visit to a foreign country. There is a good chance that you will tell everybody: "They have an awful lot of wooden legs over there!"

There is no such thing as a Dutch identity and yet there is. No, we are not the country where tulips bloom everywhere and where everyone wears wooden shoes. And yet there are more tulips here than in any other country and I have never seen an Italian wearing wooden shoes. But what defines this identity and who is defining? How broad is this national identity? We joke about the Belgians, defining ourselves as being different from them. But we feel like brothers and sisters once confronted with Asian colleagues. We even joke about some of our own fellow countrymen, defining an "us" that somehow excludes "them." And are we in Utrecht not different from people living in Rotterdam? The circles tend to get smaller and smaller until, in the end, we are alone with our own and small identity.

"Dutchness" is a very ambiguous term, like "Frenchness" or "Germanness." Once you try to grasp it, it will fade away. Once you deny it, it will present itself. It boggles the mind. But isn't this what the mind is for? For trying to understand ambiguities, for looking at the same thing from different angles, for constantly wondering? By traveling, either in real life, or by way of books.

Last year I was traveling by train in Germany. A man in his fifties, noticing me reading a Dutch history of German literature, adamantly tried to convince me that the Dutch language was a German dialect. I spent an entire hour trying to explain that he was mistaken. By the time we arrived in Cologne, I had to admit that my efforts had been fruitless. When the train stopped at the station, he said, shrugging his shoulders, that he disliked literature anyway and that there was only one true author: William Shakespeare. Did I know him? "Who, William Shakespeare? Never heard of him," I replied and left, pledging to myself that if there is going to be a next life, I would become a salesman. Of wooden legs.

Society

Chapter 1

Citizens, Coalitions and the Crown

Emmeline Besamusca

The Netherlands is often described as a country of paradox. Born in the sixteenth century as a republic within a world almost exclusively dominated by monarchies, it is now one of the few constitutional monarchies left in a world in which the republican form of government is the rule rather than the exception. In a nation that is thoroughly modern and democratic, the monarchy – which seems an embodiment of tradition and authority – enjoys surprisingly broad and stable public support. In fact, although the Dutch almost pride themselves on the absence of patriotism and flag-waving, it is only the monarchy that evokes symbols of nationalism comparable to that of other nations, and citizens gladly unite under the orange color of the Dutch royal house.

The Dutch political stage does not particularly contribute to a sense of political unity, since it is highly fragmented into a large number of political parties and movements boggling the mind even of the most invested local insider. Such fragmentation is enhanced by an electoral system based on the principle of proportionality, allowing all voices to be heard in elections. With turnout rates for national elections around eighty percent on average, the Dutch electorate seems to consider it important to participate and be represented. It may seem paradoxical then that actual government formation can lead to outcomes which seem to contradict the public voice, as it is subject to negotiations between political parties. Furthermore, the prime minister is not elected, but appointed by "royal decree," and so are the heads of the provincial governments and the city mayors.

The Dutch political structure seems thus determined by a delicate but self-evident balance between active citizens' participation in political elections and governance by coalitions and appointed executives. Amidst this paradoxical interplay of political forces, the hereditary monarch serves as a symbol of national unity and represents the continuity of the nation.

The Orange Dynasty

The Netherlands was a republic until the early nineteenth century. The Republic of the Seven United Netherlands, which surrendered to French rule under Napoleon in 1795, was replaced by a Batavian Republic, which in turn made way for a Kingdom of Holland under Louis Bonaparte – the emperor's brother – in 1806. When the French occupation ended in 1813 the European powers – convinced that monarchies would secure the desired stability after the Napoleonic period – preferred the Netherlands to remain a monarchy. The monarchy was therefore not an entirely Dutch choice. The candidate for the Dutch throne seemed undisputed though: the son of the last stadholder, who had fled to England upon the approach of the French armies, accepted the throne as King William I.

The House of Orange has been part of Dutch history from the beginning of statehood, when William of Orange-Nassau, fondly called "the Father of the Fatherland," became the leader of the Dutch Revolt, which ultimately resulted in the birth of a Dutch State. Neither William of Orange nor his direct successors were monarchs, but they played a crucial role in the Dutch Republic as hereditary stadholders, especially in the public mind. Here lie the origins of the so-called "Orange Myth," which holds that the Oranges are protectors of freedom and act in service of the people.[1] This perception certainly accounts for the popularity of the royal family still today. The many letters citizens write to the queen, requesting her particular assistance or support, give testimony of this unwavering faith in the House of Orange in general, and the person serving as king or queen in particular.

The constitution stipulates that the Dutch throne is held by William I of the Netherlands and his lawful successors, and carefully defines the line of succession. It also stipulates that his heirs need to obtain parliamentary consent to a proposed marriage in order to maintain their right to the throne. Given this official public involvement, royal marriages can be regarded as a sort of social thermometer. In the early 1960s, no parliamentary approval was given to the marriage of Princess Irene, second in line only after her sister Beatrix, to the Spaniard Hugo de Bourbon Parma, who made serious claims on the Spanish throne. The fact that Irene converted from the traditional Protestantism of the Orange Family to Catholicism caused an enormous stir in a society still strongly segregated along religious and ideological lines. The marriage of Princess Beatrix to the German diplomat Claus von Amsberg in 1966 was surrounded in clouds of smoke bombs thrown by rioters for different reasons: apparently, it was too soon after the Second World War for the Dutch public to embrace a German spouse.[2] In the next generation, religion no longer proved to be an issue in marriage approval, nor the fact that none of the chosen partners were of noble descent. Yet, Prince Friso, second in line of succession, did not receive parliamentary consent after it became known that his fiancée had not been entirely honest about her past.

As the person fulfilling the position of king is not selected based on personal merit, he or she needs to stay hidden behind the function. However, it is inevitable that the person colors the function. In the absence of male heirs, the Dutch throne has continuously been in female hands since the end of the nineteenth century. The respective personalities of each of the queens seem to have suited their time remarkably well. The unflinching and headstrong personality of Queen Wilhelmina, who formally ascended the throne when she became of age in 1898, served her well during the years of occupation in the Second World War, which she spent in London. She was a beacon of hope for many in occupied territory, who would regularly listen to her voice in broadcasts of "Radio Orange." Her only daughter, who assumed the throne in 1948 as Queen Juliana, wanted above all to be "normal." In a famous picture, she is riding a bicycle, her purse strapped on the carrier. She was "the anti-authoritarian mother of the fatherland," who used to invite the Dutch public to her "house" on her birthday on April 30, Queen's Day (*Koninginnedag*), where they would parade by her, standing on top of the stairs of her palace at Soestdijk amidst her family. In 1980, Juliana abdicated in favor of the eldest of her four daughters, Beatrix, the "professional," who has transformed her position into a "job." On Queen's Day, she no longer invites the public to come to her palace; instead, she pays a visit to two carefully selected locations, accompanied by other members of the royal family. She is regularly portrayed behind a desk in her "working palace" Noordeinde in The Hague, and is said to be extremely dedicated, well-informed, and well-prepared. Undoubtedly, the support for the monarchy is not only to be attributed to the long-standing history between the Oranges and the Netherlands, but to the personal qualities of the queen and the family of Orange as well.

Princess Máxima: Enchanting the Monarchy

In 2002, Crown Prince Willem Alexander married Argentinean-born Máxima Zorreguieta. With her engaging personality, natural spontaneity and stylish appearance, she has rapidly become the most popular member of the royal family.

The start of Máxima's relationship with the Netherlands was not without difficulties. She became subject to a fervent public debate because her father had served as Minister of Agriculture during the exceptionally cruel military regime of General Videla (1976-1981). This made it seem questionable whether her marriage to the crown prince would receive the parliamentary consent that is constitutionally required for a marriage of all members of the House of Orange in line of succession. Yet, Willem Alexander stubbornly refused to give up his intention to marry Máxima, even suggesting he would prefer love above the Dutch throne. A political debate was ultimately prevented after Máxima's father was persuaded not to attend the wedding.

In her first public appearances in 2001, Máxima stole many hearts with her presence, her radiant smile, and her charming Dutch, flavored with a Spanish accent – proving her talent for the public aspect of her future role. And as she shed a few tears during the wedding service upon hearing the tango *"Adios Nonino"* – which Astor Piazolla wrote for his father – the public realized she was not just a princess, but also a young woman giving up her country, and a daughter without her father present on her wedding day.

Máxima has since disarmed any opponents left and greatly contributed to the popularity of the monarchy, adding a charm to the royal appearance, which is invaluable to the royal family's media presence. Part of her strength is that she seems to sincerely enjoy her public functions. With an academic degree in economics she promotes microcredit projects abroad. At home, she shows particular interest in the position of immigrant women (as she herself is), incessantly stressing the importance of learning Dutch and acquainting oneself with Dutch culture. Her contribution to the presentation of an official report on "Identification with the Netherlands" was received rather critically though, not only because of its content – she stated that "Dutch culture does not exist other than in many different contours and colors" – but also because it was generally considered too outspoken for a member of the royal family.

In order to secure the continued public favor on which it depends, the monarchy needs to strike a balance between *dignitas* and *humanitas*, royalty and normalcy. The members of the Orange family need not only to be seen in official functions, but to be personally "known" and liked as well. Even though the public at large does not actively seek royalty news as disseminated by the – rather modest – tabloids, Dutch media regularly present carefully directed moments in the family's life, such as skiing holidays or the first schooldays of the children. In all the media attention surrounding her, Máxima convincingly manages to balance her "royal" and her "normal" image, combining her public role with that of working mother of three daughters, and a loving wife of her husband.

King and Crown

The Kingdom of the Netherlands consists of the Netherlands and six islands in the Caribbean: five islands united in the Netherlands Antilles, and a sixth island, named Aruba[3]. The relation between the Netherlands and the Netherlands Antilles was formally constituted with a charter in 1854, which also included the small nation of Surinam in South America until its independence in 1975. The Dutch king is thus head of state not only of the Netherlands, but also of two countries in the Caribbean, which represent less than two percent of the population of the Kingdom.

Contrary to many of the West-European constitutional monarchies, the Dutch government is formed by the king and his ministers, together called "the Crown." However, the king has no political responsibility nor any formal power; since the Constitution of 1848 the rule is maintained that "the king is inviolable; the ministers are responsible." This principle of "ministerial responsibility" – which pertains to the other members of the royal house as well – is central to the Dutch constitutional monarchy. It renders all actions of the king subject to ministerial approval, and bills and all other "royal decrees" need a minister's signature. In this context, "royal" does therefore not refer to the king's personal decision, but rather represents the unity of the Crown.[5] The king's signature is required as well, but as he is to remain neutral and stand above the parties, his refusal to sign remains a rather theoretical scenario.

One of the most visible moments when the king acts as head of the government is during the opening of the parliamentary year, on the third Tuesday of September. Tradition has it that the monarch arrives at the government center in full royal pomp in a golden carriage pulled by eight horses and escorted by court dignitaries and a military escort of honor, with people cheering and waving along the route. As stipulated in the constitution, the king then addresses the joint session of the two Houses of Dutch parliament seated on a large throne in the Ridderzaal in The Hague. Since the "Speech from the Throne" (*troonrede*), which outlines the plans of the government for the coming parliamentary year, is written by the office of the prime minister, it is the voice, but not the words or opinions of the king that are heard.

Yet, the king is an unavoidable factor in the political process, given his position, the average length of his reign and the royal privileges which the nineteenth-century British economist Walter Bagehot famously defined as the right "to be consulted, to encourage, and to warn the government."[6] To that end, the king regularly consults with the prime minister, and thus is one of the best informed people, and one who is assured of popular support Dutch politicians can only dream about. Therefore, ministers are well advised to at least listen carefully to any comments the king may have.[7]

During the often complex negotiations to form a new government after parliamentary elections, the king plays a central, yet largely invisible role by appointing the senior statesmen who coordinate this process. This role has given argument to the suggestion to exclude the king from government, which could be effectuated by amending the constitution. However, political parties favoring such a point of view have thus far been reluctant to press the issue, knowing that there is little support among the Dutch public at large for a reduced role for the king.

Government by Coalition

The actual government is left to the Council of Ministers. This "Cabinet" – headed by the prime minister, who is theoretically equal to his colleagues – is an executive council which initiates laws and policy and is collectively responsible to the parliament. Since any government needs the support of a majority in parliament – traditionally divided by about a dozen different minority parties – it is usually formed by a coalition of two or more different parties. Consequently, in the Dutch political vocabulary the term "coalition" has become synonymous with "Cabinet of Ministers."

The necessity for coalitions certainly has its advantages. Since it is almost unavoidable that some parties participate in various consecutive coalitions, they represent a certain continuity. Furthermore, coalitions guarantee that a broad spectrum of political voices is represented in the government. By the same token, the differences between the coalition partners call for continuous negotiations, which may prove to be difficult, lengthy or simply impossible, in which case the debate is stalled, given to a committee to be studied, or any other strategy to avoid the coalition having to hand in its resignation before the full term of four years is served. The necessity for coalitions has other weaknesses too. Forming a coalition in such a fragmented political field is usually a cumbersome and time-consuming process, in which the country is virtually left without a new government. Furthermore, voters can never be sure whether or not their party will actually end up participating in the coalition, and adamantly proclaimed positions in the election campaign may be given up during coalition negotiations. Consequently, this process renders the electoral results rather inconclusive, as the electorate does neither directly determine the formation nor the agenda of the new government. Also, the public does not directly influence the selection of the ministers, not even that of the prime minister, as the candidates are put forward by the negotiating parties. This means that a new government leader can rise out of total obscurity as was the case with Christan Democratic backbencher Jan Peter Balkenende who ended up leading several successive governments. It has been suggested that the prime minister be directly elected; however, such a proposal is far from gaining a parliamentary majority.

The mechanism of appointed instead of elected heads of government also applies to the provincial governments, which are led by a "Commissioner of the King" (*Commissaris van de Koning*) and to the municipal government, which is headed by an appointed mayor. This appointive principle is traditionally defended in terms of quality: appointment procedures allow selecting well-qualified candidates, without being blinded by other, rather irrelevant factors that may influence public elections. Furthermore, it is argued that a mayor should stand above the parties and is thus best appointed instead of elected. City councils therefore present candidates based on their personal merit, skills and experience, although a careful balance among the major political parties is maintained, especially in the largest cities; the mayor of Amsterdam for instance is traditionally a social democrat.

Binnenhof: Traditional Heart of a Modern Democracy

The Binnenhof, or "Inner Court," physically represents the political heart of the Netherlands. The parliamentary buildings surround an enclosed square which is accessible to all citizens, allowing them to accidentally meet members of parliament or ministers, or to offer petitions or messages in carefully directed protest gatherings. The exterior of the complex is generally used as visual reference to national political events on the Dutch television news.

Centerpiece of the Inner Court is the Hall of Knights, or Ridderzaal, which was built in the thirteenth century by Count Floris IV and completed by his son Floris V, as part of a hunting lodge. The village which developed around this residence was named 's Gravenhage (literally: the count's forest). In the late sixteenth century, this village became the meeting place of the States General of the Dutch Republic,

a choice intended to avoid favoring any particular city over another. Den Haag, as the city became known, has remained the parliamentary center ever since – even though Amsterdam is the official capital of the Netherlands.

Since 1904 the Hall of Knights is the venue of the annual opening of the parliamentary year on *Prinsjesdag* (Princes' Day), the third Tuesday in September, an event wrapped in traditions and rituals. The queen promptly arrives just before 1 p.m. in the golden carriage, which was presented to Queen Wilhelmina by the city of Amsterdam in 1898. Seated on her throne in the Hall she reads – in exactly twenty minutes – the *troonrede*, outlining the plans of the government for the coming year. Thereupon she returns to Noordeinde Palace, where she appears on the balcony, together with other members of the royal family, waving to the invariably assembled public. Whereas the speech itself may present progress and new ideas, the ritualized format of the event secures the continuity which the monarchy is to represent. Meanwhile in parliament, the Minister of Finance presents the budget accompanying the new plans, thus illustrating that not the king, but the ministers are responsible for the plans of the government.

A new meeting hall for parliament was completed in 1992. The architect Pi de Bruin masterfully managed to position it in-between the already existing buildings – thus leaving parliament where it should be – and incorporating the original outer walls into the new structure, creating a symbolic bridge between past and present. The principle of dualism between the executive branch (government) and legislative branch (parliament) is architecturally translated in the design of the meeting hall: seated in a semi-circle, the members of parliament are not facing each other, but face the ministers who are seated in the opposing governmental "box."

The council of ministers is chaired by the Minister President or *Premier*. His office is located at the Inner Court, in a small tower affectionately known as "Het Torentje" where traditionally he could be seen working through the cameras of the national evening news. However, for security reasons its windows are now permanently blinded and fences are erected. But the Inner Court is still open and accessible, symbol of an open democracy.

Decentralized Unitary State

The administrative and electoral structure of the Netherlands is divided into the national, the provincial and the municipal level. Additionally, twenty-seven so-called water boards (*waterschappen*) are responsible for issues related to water management. As the constitution assigns the legislative competencies to the national level only, the Netherlands – notwithstanding the plural in its name – is formally a unitary state.[8] However, some of these competencies are delegated to the lower levels, whose role can thus be described in terms of co-governance and autonomy: serving as a link between national legislature and local reality, implementing national legislation at the local levels. For instance, it is the city council who, within the general framework as outlined in the national law, designs a local policy with regard to opening hours of shops on Sundays. This local autonomy may result in differences between the various cities: whereas in some cities shops can be open twelve Sundays a year – as is the legal maximum – other municipalities choose not to allow shops to open on any Sunday.

The national parliament – or the "States General" in the terminology dating back to the period of the Republic of the United Provinces – consists of two houses: the House of Representatives or lower house (*Tweede Kamer,* second chamber), and the Senate or upper house (*Eerste Kamer,* first chamber). The role of parliament is to represent the public, to control the government and to pass new legislation.

The fact that the House of Representatives is often loosely referred to as "parliament" indicates that it is perceived as the center of the political process. The hundred-and-fifty members are directly elected every four years, according to the principle of proportionality, "one man one vote." Given the absence of any specific electoral threshold, only 0.67 percent of the votes – the number of votes cast divided by the number of seats in parliament – is necessary to gain a seat. Depending on turnout, usually around eighty percent, this roughly amounts to about sixty thousand votes nationwide.[9]

The provincial councils (*Provinciale Staten*) and the municipal councils (*gemeenteraden*) are elected every four years as well. In the absence of prominently featured local politics, the municipal elections – taking place simultaneously throughout the nation – mostly give an indication of the relative positions of the national parties. Participation is generally around sixty percent. The elections for the provincial councils attract considerably fewer voters. As intermediaries between the local and the national authorities, provinces deal more with authorities and representatives than with citizens and are thus less visible and consequently less appealing to the public.

Two Ideological Dimensions

Although a proportional electoral system does not necessarily cause a fragmented political field, it is safe to say that it favors small parties. The Dutch political spectrum is characterized by fragmentation and minority parties. The position of these parties can traditionally be understood by considering two ideological dimensions, which created three distinct ideological "party families:" social democrats, liberals, and Christian Democrats. It should be noted that, as these ideological dimensions indicate differences between parties, they present the relative positions and not absolute measurements. The different positions can be illustrated by indicating how the parties stand towards the issue of regulating shop opening hours – an issue which has been on the political agenda repeatedly throughout the twentieth century.

The first dimension, dividing parties into left-wing and right-wing positions, is related to socio-economic issues and the preferred role of the government in this domain. On the left hand are the social democrats – the Labor Party (*Partij van de Arbeid,* PvdA) – who consider it a fundamental responsibility of the government to redistribute the available means equally and justly. With traditional support among the working class, the Labor Party considered regulating shop hours to be a possible instrument to protect the rights of employees. More recently however, it is also viewed as a possible facilitator in increasing labor participation, especially of women. The liberal parties on the right hand – the People's Party for Freedom and Democracy (*Volkspartij voor Vrijheid en Democratie,* VVD) and the more progressive Democrats '66 (*Democraten '66,* D'66) – prefer to limit the hand of the government in the lives of individual citizens, thus allowing for the freedom necessary for creative entrepreneurship to attain full bloom. On the issue of shop opening hours they argue that a healthy market is best served by lifting restrictions as much as possible.

A second dimension distinguishes between confessional and secular political thinking. Confessional parties – the Christian Democratic Alliance (CDA), the Christian Union (*Christenunie,* CU) and a small orthodox Protestant party (*Staatkundig Gereformeerde Partij,* SGP) – take religious principles as a guideline in political thinking. The government should serve as a protector of the same values the church instructs. This becomes most apparent in ethical, non-material issues: the confessional parties support a distinct government's position, whereas for the non-confessional parties – social democrats and liberals alike – such issues should primarily remain subject to private, individual decisions. On the issue of shop opening hours one may expect the confessional parties to argue in defense of Sunday as a traditional Christian resting day. In addition, they stress the need to consider regulation of shop opening hours in relation to the local social fabric in a neighborhood, the cornerstone of a "caring society."

With the decline in ideological thinking and an increasing secularization in the last decades of the twentieth century, the dividing lines between the parties have begun to fade. In 1994 the first coalition with social democrats and liberals was formed – the so-called "purple coalition" – illustrating that the traditional distinction between left and right was not as divisive as it had been. On the other hand, with the ongoing secularization and general decline of ideologically based political thinking, the confessional parties were losing votes and for the first time ended up in the opposition.

New parties were established as well, such as Green Left (*Groen Links*), a merger in 1989 of four former small progressive parties. The Socialist Party (SP), a split from the former Communist Party in 1972, entered parliament in 1994. In addition, some one-issue parties emerged – such as the Elderly People's Party in the 1990s, and a Party for the Animals (*Partij voor de Dieren*, PvdD) in 2006. Such parties can perhaps best be seen as politicized action groups. They are sometimes accused of lacking a coherent political ideology and instead presenting a collection of opinions and statements.

From Structured to Open Electoral Model

For a major part of the twentieth century, the three so-called "heartlands" of the main party families determined electoral behavior. Many voters identified with one of the party families and voted accordingly. Today, this structured model of voting behavior is no longer as powerful as it once was.[10] Party identification is a decreasing factor in electoral behavior, as is also illustrated in declining party-membership. Voters may change preference from one election to the next, and increasing numbers of people work their way through online questionnaires to identify the party which best suits their opinions.

The significant increase in electoral volatility and floating voters has forced political parties to compete for votes – especially the undecided voters in the so-called "battlefield" – which has put more pressure on election campaigns. As increasing numbers of voters are not necessarily convinced by political analysis only, more emphasis is placed on the personality of the candidates to secure public support.

In a structured model of voting, the role of the candidates was rather modest. The participating political parties present a list of candidates, carefully drawn up, balancing men and women, various regional, social and ethnic backgrounds, age groups and – within the Christian Democratic Party (CDA) – the various "blood-groups," in other words candidates with various religious affiliations. A voter may give a vote of preference by indicating a specific name on the list: women are for instance known to vote for the first female candidate of the party of their choice. Yet, most voters routinely give their vote to a party by simply indicating the first name on the list. It is thus in fact the party, and not the voter, assigning seats in parliament.

Increasingly, political personalities play a role in election campaigns. Certainly the role of visual media as an instrument in election campaigns is important here as well. The candidates – especially the person heading the list (*lijsttrekker*) – should personify the party and be trustworthy to the voters. In 2002, the first political group was formed around a personality altogether: the List Pim Fortuyn (LPF). Similarly, in 2006, the Freedom Party

(*Partij voor de Vrijheid,* PVV) formed around Geert Wilders, and another political movement was presented by Rita Verdonk, Proud of the Netherlands (*Trots op Nederland,* TON), in 2007. In concentrating on issues related to immigration and assimilation, these parties seem to confirm the suggestion that a new, third ideological dimension is forming in the Dutch political field.[11]

Changes and Continuity

In a parliamentary democracy, elections represent the most commonly known citizens' participation in decision-making. However, parallel to a diminishing position of the political parties, a certain public dissatisfaction has surfaced, concentrating on the widening gap between politics and public. At the local level such sentiments lead to the formation of so-called *Leefbaar* ("liveable") parties in various cities, addressing issues of direct public concern – such as safety, or even chewing gum, in the streets – instead of abstract bureaucratic debates beyond daily realities.

But public discontent was also caused by a perceived lack of direct involvement of the public, strengthening the call for directly electing members in the executive branches. In selecting a new mayor, some municipal councils have asked the population for their preference in a consultative referendum. An elected mayor, though, is still hidden in the future, as is a directly elected prime minister. It has also been suggested to introduce a decisive referendum, asking the citizens their view on new legislation, as the ultimate means of direct influence on national policy. However, no political majority exists for the necessary constitutional reforms to introduce such a referendum, or even a corrective legislative referendum, allowing for the public to express an opinion on laws as agreed on by parliament. Direct public impact on the political process remains limited to elections.

Yet, it cannot be concluded that the Dutch parliamentary democracy lacks in general public trust. Rather than in declining voters' turnout at elections, dissatisfaction is materializing in volatile electoral behavior, a phenomenon which has made Dutch political life more attractive and the electoral campaigns more interesting.

Amidst this increasing political volatility and continuously changing coalitions the role of the monarchy continues to enjoy broad support in society, including the new, immigrant citizens as well.[12] Perhaps it is the very strength of the monarchy that it is not the product of political elections and subject to political campaigning. Solidly rooted in the collective memory of the citizens and supported by occasional displays of tradition, the monarchy represents the continuity of the nation. Additionally, the neutrality of the king allows all citizens equally to unite in the so-called "orange-sentiment" (*het oranjegevoel*). As such, the monarchy can be regarded as the embodiment of the heart of the nation.

Further Reading

Andeweg, Rudi B. "The Netherlands. The Sanctity of Proportionality." In: *The Politics of Electoral Systems*, edited by Michael Gallagher and Paul Mitchell. Oxford: Oxford University Press, 2005.

Andeweg, Rudi B. and Galen A. Irwin. *Governance and Politics of the Netherlands*. Third revised edition. London: Palgrave Macmillan, 2009.

Holsteyn, Joop J.M. van and Galen A. Irwin. "Never a Dull Moment: Pim Fortuyn and the Dutch Parliamentary Election of 2002" *West European Politics* 26, no. 2 (April 2003): 41-66.

Rochon, Thomas R. *The Netherlands: Negotiating Sovereignty in an Interdependent World*. Boulder: Westview Press, 1999.

Special issue on the long year 2002, *Acta Politica* 38, no.1 (2003).

Chapter 2

The Economy of the Polder

Jan Luiten van Zanden

The Dutch sometimes think they are different. They like to talk about things being "typically Dutch." Similarly, economic historians have suggested that the way in which the economy is managed is rooted in the particular past of the Netherlands – in its Golden Age, from which it inherited, for example, a strong focus on the outside world, or, as we will discuss, the "poldermodel." In many ways, however, the Dutch are very similar to other Europeans – and should be placed between Germany and the United Kingdom, in more ways than mere terms of geography. Accordingly, the history of the economy during the twentieth century can be understood as just another example of the rapid growth and modernization that occurred in the whole of Europe.

If one looks more closely, there are some "typically Dutch" features as well. This does not primarily concern windmills or flower bulbs, but the way in which the economy is managed, the particular "business system" of the Netherlands. With this concept economists and sociologists have tried to develop the idea that business firms are rooted in the culture of their society and therefore function differently in different cultures. It has been argued that the way in which not only specific companies but also the economy as a whole is governed, reflects the underlying values of a society. The "business systems" of Japan, Italy, or the United States are different from those in Germany or the Netherlands. The "poldermodel" is perhaps the best known concept that describes some of the features of the business system of the Netherlands.

Bulbs, Flowers and Cheese:
The Agricultural Face of an Urban Economy

It is a bit of a paradox that one of the most densely populated and urbanized societies in the world is also one of the largest exporters of agricultural products. Dutch farmers export huge quantities of cheese, meat, tomatoes, flowers, and bulbs, and are in this field only beaten by the United States and France – two huge countries by comparison. Again, the explanation lies in a distant past, in the Golden Age.

Before the Industrial Revolution proximity to markets was a key ingredient of the success of farming. From the late Middle Ages onwards, Dutch society was highly urbanized. Farmers learned to cater to the needs of urban citizens, and increasingly specialized in high-value products such as milk, butter, cheese, vegetables, and bulbs. Ecological conditions also played a role. In the low parts of the country – Holland, Utrecht and Friesland – conditions for growing bread grains were rather unfavorable; instead, farmers concentrated on livestock farming, and bought (imported) rye and wheat on the market in return. When England and Germany began to industrialize during the nineteenth century, Dutch farmers switched to export production of the same commodities.

These trends continued in the twentieth century. What was added was a relatively efficient system of agricultural research, education and extension services, largely managed by the agricultural sector itself, and sponsored by the state. Also, cooperative agricultural banks emerged – which merged into today's Rabobank – supplying funds at low interest rates to the farming communities. And when the Great Depression of the 1930s struck the Dutch economy, it was agriculture that was supported first by the government. A set of policies to guarantee minimum prices was established, which eventually developed into the European agricultural policy that became an important feature of the EU.

The new agricultural system concentrated on the further increase of the productivity of agriculture. It became quite good at increasing the quantity of output – more cheese or tomatoes produced at lower prices – but until recently was less successful in improving the quality of output. And the concentration of large scale agricultural activities in such a tiny country also lead to growing environmental problems, especially in regions where the "bio-industry" (pig and chicken farming) was concentrated. Having such a dynamic agricultural sector has therefore become a bit of a mixed blessing.

Long Term Trends in the Twentieth-Century Economy

Sometimes one picture can tell more than ten sentences. The graph in figure 1 describes the evolution of income per head of the population in the Netherlands and the United States between 1900 and 2006. Already at the

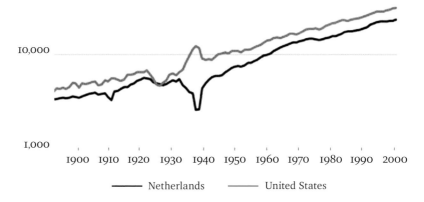

100,000
10,000
1,000
1900 1910 1920 1930 1940 1950 1960 1970 1980 1990 2000

————— Netherlands   ————— United States

Figure 1 – GDP per capita in the Netherlands and the United States,
dollar value of 1990 (after Angus Maddison)

beginning of the twentieth century there was a gap: people in the United States were on average better off than those in the Netherlands. Dutch economic modernization had been rather slow during the nineteenth century. This was the period of the Industrial Revolution, the period of the steam engine, which began in the United Kingdom in the eighteenth century. The Netherlands however continued to rely on its service sector and its highly productive agriculture – both part of the heritage of the Golden Age. During the "Second Industrial Revolution" of the 1880s and 1890s, new technologies linked to electricity and oil began to fundamentally change the economy. Although these new technologies originated in the United States and Germany, Dutch companies were rather quick to adopt them and sometimes even took a lead in the new industries that emerged. The companies Philips and Royal Dutch Shell are the best examples of this renewed "awakening" of the economy. The graph also shows that the gap between the Netherlands and the United States – then the richest country in the world – clearly narrowed between 1900 and 1930. The depression of the 1930s struck the United States even harder than it did the Netherlands, and in the worst years of the 1930s the disparity between the two completely disappeared. But soon a new gap emerged: during the Second World War the economy of the United States expanded rapidly – its highly successful war economy was one of the reasons why the allies were able to defeat Germany and Japan. The Netherlands, quickly conquered by Nazi Germany in May 1940, suffered quite badly during these years – although Dutch estimates after the war perhaps tended to somewhat exaggerate this.

When in 1945 the Second World War ended, the two economies were therefore at quite different points: the Dutch were impoverished while the American economy had grown spectacularly during the war years. In 1947, when the recovery of the European economy was barely underway, the US Secretary of State Alfred Marshall announced a plan to come to the rescue of

Europe, the famous Marshall Plan. It consisted of large donations of US commodities and funds to Western Europe. Because the Dutch economy was in such bad shape, and its deficit on the balance of payments was so high, the Netherlands profited considerably from the European Recovery Program, as it was officially called. The program was an attempt to link these two fates: oversupply of goods in the United States versus the scarcity at the other side of the Atlantic. Similarly, the post-war years were very different too: the United States rapidly moved into "mass consumption" during the 1950s, while the Netherlands and other European nations, although they recovered very successfully, did not enter a phase of mass consumerism until the 1960s. Due to the big gap between the two regions, Europe tried to emulate the American example in almost all fields: technology, management ideas and marketing skills all were eagerly adopted from the other side of the Atlantic. The American challenge was also taken up in the political field: European countries – sometimes gently induced by the United States – began to cooperate more intensely, which ultimately resulted, amongst others, in the present European Union.

During the 1950s and the 1960s the gap declined sharply: Europe was catching up, partly by copying and adapting the technologies developed in the United States. But Europe also did things in its own way: it expanded its welfare state dramatically – the Netherlands took the lead in this process in the 1960s and 1970s. During the golden years before 1973, the view developed – thanks to the ideas of the British economist John Maynard Keynes – that growth could permanently be secured by, on the one hand, the welfare state, which would stabilize the economy because people would not lose their income when unemployed, and on the other hand by a better management of the demand side of economy (via Keynesian budget policies). As a result, politicians thought that taxation and real wages could be increased almost without limits. The general euphoria was further stimulated by the discovery of rich fields of natural gas in the north of the country, which meant a tremendous boom to the Dutch economy. The expectation of endless growth ended suddenly in the 1970s. Due to high inflation, high wage costs, high levels of taxation, and, as a result of all this, low profits for enterprises, a period of slow growth began. Unemployment – which had been close to zero in the 1960s – increased again and many workers retired early or moved to other forms of welfare. The economy only recovered very slowly.

Again, during the 1990s and the first decade of the twenty-first century, the United States was considered exemplary. Here, the "Third Industrial Revolution" began – the revolution of information technology, personal computers and the internet. American companies such as IBM, Microsoft, Intel and Google took the lead, and European firms found it difficult to emulate their example. Philips – one of the few electronics companies that survived the onslaught of Japanese competition in the 1970s and 1980s – was only moderately successful in this, and after 2000 decided to move into other directions, such as lighting and medical equipment. The gap between the Netherlands and Western Europe in general on the one hand and the United States on the other remained more or less constant in these years. Although the difference in productivity had been relatively small since the 1970s, the gap remained because Europeans preferred to work less hours – they enjoy longer holidays, but also have more people dependent on unemployment and disability benefits (WW and WAO). The relatively well-developed welfare state meant that inequality did not increase significantly during these years, whereas in the United States and in the United Kingdom income differences grew very rapidly.

What is equally striking about the graph is, of course, the consistent increase in income levels. The Gross Domestic Product per capita increased by a factor of almost seven between 1900 and 2006, which meant that, on average, the Dutch can now buy about seven times the number of consumption goods that our (great)grandparents had at their disposal when they were young. This process of "modern economic growth," which began during the Industrial Revolution, was accompanied by structural changes in the economy. The agricultural sector declined rapidly, even though the Netherlands had already since the seventeenth century been a predominantly urban and service oriented society, whereas at the same time the industrial sector expanded and large industrial companies emerged. After the process of industrialization came to a halt around 1960, it was the service sector that grew most rapidly: new employment emerged in such sectors as education, medical services, government, banking, insurance and tourism. Industrial products were increasingly imported from "low wage economies" – Japan at first, Korea, Taiwan, Malaysia later on, and most recently, mainland China.

At the same time, a process of globalization occurred, although this was much less of a change for a small and open economy such as the Netherlands than for large and closed economies such as the United States. International capital markets expanded dramatically and – until very recently – firms operated increasingly on a global scale and were constantly involved in "restructuring" their activities. Much employment moved from the West to East or South Asia. Yet, in spite of globalization, national economies continued to have their own development paths; the Dutch *poldermodel* is a good example of such a national turn in the phase of globalization.

Royal Dutch Shell:
Corporate Legacy of Colonialism

One of the distinctive features of the Netherlands in the centuries before 1949 was its huge colonial empire, which consisted mainly of present day Indonesia, then called the Netherlands East Indies. This comparatively huge colony – with a population many times that of the Netherlands itself – contributed much to the economic development of its "mother country" (although it is a slightly more complex question whether Indonesia also profited from being a colony). Part of this legacy is, arguably, one of the most successful companies of the twentieth century, Royal Dutch Shell. In 1907 this company was established as a result of a merger between Royal Dutch, a Dutch-owned company with large oil concessions in Indonesia (mainly on

Sumatra), and the "Shell" Transport and Trading Company, a British company with oil possessions in the same colony, but on another island, Kalimantan. Since Royal Dutch acquired a sixty percent share in the new company they tended to see it as a "Dutch" company. Because it mainly used the brand of Shell in its marketing, the British could likewise see it as "their" business. When its American subsidiary became larger and larger, and also started to sell its own shares on the New York stock exchange, it adapted so well to the United States that it was often also considered to be an American company.

From small beginnings – the two companies who merged in 1907 were set up in 1890 and 1898 as relatively modest businesses – Royal Dutch Shell became the main challenger of the biggest company on earth, Standard Oil Company and Trust, the corporate empire of John D. Rockefeller and his associates. It was relatively successful, also because anti-trust legislation in the United States led to the partition of Standard Oil into a number of different companies (in 1911). After 1907 Royal Dutch Shell rapidly spread its activities from Indonesia to all other continents, bought oil concessions in the United States, Russia, Romania, Venezuela, and Egypt (before 1914), and set up marketing organizations in all parts of the world (including China, India, and Africa). Between 1907 and the mid-1920s it became the largest oil company in the world, with a truly global presence. Afterwards, competition with Standard Oil of New Jersey increased again, and the two companies continued to battle over the dominance in the oil industry in different parts of the world.

For a small country like the Netherlands, Shell (as it usually is known) was really a huge company. During the two world wars

tensions within the company surfaced, but somehow the management teams that controlled it were able to keep things together. In more recent times Shell caught the attention of the world by being involved in Third World conflicts (in Nigeria, Zimbabwe and South Africa), or by policies which were considered not to be very environmentally friendly (such as the "dumping" of the oil storage buoy Brent Spar). The Dutch still own a relatively large portion of its shares, its international headquarters is in The Hague, and it still has a large impact on – for example – Research and Development that is carried out here. In these respects it is still one of the most visible legacies of the colonial past of the Netherlands.

The *Poldermodel*

Growth and structural change were normal features of the Western European economies in the twentieth century. But in some respects the Dutch economy was different. In the 1990s economists and sociologists began to develop the idea that there are various roads to economic modernity, and that economies can be organized in different ways, reflecting the institutions and cultural values of these societies. They argue that markets and the actors in those markets – such as firms, unions, and the state – are embedded in the culture of their society. A labor market in Indonesia is different from one in the Netherlands, and the same applies to the way in which business is organized, the state intervenes in the economy or trade unions play their role. Within the "developed" world, two major types of "business systems" have been distinguished. Continental Europe generally has the *coordinated market economies* (CME), of which Germany is perhaps the best example. They contrast with the *liberal market economies* of the Anglo-Saxon world. In the CMEs of Western Europe the state plays a large role in the economy, trade unions are also quite important, and banks and companies engage in long-term relationships. The stock market, on the other hand, is much less important than in the Anglo-Saxon world.

The Netherlands is an example of a CME with some peculiar sets of institutions and values. The concept of the *poldermodel* is often used to typify the special features of this economy. What is the *poldermodel*? The most heroic, but historically disputed interpretation of this concept is that the Dutch, in their incessant battle against the water, set up their own institutions, the water boards (*waterschappen*), to cope with the management of water. Because of the vital and comprehensive nature of the problem – every citizen had a clear interest in keeping the water out – relatively democratic institutions developed already during the Middle Ages to handle this. Farmers with land in the polders convened at meetings where they discussed the problems that had to be solved and tried to make decisions on the basis of consensus, and where they elected the managers of these polders that had to execute the decisions made. As a result, a bottom-up process of democratic decision making emerged, based on meetings and elections, which was – so the story goes – to form the basis for the political system of the country. The fact that the Dutch still convene in many a meeting, that decision making is still largely based on consensus and compromise, and that trade unions, employers organizations and the state still attempt to monitor the economy in this collective fashion – all these facts are explained with reference to these medieval roots.

Historians do not completely agree on this picture, however. There is some debate about how democratic these polders actually were in the Middle Ages. More importantly, it is not clear how to link these institutions of water management to current political traditions. Probably there is a much stronger tradition in "democratic" decision making related to the governing politics of the cities that emerged in the same period. The Netherlands from early on was also a heavily urbanized country – in particular the west – and the urban communities that arose in the Middle Ages were governed in a similar way. Moreover, they continued to dominate Dutch political life in the early modern period, and produced the urban bourgeoisie that was the backbone of Dutch politics from the sixteenth century onwards. The "poldermodel" therefore may well have originated in the medieval citizenship of Dutch cities rather than in its water boards.

The way in which the *poldermodel* has been reinvented as an idea in the 1980s and 1990s, refers to only a small – yet strategically important – part of the governance of the economy. In the 1970s, similar to the rest of Western Europe, the Dutch economy went through a difficult period: unemployment increased, wages and taxes were probably too high, and profits too low. Although trade unions were initially not eager to change this situation of high wages, they gradually became convinced that something had to be changed. Their power was undermined because they were losing members as a result of growing industrial unemployment, and the Central Planning Bureau (CPB, a government agency that published analyses of the causes of the economic problems), managed to convince the unions that wage costs were too high.

To meet these economic challenges, the government, the trade unions and the employers' organizations reached the famous Wassenaar Agreement in 1982. The unions now agreed to moderate the demand for wage increases, the employers promised to shorten the workweek to stem the tide of rising unemployment, and the government agreed not to interfere with the new compromise. From 1982 onwards this policy of wage moderation was suc-cessfully implemented. Wage costs increased much less than elsewhere in Western Europe, in particular compared to Germany, and this strongly in-creased Dutch competitiveness in comparison with its major trading partners, again, especially compared to Germany, its most important neighbor.

As a result, employment increased rapidly from the early 1980s onwards, particularly in the new service industries that became increasingly important in these years. Also, the unions agreed on various measures which improved the flexibility of labor markets such as stimulating part-time work and an increasing role played by temp agencies. At the same time, the various Dutch governments were quite successful in lowering taxes and achieving a gradual liberalization of the economy – very similar to what was happening in Great Britain and in the United States at the same time. In short, due to the cooperation between the three "social partners" – trade unions, employer's organizations and the government – the Netherlands was quite successful in adapting to the changed conditions of the 1980s and 1990s, to the "post-industrial society" and the age of globalization.

This all sounds perhaps too good to be true – and there are of course disadvantages of the *poldermodel* as well. It has been pointed out that an advanced country such as the Netherlands should not compete with low wage costs. It cannot really compete with countries like India and China anyway. Low wages also make industry lazy – because there is insufficient inducement to develop labor-saving technology or new products. More in general, given its high level of development, the Netherlands should concentrate on high-tech products based on new Research and Development (R&D), and on its highly skilled labor. Government policies should aim at increasing R&D, which is quite low in the Netherlands by international standards. This being said, as a solution for the problems of the 1980s the policy of wage moderation was initially quite successful.

The Wassenaar Agreement did not come out of the blue. First of all, already in the 1950s and early 1960s a similar policy of wage moderation – again with the full cooperation of the trade unions – had been carried out with the same purpose, creating full employment and enhancing economic growth. More importantly, directly after 1945 new institutions had been created which facilitated the negotiations between the "social partners" that formed the basis of the policy of wage moderation. The most important of these institutions is the Social and Economic Council (SER), where the three parties meet and freely discuss all important economic and social issues. It was the SER that laid the basis for important new agreements such as the Wassenaar Agreement. Another innovation of the post-1945 period, initiated by Jan Tinbergen, the famous economist and Nobel laureate, was the Netherlands Bureau for Economic Policy Analysis (*Centraal Planbureau,* CPB), initially meant as a "planning agency" to map out the reconstruction of the economy after 1945. Its powers were rather limited however, especially when compared with "real" planning agencies of the communist world, and it developed into a more or less independent think tank, that produces annual and even three-monthly forecasts of the economy and "white papers" analyzing main economic issues.

The *poldermodel* is based on traditions of bargaining and consensus decision making, still relevant even today. Dutch governments, for example, are always composed of different political parties, as no single party ever has had an absolute majority in parliament. Before a coalition is formed, a number of parties have to negotiate a "coalition agreement," and once the coalition has been appointed, some kind of balance between the political parties involved has to be maintained, because estranging one of them may imply that the coalition will lose its majority support in parliament. This is just one – albeit an important – example of the significance of bargaining in society. We see similar practices in business. Large companies in the Netherlands were usually not led by a single Chief Executive Officer (CEO) who takes all major decisions – as is usual in the United States – but were managed by boards of directors, teams of managers of whom the chairman was not more than the first among equals ("primus inter pares"). This may sometimes have delayed decision making, as consensus is needed, which means long meetings and detailed discussions. But one can also argue that this must have enhanced the quality of the decisions made since they are based on more information, coming from all managers involved. Perhaps even more important, it may have lowered the costs of implementing these decisions, as all managers feel responsible for the decisions made, and therefore more committed to the outcome of the decision making process.

However, a tendency in the 1990s to adopt Anglo-Saxon examples has meant that in the Netherlands the model of the all-mighty CEO has become more fashionable too. In at least one example, the downfall of ABN-AMRO bank in 2008, it has been demonstrated how risky such a strategy can be: if the CEO fails, the whole company can go down.

The 1990s not only witnessed the successes of the *poldermodel* – the Dutch "job machine" became famous for producing very high levels of employment – but also growing criticism of the *poldermodel*. Decision making was supposed to be very slow and not very transparent. After all, who was really in charge of a certain firm: the chair of the board or a team of managers? This decision-making model was therefore considered unfit for the demands of a globalizing world. With the growing power of shareholders in the international economy – who preferred transparency – there was a growing tendency to implement aspects of the Anglo-Saxon system, both in business and in government. One can also argue that to some extent Dutch society accommodated these pressures in a typically Dutch way – flexibility and openness to the outside world have also been long-standing features of the business system. It appears that the financial crisis of 2008 has put an end to this pressure to copy the "superior" American or British way of doing things – the future is open again.

Summing up, the development of the Dutch economy during the twentieth century has in many ways been similar to that of Western Europe in the same period. In terms of growth and structural transformation it was not much unlike that of Belgium, Germany, Denmark or the United Kingdom. Compared with the US, there was a process of rapid catching up going on in the years 1950-1973, but since the 1970s the differences between both sides of the Atlantic have more or less stabilized. If we dig somewhat deeper we discover a particular business system that is unique to the Netherlands. It is based on old traditions – although it is still unclear if the *poldermodel* was really invented "in the polder." But this version of the Coordinated Market Economy has adapted successfully to the challenges of the twentieth century. New institutions were created that facilitated cooperation between employers and trade unions both in the post-1945 world of rapid economic recovery, and in the post-1980 period of advancing globalization. With the crisis of 2008/2009 it appears that the world economy is going through another phase of rapid changes – it may well be that the *poldermodel* will again make it possible to adapt to these shocks too.

Further Reading

Sluyterman, Kate Eveline. *Dutch Enterprise in the Twentieth Century: Business Strategies in a Small Open Economy*. London: Routledge, 2005.

Visser, Jelle, and Anton van Hemerijck. *A Dutch Miracle: Job Growth, Welfare Reform and Corporatism in the Netherlands*. Amsterdam: Amsterdam University Press, 1997.

Zanden, Jan Luiten van, Stephen Howarth, Joost Jonker and Kate Eveline Sluyterman. *A History of Royal Dutch Shell.* 4 vols. Oxford: Oxford University Press, 2007.

Zanden, Jan Luiten van. *The Economic History of the Netherlands in the 20th Century.* London: Routledge, 1997.

Chapter 3

Dilemmas of the Welfare State

Lex Heerma van Voss

In 2007 American journalist and writer Russell Shorto settled in Amsterdam to become Director of the John Adams Institute. Over the following months and years, he submerged himself in Dutch society. Among his experiences were receiving unsolicited payments: some € 500 every quarter with the one-word explanation *kinderbijslag* (child benefit). Upon first receiving this money, Shorto looked up the website of the benefactor, the *Sociale Verzekeringsbank* (Social Insurance Bank), where the reason for this financial transaction to every parent residing in the Netherlands was explained as follows: "Babies are expensive. Nappies, clothes, the pram ... all these things cost money. The Dutch government provides for child allowance to help you with the costs of bringing up your child." Similar surprises continued to materialize over the subsequent months. At the start of a school year the Social Insurance Bank transferred € 316 to his account for every schoolgoing child, to help pay for books. Other American expats who settled in Amsterdam had equally grown to appreciate Dutch social security. Shorto's friend Julie discovered that Dutch universal health care did not only cover the cost of the midwife when she gave birth – at home, following Dutch tradition – but in addition a week-long maternity assistance after having given birth, as well as regular checkups at a public health clinic. Day care for Julie's children was subsidized, so she could afford to continue her writing career. Another friend learned to appreciate the benefits of social housing, which allowed living in an affordable place.

Although Shorto seems to have taken a liking to the Dutch system, he realizes that some of its features will make many foreigners view the Dutch welfare state as a form of socialism. And at least one aspect of it seemed to confirm this. Shorto: "For the first few months I was haunted by a number: 52. It reverberated in my head; I felt myself a prisoner trying to escape its bars. For it represents the rate at which the income I earn, as a writer and as the director of an institute, is to be taxed."[1]

What Shorto so vividly described is the difference between the Dutch welfare state and the arrangements he grew up with in the United States. His experiences illustrate the well-known division between three types of welfare states that Danish sociologist and welfare state specialist Gøsta Esping-Andersen categorizes as liberal, social-democratic and conservative.[2]

Along with for instance Australia and Canada, and in some ways also the United Kingdom, the United States represents a typical liberal welfare state.

Liberal welfare programs are lean and avoid interference with the market. They primarily target the very poor. Entitlement rules are strict and to be a welfare recipient generally carries a social stigma. Middle-class citizens cover their own risks and save for their own pensions through private insurance. Hence, the liberal welfare state is relatively cheap and taxes can be low. However, the resulting transfer from rich to poor is limited, and differences in income between these two groups remain substantial.

Social-democratic welfare states, such as found in Scandinavia, are so termed by Esping-Andersen because social-democratic parties took the lead in establishing them. However, since they did so in cooperation with farmers' parties, more than lower-class interests are taken into account. Hence, recipients include the middle classes. As entitlement is nearly universal, receiving a welfare payment does not necessarily carry a stigma. As everyone is entitled to relatively high levels of welfare, market involvement is limited and social and economic differences between citizens remain small. However, high taxes are needed to pay for all this.

Esping-Andersen's third category is found in continental Europe. He calls it conservative because rights are linked to social status, and the welfare state is used to sustain distinctions, not to make them disappear. Catholic parties were often responsible for putting this type of welfare state in place. Consequently, social security is targeted at keeping mothers at home and hence day care, for instance, is typically underdeveloped. The state aims to fund only those programs that are not already well organized by civil society. As the level of benefits is positioned between that of the two other types, so does the tax level. The Netherlands is usually counted among the latter welfare states. Yet, as the Dutch system includes some traits of the social-democratic type, it is sometimes considered to belong to that group.

Labor Productivity:
Balancing Work and Leisure

Dutch productivity per hour is among the highest in the world, but due to the low number of working hours, Dutch productivity per work year is less impressive. Long holidays and short working weeks mean that the number of working hours Dutch employees put in, both during a year and during their whole working life, is much lower than in most developed countries.

Included in the money transferred to American writer Russell Shorto's bank account was "vacation bonus." In May his employer paid him roughly an extra month of salary. Shorto: "This money materializes in the bank accounts of virtually everyone in the country just before the summer holidays; you get from your employer an amount totaling 8 percent of your annual salary, which is meant to cover plane tickets, surfing lessons, tapas: vacations. And we aren't talking about a mere 'paid vacation' – this is on top of the salary you

continue to receive during the weeks you're off skydiving or snorkeling."

Labor participation is also low because many women prefer part-time jobs, in order to combine a career with actively raising children, since – compared to other Western countries – school meals, day care facilities, nannies and au-pairs are rare in the Netherlands. Until the 1960s, married women in the Netherlands only seldom had paid jobs. This changed from the 1970s onwards and nowadays the Netherlands is among the leading European countries in female paid employment. However, many economists and politicians argue women should seek full-time jobs, both in the interest of their careers as well as the national GDP.

Something similar applies to retirement. In the 1980s, when unemployment was high, schemes to enable employees to retire early were popular. The Dutch usually consider that working until one's early sixties is enough, allowing for a couple of years to enjoy retirement in fairly good health. In most branches of the economy, it has become possible to take early retirement from age 60 or 62. In fact, in some jobs, like garbage collecting, bus driving or primary school teaching, virtually no-one reaches the mandatory retirement age of 65.

The effect of the Dutch welfare state is that the Dutch are able to refuse low paid jobs. This is immediately visible to anyone visiting the Netherlands. Compared to an American restaurant, a Spanish bank or a Hungarian department store, the Dutch equivalent is poorly staffed. As the Dutch nevertheless eat out, do financial transactions and buy goods, these low staff levels turn up in the economists' statistics as high productivity per hour. The welfare state allows the Dutch to have a preference for paying people to stay at home instead of working in humble jobs. This has become a real preference, with many Dutch feeling ill at ease when they are in overstaffed banks or restaurants. Whether it would not be better for people to work in low paid jobs rather than getting paid to do nothing, is a matter of debate.

Roots in the Golden Age

Towns intensify the problems of poverty. Rural poor are drawn to towns because they hope to find work there, whereas family farms inherently offer opportunities to the old and the invalid to carry out useful tasks, and produce food and shelter for family members. By moving to a town, rural poor cut themselves off from these means of survival and often from family ties.

During the seventeenth century – its Golden Age – the Dutch Republic already was one of the most urbanized countries in the world. The towns had to provide other ways of taking care of the poor, the destitute and the diseased. Whilst in small villages this was achieved informally – the rich giving alms directly to the poor as they met each other in the street, or the village community deciding to support the poor with food or some land – more elaborate arrangements were necessary in towns. Specialized institutions were established to take care of impoverished subpopulations. It was not unusual for rich citizens to leave money in their will to found almshouses around small courtyards (*hofjes*) that would house a limited number of the elderly without other social support. Well into the twentieth century, these *hofjes* – more than two hundred were built in Dutch towns over the past centuries – generally functioned exactly as intended. Currently they are sought after dwellings with a historical flavor and have developed into tourist attractions. For orphans and the elderly, towns built larger institutions, which were so magnificent that they already drew tourists as early as the seventeenth century. Even today, former poor houses in Amsterdam are impressive enough to serve as housing for university administrations or prestigious museums.

All these charitable organizations were funded by a variety of sources: individuals leaving money to charities, door-to-door collections, offertory-boxes in churches, and money confiscated from convents and other religious institutions at the time of the Reformation. If urban charitable institutions were short on money, the towns expected the religious communities to take care of their needy fellow believers. This added to the variety and quantity of institutions, as separate Protestant, Catholic and Jewish relief agencies for the poor were established. Additionally, it was not uncommon for guilds and other professional organizations to take care of illness and poverty among their membership. Others copied these mutual arrangements and created separate widow funds or health insurances, some of them as fully commercial enterprises and others non-commercial in every sense of the word. Some of the municipal or religious programs distinguished between different social categories of recipients. Orphaned children of citizens were fed and housed better than those of town inhabitants without citizen status. "Deserving" middle-class recipients could receive their relief at home, in secrecy, so the stigma of being on the dole would be avoided. The poor from the working class would receive relief only if they agreed to move to the poor house.

By the nineteenth century, this mechanism had resulted in a patchwork of welfare institutions and arrangements. Some of the needy were able to work this system to their advantage, receiving dole money from several charities, or even bargaining to change from one Protestant denomination to the other if they would receive more poor relief. Consequently, a number of proposals were put forward to streamline the system and make relief rules more rational and uniform. However, some had a vested interest in maintaining the system, among whom the voluntary officials of private charities and churches who felt that they were doing an important job, or the churches that looked at poor relief as an important service to members of their congregation and as a way to keep their poor on the straight and narrow path. Typically, attendance at the Sunday service was expected of those on relief. Social theorists – representing especially orthodox Protestant circles, but also other churches – felt that what had developed organically in civil society was to be preferred over a system governed through state bureaucracy and the state was only to interfere with church and/or private charity when these proved unable to take care of "their" poor.

The notion that the role of state relief should only be subsidiary to private charity was ideosyncratic to Dutch society and was maintained as an ideal well into the twentieth century. By that time essential social services, such as education, health care and poor relief, had become so expensive that the churches were no longer able to pay for them. Yet, by public funding for private welfare arrangements, Dutch politics managed to keep the ideal of civil society charity intact. Thus, Catholic hospitals or Protestant schools were factually funded almost completely by the state, as long as they met certain basic standards.

The Dutch state preferred to act only in a subsidiary way and deliberately not only called upon private, often denominational, organizations to execute part of the welfare provisions, but also offered ample political room to organized employers and trade unions. These organizations claimed that they had a better insight in the economy and consequently were in the best position to administer welfare funds, especially those related to employment, which were funded by contributions from employers and workers anyway. Consultation with all social organizations concerned, the so-called *polder-model*, became a hallmark of Dutch politics.

These ideals notwithstanding, during the first three quarters of the twentieth century, the national state rationalized this organically grown patchwork of private charities, denominational boards, employers' and workers' representatives administering funds and arrangements run by local, regional, and national authorities. During the First World War and again during the economic crisis of the 1930s, the government felt compelled to actively interfere in an attempt to prevent the existing unemployment relief from collapsing under extraordinary demands. Between 1945 and 1963 an extensive welfare state was created. Within less than two decades, state pensions at age 65, unemployment and disability benefits, child allowances (that so surprised Shorto) and better health-care arrangements were put into place. The capstone of this new social building was the General Relief Act of 1963 (*Algemene Bijstandswet*), which aimed at supporting everyone not covered by one of the other arrangements. Whereas up until then relief had been a favor, offered by a private or denominational charity, Dutch society now recognized that everyone, being for whatever reason unable to earn their own income, was entitled to an income paid by the state. The change from a favor to a right immensely improved the position of people on relief. The minister, who introduced the General Relief Act, argued that the poor should have enough income to "put some flowers on the table now and then." Although especially the socialists and Catholics were most ardent supporters of these social programs, they could count on broad support within Dutch society and politics.

A similar broad support for the idea that married women should stay at home prevailed in Dutch society and politics. Compared to other countries, married women were hardly represented on the labor market; until the 1950s, female teachers and civil servants were even fired upon marrying, as was the norm rather than the exception in many other jobs as well. Welfare arrangements reflected this: child allowance was offered to support families in raising their children, but no program existed to finance day care. However, by increasing the agency of individuals to act, the welfare state also entailed unintended side-effects. The General Relief Act of 1963 is a good example. Previous to this Act, the lack of a regular income often discouraged women to divorce their husbands even in case of insurmountable marital problems, as so few married women held paying jobs. The General Relief Act entitled women to an income, even when their former husbands were not ruled to pay alimony. This unforeseen consequence of the welfare state enhanced the freedom of women to file for divorce if they wanted to.

Overall, the entitlements created by the General Relief Act were much larger than had been anticipated. In 1965, some 140,000 people received welfare (*bijstand*). By 1985 this number had risen to 580,000, a more than fourfold increase in twenty years. The spectacular growth of the Dutch economy between 1945 and 1973 allowed for a growth of the welfare state after the introduction of the General Relief Act, resulting in ongoing improvements in social legislation until the 1970s. Programs that had originally only been targeted at wage workers were expanded to cover all Dutch citizens. In 1960 thirty out of every hundred people received some sort of relief. Ten years later that number had risen to forty-five. The expense involved had increased from ten percent of the national income in the 1950s to twenty-five percent in 1974. In the 1970s, however the economic downturn kicked in and as a result in 1980 almost seventy people were receiving some sort of welfare support for every hundred working, and by 1990 eighty-five.

By the 1970s the welfare state was complete. But almost as soon as its construction was finished, it came under attack. The aforementioned increase of recipients and the percentage of the national income involved in social security led to constant debate and reconstruction, especially since the Dutch welfare state faced a number of acute dilemmas.

Does the Welfare State Work?

The general dilemma is whether the overall experience with the welfare state has been positive. In the 1980s and 1990s many economists argued in favor of trimming the welfare state, if not abolishing it altogether. The welfare state was said to stifle "bottom-up" initiatives. The unemployed had no incentives to find a job or set up a business, nor were welfare recipients inclined to improve their positions themselves, while high taxes prevented businesses and the rich to spend money in the way they saw fit. All of this would slow down economic growth. It would appear the welfare state was just a cumbersome detour to poverty.

One way to test this assumption is to look at the overall development of the Dutch economy and compare it with the development of a liberal welfare state. The graph in figure 1 in the previous chapter does just that: it compares income (technically: GDP) per capita in the Netherlands and the United States. The graph shows that income per head in the Netherlands has almost always lagged behind that of the United States, but also that economic growth has on the whole been very similar. The growth of the Dutch welfare state after 1945 has not visibly constrained the Dutch economic growth compared to that in the United States.

Furthermore, the Dutch welfare state delivers. Not only to Russell Shorto's bank account, but also in terms of its own goals. Inequality in income is reduced. For instance, comparative research conducted in the Netherlands over the 1985-1994 period has shown that in any given year about twenty percent would fall below the poverty line without transfers through the welfare state. Dutch welfare brought that figure down to five percent. In the United States, which would have a comparable percentage of poor people without interference, welfare only reduced this to eighteen percent.[3] The system was also popular with the Dutch population. From the mid-1980s onwards and following international trends, lower benefits and cutbacks on social security slowly reduced the degree to which the welfare state decreased income differences in the Netherlands. During all this time the majority of the Dutch population wanted exactly the opposite: smaller, not larger differences between rich and poor.

In the 1980s some Dutch political philosophers predicted that the welfare state would lead to "ego-centrism, immorality and consumerism." In fact, this is not what has happened. The majority of the Dutch continue to cherish a strong work ethic. They prefer work over relief and think that those on welfare should try to find a job. This consensus includes the recipients of welfare themselves. Only elderly unemployed with little schooling consider attempts to get a job a waste of time. For this particular group, this attitude is a sign of realism, rather than a lack of work ethic.

Pensions: Well-Deserved and Well-Funded

Dutch pensions are funded in three tiers. At age 65, every Dutch citizen is entitled to basic AOW, an acronym which stands for *Algemene Ouderdomswet* or General Pensions Act, but has come to be a shorthand for retirement pay. Old-age pensions for all citizens over 65 were introduced in 1947, a feat perennially linked to the name of the minister of Social Affairs, Willem Drees, a social democrat. It is paid from tax money: those currently working pay for those currently retired. If a couple lives together, both receive fifty percent of the net minimum wage. An individual old age pensioner receives seventy percent. In 2009 this was slightly less than € 1,000 per month.

A majority of the people who retire receive a pension in addition to the AOW. Some pension funds cover a branch of the economy, others are limited to the employees of one large firm. Pensions are saved throughout a working career. Pension funds typically raise total retirement pay to seventy percent of the average wage earned over one's working life. In 2008, the Dutch pension funds together held some € 700 billion.

This immense amount of capital means that Dutch pensions are among the most solidly financed in the world. In 2006, the capital of the Dutch pension funds equaled some 140 percent of GDP, compared to ninety percent in the United Kingdom, twenty percent in Germany or ten percent in France. From the 1990s onwards, pension funds tried to raise their income by investing more in stocks, which made them more vulnerable to market downturns. In the 2008/2009 credit crunch they lost considerable sums and many fell below the level to which their expected claims should be covered by their capital.

About fifty percent of the money paid out as Dutch pensions are AOW payments, forty-five percent is paid out by pension funds. The remaining five percent are individual private investments. These have grown over the last decades, as many foresee that old age entitlements will dwindle. A strong point of the current Dutch system is that it predicts pension levels. This frees the individual from worrying about his or her investments, but of course it only transfers this worry to the pension funds.

The pension system is a prime target for welfare state reform. Raising the mandatory retirement age will make it easier to finance pensions, and at the same time increases the number of people working and thus paying taxes and social insurance premiums. With that in mind, for the last ten years the government has struck down measures that promoted saving up money to finance early retirement. It now seems likely that in the near future the retirement age in the Netherlands will go up to 67.

Another measure that has been debated over the past years is making the retired pay more taxes. However, most political parties are weary of proposing this, fearing that they may chase away the elderly, who are an increasing percentage of the electorate.

Costs and Management

This rosy picture, however, should not detract from the fact that there are real dilemmas. One is associated with the costs of a welfare state. As already argued, the Dutch are essentially willing to shoulder the costs of their welfare state. But even so, paying too much for welfare could be detrimental. In the 1980s the debate focused on the "wedge" between income before and after taxes. If employers and workers have to fork up the costs of social insurance, the wedge might become too large and production could be transferred to countries with smaller wedges, and therefore smaller gross wage costs.

One prominent example is the contribution to the disability insurance. When the Work-Disability Insurance Act (*Wet op de Arbeidsongeschiktheids-verzekering*, WAO) was introduced in 1967, the premium added just over four percent to what companies paid in wages, but this had risen to more than twenty percent by 1983. Why did the disability insurance grow so much? The WAO was administered in each branch by a bipartite industrial insurance board (*bedrijfsvereniging*), in which trade unions and employers were represented. If there was a groundbreaking decision on eligibility to be made, it was referred to a committee of representatives of these organizations. There were good grounds for this procedure. The funds had been raised by workers and employers. The organizations simply represented their members by administering their money, as they represented them in many other ways. Furthermore, the representatives were knowledgeable about work in their branches and thus considered themselves to be in a good position to judge which handicaps prevented workers from making a living in their branch of industry.

However, they had also other interests to look after. By the 1980s, the Dutch economy had been hit by two oil crises, and unemployment was on the rise. In several ways it was more attractive for workers to get disability relief than to be put on unemployment relief. Disability pensions were somewhat higher and unemployed workers were supposed to find a new job. The representatives of workers and employers often were able to strike a deal by which older and superfluous workers received WAO benefits. The industrial insurance boards were very efficient in remitting the right amount to the right bank accounts every month, and they never had to bother about getting their clients back to work. As a result, by the early 1980s, the number of people on disability pensions threatened to reach one million. Politicians were worried about the costs of the welfare state. Relief payments were cut back. Unfairly, the industrial insurance boards were held accountable for the fact that they had never worried about the number of people on relief. In fact, nobody had ever asked them to do so.

This situation was not unique to the Dutch welfare state, even if industrial insurance boards represent a rather Dutch institution. At the same time that the Dutch had many people on disability pensions, the Belgians had as many on unemployment relief, and the Danish and the British on poor relief. In each country unemployment was met by the kind of relief that offered the best deal in the respective welfare system. In the Netherlands, a parliamentary committee concluded that the social partners had used the disability pensions improperly. Consequently, new principles for the administration of social insurances were laid down by law in 1995. The implementation of social security and monitoring the system were separated. Workers' and employers' organizations were kept at a distance. In 2005 the WAO was replaced by a more restrictive system which paid benefits to disabled workers depending on their "earning capacity," the degree to which they were able to work (*Wet Werk en Inkomen naar Arbeidsvermogen*, WIA).

Recurring economic crises and the desire to bring down the volume of welfare entitlements led to similar changes elsewhere. Poor relief payments were cut back and municipalities were made responsible for deciding whether, out of their budget, individual welfare recipients were eligible for additional payments. Businesses were made to pay sickness benefit partly out of their own pockets, so as to stimulate them to check whether they could encourage their employees to return to their jobs. Health care insurance was revamped to stimulate competition between insurance companies, which at the same time were obliged to offer all Dutch citizens a basic insurance package at an affordable rate. Individual citizens were given the option to shoulder more risk themselves, against a lower premium.

In fact, the ongoing restructuring of the welfare state invariably revolves around a small set of undesirable outcomes that are to be avoided. It may be cost-effective to offer insurance on a commercial basis, but if the insurance companies turn away the "bad risks" social insurance will become even more unaffordable to those who need it most. Systems run by a state bureaucracy may lead to too much red tape, which makes them more expensive. If the system is run by the people who are most directly involved, they may use it in a way that is comfortable to their constituency, but costly to the economy as a whole. So far the solution is that all parties will continue to have some role, so as to create checks and balances.

The immediate outcome of the restructuring of the Dutch welfare state seems to be positive. Low wage demands from the trade unions after 1982 restored the position of the Netherlands on international markets. With this economic tail wind, employment soared and the share of people on relief fell correspondingly. In 1982 the Dutch were near the top of European nations in spending on social security, and in the percentage of people on relief. By 1998 the Netherlands had descended to the European average. There were a few drawbacks as well. As welfare payments failed to keep up with inflation, the gap between rich and poor – which had grown smaller for decades – started to grow again. The Dutch complained about appalling conditions in old people's homes and dirty toilets in schools. But on the whole, the system held well.

Long-Term Dilemmas

Although the Dutch welfare state seems to be doing well at the moment, there are other problems looming ahead. The openness of Dutch society and economy to European measures and to economic globalization are potential threats to the system. A particular problem is ageing: the percentage of the population over 65 will increase, as women give birth later, fewer children are born and people live longer. Today, for every person of 65 and older the Dutch population counts about four people in the age bracket 20-64, who must earn an income and pay for the AOW of the elderly, or take care of the pensioner's health and other needs. Around 2060 there will be only two left to work and pay for every pensioner.

But long before that date, the Dutch welfare system will be subjected to another severe test. The economic crisis in the early twenty-first century made the long-term sustainability of the system an even more pressing concern and presented the Dutch welfare state with what may well become its largest challenge ever. In fact, with its historical roots in the crisis of the 1930s, this is exactly what the system was designed for. The crisis also showed that, although a welfare state is a way to cope with the uncertainties of the future, that future is never wholly predictable. A few years ago an ageing population seemed the largest risk for the welfare state, but in the shorter term, the fact that the Dutch population is getting older results in far fewer fresh young arrivals on the labor market than in the 1930s, thus easing the strain of unemployment. Hence, the only thing one can really be certain of is that the Dutch welfare state will remain for some time a welcome surprise to visitors like Russell Shorto.

Further Reading

Gier, Erik de, Abram de Swaan and Machteld Ooijens, eds. *Dutch Welfare Reform in an Expanding Europe: The Neighbors' View*. Amsterdam: Spinhuis, 2005.

Mooij, Ruud de. *Reinventing the Welfare State*. The Hague: CPB Netherlands Bureau for Economic Policy Analysis, 2006.

Swaan, Abram de. *In Care of the State: Health Care, Education and Welfare in Europe and the USA in the Modern Era*. New York: Oxford University Press, 1988.

Visser, Jelle and Anton Hemerijck. "*A Dutch Miracle*": *Job Growth, Welfare Reform and Corporatism in the Netherlands*. Amsterdam: Amsterdam University Press, 1997.

Chapter 4

Randstad Holland

Ben de Pater & Rob van der Vaart

Some forty percent of the Dutch population and almost fifty percent of the jobs are concentrated in an area that is about twenty percent of the national land surface: the urbanized ring connecting the four largest cities of Amsterdam, The Hague, Rotterdam, and Utrecht, located in the three provinces North Holland, South Holland and Utrecht. Without any doubt "Randstad Holland" (literally: "Rim City" or "City on the Edge"), as this area is called, is the country's core region.[1] The image of this area as the center is reinforced by the common international practice to use "Holland," the name of the largest two provinces in the *Randstad*, as an equivalent for the Netherlands.

The economic, political and cultural dominance that this part of the Netherlands has exerted for more than four centuries has manifested itself in a variety of domains. The standardized language that is now spoken in the Netherlands originated in Holland and gradually became the official language over the last two hundred years. This powerful *Randstad*, which not only dominates the Netherlands but is also one of the largest conurbations in Europe, justifies special attention in this chapter.

Urban Demography

A topographical map of the Netherlands from around 1900 presents an empty and scarcely populated country where only about five million inhabitants lived. The map shows vast stretches of uncultivated land, innumerable and generally tiny fields and meadows, many unpaved roads, here and there a railway or a canal, and many small villages. Cities are compact and relatively far apart, mostly of the same size they had two hundred years earlier.

Around 1900 the *Randstad* as we know it today was in fact non-existent. The cities of Holland had been the largest cities of the country since the Golden Age, but they were modest in size and wide apart. Only Amsterdam was an exception: with about half a million inhabitants in 1900, it was much bigger than the numbers two, three and four on the ranking list: Rotterdam, The Hague, and Utrecht. Table 1 shows that the top-four has not changed in order since then, although Amsterdam is not as far ahead as it once was. Rotterdam has benefited from its excellent water-connections with the fast-industrializing Ruhr region in Germany and has become a globally important harbor. With the seat of the government, The Hague also grew quickly, due to the rapidly growing number of civil servants in a modernizing and expanding state system. Many retiring people, returned from colonial service, chose to live in The Hague as well. Utrecht benefited from its central location and its improving connections in all directions by water, road and rail. As important

Table 1: The ten largest cities of the Netherlands in terms of population (x 100,000): 1795, 1899, 2000

Ranking 1795	Inhabitants 1795	Ranking 1899	Inhabitants 1899	Ranking 2000	Inhabitants 2000
1. Amsterdam	221	1. Amsterdam	511	1. Amsterdam	1003
2. Rotterdam	57	2. Rotterdam	320	2. Rotterdam	990
3. The Hague	38	3. The Hague	206	3. The Hague	610
4. Leiden	31	4. Utrecht	102	4. Utrecht	366
5. Utrecht	31	5. Groningen	67	5. Eindhoven	302
6. Groningen	23	6. Haarlem	64	6. Leiden	250
7. Haarlem	21	7. Arnhem	57	7. Dordrecht	241
8. Dordrecht	18	8. Leiden	54	8. Heerlen	218
9. Maastricht	18	9. Nijmegen	43	9. Tilburg	215
10. Delft	14	10. Tilburg	41	10. Groningen	192

Data: Central Bureau of Statistics. Municipal data for 1795 and 1899; urban agglomeration data for 2000 – agglomerations are defined as central city plus adjacent urbanized municipalities.

location factors for many factories, offices and institutions, Utrecht, too, experienced considerable population growth after 1900.

Amsterdam may have remained the largest Dutch city, but in a European context it has clearly lost position. Still the fourth largest European city in 1750 (after London, Paris and Naples), it slid to a sixteenth position in 1850 and even a twenty-fifth position in 1950.[2]

In 1900 the population density of the cities of Holland was very high. Inconveniences such as noise and air pollution were an accepted fact of urban life, particularly during the summer. As a result, the wealthier urban classes started to move to villages in the surrounding countryside, where more spacious dwellings were constructed in a green and pleasant environment. These migrants were in fact the first commuters: wealthy people from Amsterdam, for example, living in villa villages in the forest area of "Het Gooi" (southeast of Amsterdam) and using the train or streetcar to get to their work in Amsterdam. Initially, these urban classes used their suburban

The Amsterdam Canal Ring: Urban Heritage of the Golden Age

The semi-circular canals Herengracht, Keizersgracht and Prinsen-gracht, in the center of today's Amsterdam, are easily recognizable on the city map. This canal ring is a fine example of seventeenth century Dutch urban design. In 2008, the government nominated the canal ring for the UNESCO-World Heritage status as "an international icon of urban architecture." The canal ring is part of the city's response to the need for urban expansion and development, during a phase of massive immigration, housing shortages and lack of urban space.

Already at the end of the sixteenth century, the urban govern-ment hesitantly took its first steps towards urban expansion. But large-scale development only started in 1613, following a master plan that had been designed by the town carpenter, Hendrick Jacobszoon Staets, and approved by all layers of government: urban, regional, Republic. The master plan took all conceivable aspects into account: dispossession and repossession of land, expansion of the urban defenses, financing, a geographical separation of functions in the newly developed urban zones and aesthetic principles of design.

The above-mentioned canals – in fact their western sections up to the current Leidsegracht – were part of the plan and designed as a residential zone for the well-to-do. Port expansion, on three rect-angular islands to the west, and a new popular housing and artisan district (Jordaan) were other elements of the master plan. All these elements were realized, but within forty years it became evident that further expansion was needed.

Between 1656 and 1662, a further extension of the canal ring towards the east took place, among the same circular lines, to the other side of the river Amstel. It was in this zone that some of the most grandiose canal houses were built. The so-called "Golden Bend" of one of the canals, Herengracht, is probably the best example of the wealth that had been accumulating in the city during the Golden Age of Dutch hegemony in colonial trade. Large houses, in fact urban palaces, line up along this section of Herengracht, built by rich merchants, bankers, patricians, and other wealthy inhabitants. However, during this new phase of urban development it became evident that Holland's trade hegemony was in decline. Economic development slowed down and some of the new urban spaces remained underdeveloped until well into the nineteenth century.

The canal ring today not only demonstrates the urban wealth of the seventeenth century. Since the "grachtengordel" has also become a desirable residential area for Dutch celebrities from the world of art and politics, it is among the Dutch public sometimes known as a symbol of intellectual pretentiousness. However, to the observer, it first and foremost exemplifies typical Dutch urbanism – the omnipresence of water, relatively small-scale development, and the sight of bicycles everywhere.

---

homes only during the summer, but gradually it became more common to live in the countryside throughout the year. Such suburbanization is a phenomenon that gained enormous dimensions during the twentieth century.

The cities of Holland not only expanded, but urban density decreased simultaneously. The use of space gradually became less intensive. In 1850 the nine largest cities of what we now call the *Randstad* had an average population density of 21,600 inhabitants per square kilometer.[3] By 1940 the average density had declined to 11,800 inhabitants per square kilometer, and the figure continued to go down to 7,100 in 1970 and 4,600 in the year 2000. The built-up surface of these nine cities multiplied by a factor twenty-two between 1850 and 2000, whereas the population of these cities only grew by a factor 4.6. Today the urban density of the cities of Holland is still very high in comparison with, for example, the urban zones in the southwest of the United States. But Holland's urban population density in around 1850 was at the same level as in many cities of China today, or cities of what is still often called the "third world."

The long-term population growth of the three provinces in which the *Randstad* is located (North Holland, South Holland, and Utrecht) shows the combined effect of urbanization and suburbanization. These provinces had 1.2 million inhabitants in 1850 (or thirty-nine percent of the national population) and seven million inhabitants in 2000 (forty-four percent of the national population) – an increase of almost a factor six over one and a half century.[4]

This is the result of a concentration process in the distribution of the national population, with the *Randstad* gaining population and other parts of the country losing inhabitants in relative terms. The regions commonly called "the North," (provinces of Groningen, Friesland, and Drenthe, see the map on page 9) and "the Southwest" (province of Zeeland) lost position throughout this period. They jointly housed twenty-two percent of the Dutch population in 1850 (0.7 million people) and only thirteen percent of the population in the year 2000 (two million inhabitants). More than before, these regions are now the periphery of the Netherlands, with population densities that are relatively low by Dutch standards (approximately two hundred inhabitants per square kilometer), an ageing population, few employment opportunities, and a surplus of out-migration. Until the late 1950s, mainly unemployed farm laborers moved from the periphery to the West; nowadays, many well-educated young people move to the *Randstad* area where most knowledge-intensive economic activities are located. In reaction to this concentration trend, the provinces of the North and Southwest try to create counter-images to the hectic, expensive and overcrowded *Randstad* and present themselves as places of leisure and open space, thus trying to attract new inhabitants.

It should be remarked here that extensive and languishing peripheries do not exist in the Netherlands. In terms of scale and intensity of periphery problems, no Dutch region compares to places such as the Scottish Highlands, the north of Scandinavia, inland Spain, Southern Italy or many Eastern European regions.

The two other parts of the country, "the South" (provinces of North-Brabant and Limburg) and "the East" (provinces of Gelderland, Overijssel, and Flevoland), have maintained their relative position quite well. Together, they housed thirty-nine percent of the national population in 1850 and forty-three percent in the year 2000. During the late nineteenth and particularly the early twentieth century, it was mainly the process of industrialization that explains the relative demographic vitality of these regions. Many textile factories, attracted by the relatively low wages, were located in the cities of the East (in Twente) and the South (Tilburg, Helmond). The city of Eindhoven experienced rapid population growth thanks to the employment provided by the electronics company Philips. The coal mines in the south of Limburg caused Heerlen to develop into a genuine coal city. The new industrial cities of the East and South attracted many migrants from the surrounding countryside as well as from other parts of the country. During the 1920s, for example, the lamp or radio factories of Philips attracted hundreds of families from the northern province of Drenthe. Miners from surrounding countries came to the newly established coal mines of southern Limburg. International labor migration to the industrial centers became more common in the 1960s, as was the case in all Western European countries, with the influx of so-called "guest workers," originally from countries such as Spain and Italy and later from Turkey and Morocco.

Nowadays it is no longer industrialization that explains population growth in the east and south of the country. Substantial parts of these regions are now within the sphere of influence of the expanding *Randstad*. Families as well as companies move away from the expensive and crowded *Randstad* area, and try to escape from its traffic jams and lack of space. By settling down in adjacent regions of North Brabant, Gelderland, or Flevoland, these families and businesses may still enjoy the benefits of relative proximity to metropolitan facilities and services, while escaping from the disadvantages of agglomeration. As a result, the *Randstad* is expanding towards the south and east, mainly along the motorway corridors with new industrial estates and business parks. This trend is visible along all main transportation axes: south of Rotterdam towards Breda, east and southeast of Utrecht towards Arnhem and Den Bosch, or northeast of Amersfoort in the direction of Zwolle. Increasingly, these motorways are flanked by businesses with a "sight location:" visible from the motorway and easily accessible by car rather than by public transportation.

Already during the 1980s, regional planners invented the term "Central Netherlands Urban Ring" as a proxy for the expanding *Randstad*. It is easy to identify this urban "ring" on a map: if we start in the east (Arnhem and Nijmegen) and proceed counter-clockwise, we see an oval of cities: Utrecht, Amsterdam, Haarlem, Leiden, The Hague, Rotterdam, Dordrecht, Breda, Eindhoven, and back to our starting point. The concept of a Central Netherlands Urban Ring has fallen into disuse, but the U-shaped and prolonged urban zone of the Netherlands has become more of a reality.

Suburbanization and urban expansion were not the only reason for the declining urban densities in the west. Falling birth rates contributed as well: the average number of persons per household and per house decreased dramatically. But the decline of densities and the expansion of urban space were accompanied by another important process: the geographical separation of functions. Around 1900 a spatial mix of housing and work was still the norm, with wealthy commuters as the only exception. Although the larger cities had streetcars and more and more people could afford a bicycle, the vast majority of the urban population walked to the workplace. For many urban dwellers workplace and home were the same: artisans usually lived behind their workshops; maids and servants, still numerous in those days, slept in modest rooms in the attic of the house of their employers.

But gradually society became more mobile, which facilitated the geographical separation of functions. Factories, causing inconveniences such as noise and air pollution, moved to industrial zones at the city borders. In many new housing areas the only non-residential functions allowed were retail functions. Separation of housing, work and leisure became the creed of urban and regional planners, a professional group of civil servants that gained considerable power over urban development. Motorways, public transportation, and bicycle lanes connected the geographically separated new housing zones, employment areas, and leisure zones. Distances from home to work increased. The number of commuters grew spectacularly. In 1928, only five percent of the working population was commuting. In 1947 it was fifteen percent, in 1971 thirty-seven percent. In 1986 over half the national working population (fifty-two percent) was commuting and since then the figure has gone up even more.

Urban expansion and declining urban density, a separation of functions, and increased geographical mobility: the figures are quite revealing. In 1900, a Dutch citizen traveled about 1,000 kilometers per year on average, mainly on foot. Nowadays, a citizen covers 12,000 kilometers, mainly by car. The modern map of the *Randstad* reflects this rise in mobility – a striking contrast to the situation around 1900 (see the map on page 69).

The Port of Rotterdam:
A Logistical Hub of Europe

The port of Rotterdam, one of the largest in the world, is a major gateway to Europe for global trade and the most important window to the world for European exporters. It is accessible for the largest tankers and cargo ships, and within one-days travel distance it includes a consumer market of about one hundred million people. The port zone stretches out over some forty kilometers, from its oldest parts in the heart of Rotterdam to its newest zones that were reclaimed from the sea.

During the phase of Dutch global trade hegemony in the late sixteenth and first half of the seventeenth century, Rotterdam was not at all an important colonial port. It only had a modest share in colonial trade. Investors and entrepreneurs were concentrated in Amsterdam, clearly favored for colonial port development. This was partly caused by the fact that the accessibility of the Rotterdam port from the sea was problematic.

The history of Rotterdam and its port goes back to around the year 1250. In those days, a dam was constructed in the estuary of the small river Rotte, in order to avoid salinization of the river. A small settlement developed, where goods were loaded manually from coastal ships to riverboats and vice versa. Later on, the settlement also increased its role as a fishery port.

The port of Rotterdam as we know it today goes back to the second half of the nineteenth century. The German Ruhr region began to develop as a mining area and an industrial region. Rotterdam, well connected to the Ruhr region by the river Rhine, was the natural harbor for Germany's imports and exports. Access to open sea was greatly improved by the "New Waterway" (*Nieuwe Waterweg*), a canal cutting through the dunes at Hook of Holland (*Hoek van Holland*) designed by hydraulic engineer Pieter Caland. The combination of demand and accessibility gave an enormous boost to the port.

The harbor zone was severely damaged during the Second World War; the rebuilding of it was a top priority during the post-war reconstruction years. Activity boomed because of European integration, economic growth during the 1960s, and later on of course economic globalization. From a Dutch perspective, Rotterdam is now one of the two international hubs (together with Schiphol Airport) that are crucial for the open national economy.

The neoliberal and highly competitive phase of globalization, that set in during the 1980s, not only created opportunities for the port of Rotterdam, but also many threats. Competition between ports is fierce, also within the Le Havre (France)-Hamburg (Germany) range in northwestern Europe. In order to remain competitive, ports need excellent and diverse hinterland connections – by rail, road, pipeline, and water. For this reason the Dutch state has invested heavily in the new *Betuweroute*, a freight railway connecting Rotterdam with Germany. It remains to be seen to what extent this railway, heavily contested during the construction phase by action groups, environmentalists, planners and others, will give the port a competitive edge in the future.

Territorial Planning: Between Vision and Reality

The *Randstad* was born during the twentieth century when a handful of distinct cities was transformed into a more coherent network of agglomerations, which were connected by flows of commuters, goods, and shoppers. This urban conglomerate folds around an open zone of farmland, lakes, streams and ditches, which became known as the "Green Heart" in the 1970s. In the 1950s, the concept *Randstad* was already commonplace among planners, and gradually, during the 1960s, the term became part of Dutch vocabulary. It was the British geographer and planner Peter Hall who introduced the concept "*Randstad* Holland" to the international academic and professional community of planners. His famous book *The World Cities* (1966) includes chapters about London, Paris, Moscow, New York, Tokyo, the Ruhr urban region, and also – much to the pleasure of the Dutch – about *Randstad* Holland. He praised its unique poly-centric character: he predicted (wrongly) that the typical problems of mono-centric world cities such as traffic jams would not be as intense in the poly-centric *Randstad* with its separation of functions: banks and culture in Amsterdam, national government and international governance in The Hague, harbor and wholesale functions in Rotterdam. He warned against the usurpation of the green central space by urban expansion – otherwise the *Randstad* might lose its unique character and become "another formless urban sprawl," just like so many already existing around the world.

It was certainly not the intention of the national planners to give up the Green Heart; in fact, it was their opinion that this central green space should remain as open as possible. In his book, Peter Hall complimented Dutch planners and politicians for this policy intention – he felt that foreign colleagues had a lot to learn from Dutch metropolitan planning. However, in practice it proved to be extremely difficult to maintain the Green Heart as an open space. In matters where the government had a final say, the ideal of the Green Heart indeed often had priority. One example is the decision in 1996 to construct a tunnel for the high-speed train from Amsterdam Airport Schiphol to Rotterdam, Brussels, and Paris, seven kilometers in length under one of the most beautiful parts of the Green Heart, in spite of the considerable extra costs.

But at the provincial level and particularly the municipal level, many decision makers saw no harm in, for example, residential development in the Green Heart. Constructing new neighborhoods improved their financial position, an increasing population was considered vital for local shops and other services, and a lack of new dwellings could force young couples to leave. Furthermore, since detached or semi-detached houses with a garden and a parking lot are very difficult to find in the urban areas, the demand for houses in the nearby Green Heart was huge. Businesses were more than willing to settle there as well, given its proximity to all major cities and Amsterdam Airport Schiphol. Thus, in spite of national spatial policy goals, numerous housing estates, office blocks, and industrial zones, with accompanying infrastructure, arose in the Green Heart. A good example is Hoofddorp in the Haarlemmermeer polder: until the 1960s just a small village close to Amsterdam Airport Schiphol, but today a suburb of almost American proportions.

The only policy area almost completely controlled by the government was the social housing sector. Since the construction of major new development zones was primarily financed from the national budget, national planners could enforce choices in line with national spatial policy goals, such as sparing the Green Heart. During the 1960s, 1970s and 1980s, large-scale subsidized residential development zones were therefore "bundled" in so-called "growth-nodes" on the outer ring of the *Randstad*, mostly within twenty to thirty kilometers from the cities. This resulted in major migration flows from the cities to the newly available residential areas, for example from Amsterdam to the north (Purmerend, Alkmaar, Hoorn) and northeast (Almere, Lelystad). Unfortunately, most *Randstad* companies and businesses were not inclined to move in the same direction. As discussed above, they preferred relocation to the centrally located Green Heart or to the borders of the big cities. As a result, many commuters routinely drive every workday by car from, for example, Purmerend to Amsterdam Airport Schiphol, thus contributing to the traffic jams that have become a structural and daily phenomenon – even in the "poly-centric" *Randstad*.

This policy of bundling large-scale housing in "growth-nodes" has now become planning history. Since the 1990s, large-scale housing developments are no longer planned in municipalities perhaps fifteen to twenty kilometers away, but in locations directly adjacent to cities. These new neighborhoods are known by the acronym VINEX, after the governmental memorandum that instituted them.[5] But not only the location of large-scale new housing has changed over the decades, even more important is the erosion of regulating the power of the state. In line with trends such as privatization, deregulation and more generally a stronger reliance on "the market," the government has willingly reduced its role in the (social) housing sector and consequently also lost a great deal of its power over location decisions. The largest VINEX neighborhood now under construction is called Leidsche Rijn, directly west of Utrecht. Many of its inhabitants work in Utrecht, or elsewhere in the *Randstad* area. With many of them commuting by car, they contribute to the congestion problems that characterize the complex urban space of the *Randstad*.

Since many immigrants moved into the urban dwellings that were vacated by the new suburbanites, large cities in the *Randstad* have become the focal points of the new multicultural society, with all its inherent attractive and problematic aspects. While the total number of "non-Western" immigrants in the Netherlands is about 1.8 million (one million first generation immigrants and 0.8 million second generation immigrants) or about eleven percent of the national population, they make up thirty-five percent of the population of the four big cities of the *Randstad*, even forming the majority in some neighborhoods.[6] These "concentration neighborhoods" are mainly urban areas constructed between 1870 and 1970 for either working classes or lower middle classes. Local governments, believing that geographical clustering of non-Western migrant groups hinders their integration into Dutch society, try to fight spatial segregation and to stimulate the development of mixed neighborhoods, ethnically as well as socio-economically. It is questionable, however, whether clustering and segregation are indeed a handicap to integration, since there is little empirical evidence of the relationship between geographical and social segregation.[7]

Between Unity and Fragmentation

Born almost accidentally as an idea at some point during the twentieth century, the *Randstad* urban area is clearly not a historically well-established region – a vernacular region or imagined community – that its inhabitants can easily identify with, as in the case of traditional regions such as for example Twente (in the east) or Brabant (in the south). People living in the

Randstad area may feel attachment to their city, as an inhabitant of Amsterdam, Rotterdam, or Utrecht. But there is no *Randstad* identification. A newspaper called *"Randstad Today"* does not exist, nor a soccer club named FC Randstad, since newspapers or sports clubs are linked to the individual cities and serve as instruments for local identification. In some cases, social identification is at an even lower level of scale: people may identify themselves as an inhabitant of Amsterdam-North or Rotterdam-South.

Identification with a home city or local region always implies the opposition to any other city or region: there can be no "us" without a "them." A good example of this can be found in a study among key actors in the Rotterdam art sector.[8] These art sector professionals could only talk about their city by contrasting it to Amsterdam. In their eyes, Amsterdam is a smug, provincial, navel-gazing city where people talk endlessly and do not work. Rotterdam is the city of doers, of rolled-up sleeves – "no words but deeds," as the well-known club song of soccer club Feyenoord has it. The cultural elite of Rotterdam interviewed apparently does not shy away from any cliché or stereotype.

The idea of a *Randstad* clearly does exist in the minds of people in other parts of the country, who use it as a "them" against whom to construct their own identity. The idea of a *Randstad* does exist in Brabant or Limburg, for example, where the *Randstad* is used for the "other," a bastion of the cold and businesslike "Hollanders." For many people in the rest of the country, *Randstad* is the area that is consistently favored by the political insiders in The Hague. This view seemed to be confirmed when a newspaper analyzed the hundreds of widely publicized field trips the ministers of the new government in 2007 made to get a good notion of what was going on in Dutch society. The newspaper showed that seventy percent of these working visits took place in the *Randstad* region; hardly any ministers visited the North, Zeeland, or Limburg as regional politicians from these "peripheries" angrily pointed out.

True enough, since the 1980s the national government has mainly supported the economically strong regions of the country to stimulate international economic competition. Traditional regional policy, based on the principle of solidarity, has largely been taken over by the European Union. "The Hague" now mainly invests in the *Randstad* region in order to maintain its competitive position against metropolitan centers such as London, Paris, the Flemish cities, the Ruhr region, and Frankfurt.

If the *Randstad* is hardly a unity to its own inhabitants, available research also undermines the idea that it is one powerful and real network city. Some experts continue to believe that the *Randstad* is a unity; polycentric, but nevertheless one functional whole and therefore comparable to mono-centric world cities. Others stress the co-existence of two distinct and functionally quite separated urban zones: a north wing (Utrecht-Amsterdam-Haarlem) and a south wing (Dordrecht-Rotterdam-The Hague-Leiden). A few go even further, and perceive the *Randstad* as a rather loose collection of urban areas without much geographical coherence, citing a governmental study with the telling title "Many Cities Do Not Make a Randstad" that shows that only twenty percent of *Randstad* inhabitants commute between distinct urban agglomerations.

There is also considerable political debate about the most desirable governance structure for the *Randstad* region since the governance density of the *Randstad* region is enormous, according to many even stifling. In January 2007 a blue-ribbon committee suggested to create one regional government for the *Randstad* as a whole, so that it could regain its position as a leading European urban region. Although this advice was not realized, local and regional governments created their own plans for future governance. The provinces of North Holland and Flevoland, together with the cities of Amsterdam, Haarlem, and Almere, proposed to cooperate in the "Amsterdam Metropolitan Area," which would create an attractive, competitive and eco-logically sustainable metropolis of two million inhabitants by the year 2040. Meanwhile, the national government has decided on its own course "for an integral development of the *Randstad* towards a sustainable and competitive top European region in 2040" with the construction of half a million houses over the next thirty years – forty percent of which should be realized in the existing cities – and a "Green-Blue Delta," linked to the IJsselmeer, the North Sea, and to the waters of Zeeland in the south-east, as a region where surplus water can be safely collected and controlled: the *Randstad* is to become climate-change proof.

But history teaches us that ideals are larger than plans, and these plans again are much larger than available financial resources. Inevitably, the real development of the *Randstad*, partially influenced by the private sector and by regional and local authorities, will be quite different from the govern-mental intentions. A captain may be lacking on the ship, but the *Randstad* has lots of helmsmen and helmswomen.

Further Reading

Dieleman, F.M. and S. Musterd, eds. *The Randstad: A Research and Policy Laboratory*. Dordrecht: Kluwer, 1992.

Hall, Peter. *The World Cities*. Third edition. London: Weidenfeld & Nicholson, 1984.

Kranenburg, Ronald H. *Compact Geography of the Netherlands*. Utrecht: Royal Dutch Geographical Society, 2001.

Territorial Review: Randstad Holland, Netherlands. Paris: Organization for Economic Co-operation and Development, 2007.

The *Randstad* in 2000

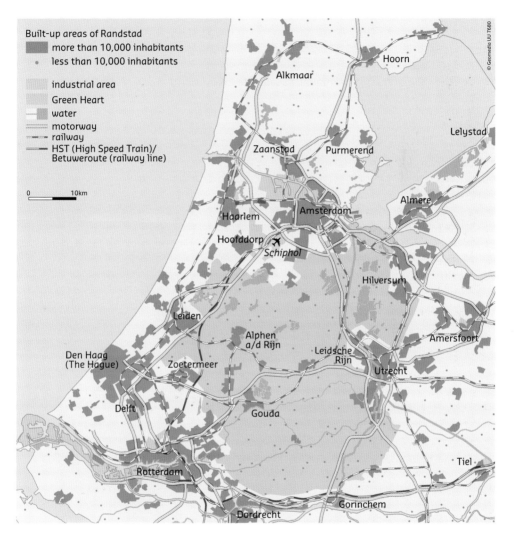

Built-up areas of Randstad
- more than 10,000 inhabitants
- less than 10,000 inhabitants

industrial area
Green Heart
water
motorway
railway
HST (High Speed Train)/
Betuweroute (railway line)

0   10km

© Geomedia UU 7680

Hoorn
Alkmaar
Lelystad
Zaanstad   Purmerend
Almere
Haarlem   Amsterdam
Hoofddorp   ✈
Schiphol
Hilversum
Leiden
Alphen a/d Rijn
Amersfoort
Leidsche Rijn
Den Haag (The Hague)   Zoetermeer
Utrecht
Delft
Gouda
Tiel
Rotterdam
Gorinchem
Dordrecht

GeoMedia, Faculty of Geosciences, Utrecht University

Chapter 5

Idealism and Self-Interest in World Politics

Duco Hellema

Although the glorious days of the Republic of the United Seven Provinces and the Dutch colonial empire are long gone, the Netherlands is still a power of some significance. After a painful process of decolonization and adaptation to the post-war realities, the Netherlands has become a prosperous Northwest-European country that is an active member of the European Union and the North Atlantic Treaty Organization (NATO). In the 1960s and 1970s, it even gained a reputation as a liberal, progressive, and tolerant society, an idealist supporter of the United Nations and a generous donor of development aid. In recent years, however, a certain unease and insecurity over the position and identity of the Netherlands has crept into the minds of the Dutch political elites, which also affects decision making in the field of foreign relations.

The Atlantic Alliance

Before the Second World War the Netherlands was a conservative colonial power, a small country with huge colonial possessions that had tried – against all odds – to pursue an independent policy of neutrality and free trade. Nevertheless, in May 1940 the Netherlands had been overrun by German troops. Almost two years later Japan occupied the Dutch East Indies, which meant the end of three hundred years of Dutch colonial rule. Directly after the war the colony proclaimed its independence as Indonesia. In spite of a considerable military effort, the Dutch were unable to turn the tide. In 1949 the Netherlands had to accept the independence of Indonesia and the fact that it was now merely a smaller Northwest-European state.

Although many Dutch politicians resented the fact that the United States had opposed them during the conflicts over Indonesia, the Netherlands enthusiastically joined the Americans in the NATO alliance in 1949. The Netherlands soon built up a reputation as a loyal ally of the United States and a trustworthy member of the Treaty Organization. This reputation was in many ways well deserved. Successive Dutch governments assumed that Dutch interests were best served by a solid military alliance that linked the United States to Western Europe. They considered the Atlantic alliance as vitally important, not only as a counterweight against Soviet expansionism but also against possible hegemonial aspirations of the European great powers. Moreover, the Americans had taken the lead in liberalizing Western Europe's economies and trading relations, and had been prepared to support Western Europe's recovery with economic and military means. The Hague therefore welcomed and appreciated American leadership and Atlantic unity.

This is not to say that there were no differences of opinion and conflicts between Washington and The Hague. On the contrary, for a country that was supposed to play the role of an exemplary loyal ally of the United States, a remarkable number of political confrontations took place during the 1950s. Most of these conflicts had to do with the former colonies and the relationship between the West and the non-Western world. In 1949, the decolonization of Indonesia had not included West New Guinea. The Netherlands stubbornly tried to defend this last bulwark of Dutch sovereignty in the Far East, which led to a serious and embittered conflict with Indonesia. In spite of all Dutch efforts, the United States forced the Netherlands to accept that West New Guinea became a part of Indonesia in 1963. The Netherlands, and especially its long-time minister of Foreign Affairs Joseph Luns, was highly critical of the American refusal to support the West-European states in their post-colonial conflicts with some of their former colonies. This resentment sometimes undermined Atlantic loyalty. When The Hague learned in May 1958 that the United States was supplying arms to Indonesia, it was even suggested that the Netherlands should leave NATO.

Regarding conflicts about the future of NATO, or about the position of the West-European member states, the Netherlands continued to advocate a solid and American-led Atlantic alliance. During the years of the Vietnam War, minister of Foreign Affairs Luns refused to openly criticize the American war effort. Atlantic unity remained the cornerstone of Dutch foreign policy during the "radical years" of student protest and anti-American demonstrations and during the social-democratic oriented government of Joop den Uyl in the mid-1970s. This Atlantic loyalty seemed to weaken towards the end of the 1970s as a result of the massive opposition to the NATO decision to deploy new middle range cruise missiles in Western Europe, forty-eight of them in the Netherlands. It brought the center-right Van Agt government and its successors in the early 1980s in great difficulties, not in the least because the Christian Democratic Party (CDA), the major coalition partner, was divided on this issue. The successive Dutch governments in those years were caught between pressure of the NATO allies on the one hand and the strong public and parliamentary opposition on the other. In 1984, the center-right government led by the pragmatic Christian-Democratic politician Ruud Lubbers decided to pursue deployment of the cruise missiles in spite of massive opposition. The coalition of the conservative-liberal VVD and the Christian-Democratic CDA now managed to close the ranks and supported its government, which meant the end of a delicate phase in the history of post-war American-Dutch relations.

Throughout the Cold War the Netherlands tried to behave as a loyal, Atlantic ally of the United States, in spite of all the colonial conflicts and misunderstandings. Nonetheless, Robert Kagan's reproachful observation that life was easy for the West-European countries, as they were being protected by American military power and firmness, is also valid for the Netherlands. Although the Netherlands duly contributed to the allied defense effort and the Dutch armed forces did not come off badly compared to other member states, the Dutch were, in fact, sheltered from the major conflicts in world politics. The Netherlands played its part within the allied military structure in Northwest-Europe, but its military capacities were never really tried. And as East-West relations became more stable during the 1960s, the chances that the Dutch army would be put to the test decreased even more. These circumstances meant that the pre-war Dutch policy of aloofness and neutrality was continued in certain respects, be it under completely different circumstances.

This passivity changed after the end of the Cold War. More so than during most of the Cold War period, the Netherlands not only supported the United States politically but became militarily active too. This is remarkable, because the Soviet threat – the widely accepted explanation for Dutch Atlantic loyalty – has lost most of its relevance. Nonetheless, the Dutch government put aside its traditional military reluctance. At the beginning of the twenty-first century, Dutch governments and Defense ministers, supported the American "War on Terror," that was unleashed after the terrorist attacks of September 2001, and they were prepared to fight, shoulder to shoulder with the American and NATO allies, although it was not always obvious which Dutch interests or humanitarian ideals were at stake.

Hollanditis: The Politics of Pacifism

In December 1979 NATO decided to introduce new Pershing and cruise missiles in Western Europe to counter the ongoing deployment of the Soviet SS-20 intermediate-range missiles. NATO's decision marked the beginning of the so-called Second Cold War. In the Netherlands, the issue became particularly volatile politically because the center-right coalition government of Christian-Democrat Dries van Agt had granted NATO permission to deploy forty-eight cruise missiles on Dutch soil, but lacked the parliamentary majority to enforce it, as members of his own party (CDA) leaned towards the opposing social-democrats' position.

The deployment of the cruise missiles was to become the most contested security issue in Dutch history. Stimulated by the impotence of the Van Agt government, a broad opposition movement was able to put great pressure upon parliament and government. In November 1981 some four hundred thousand people demonstrated in Amsterdam against the new nuclear weapons; in October 1983 probably more than half a million – according to some sources even almost a million – demonstrators took to the streets of The Hague, turning it into the largest demonstration in Dutch history. In addition, in 1985 almost four million people signed a national protest petition against deployment. Given the fifteen million inhabitants of the Netherlands, these were impressive numbers. The political problems in the Netherlands, and the possible consequences of a Dutch refusal, attracted attention from all over the world. According to the American historian Walter Laqueur, a renewed Dutch neutralism – a "disease" he labeled "Hollanditis" – was spreading over Western Europe.

The successive Dutch governments between 1979 and 1985 postponed the final decision-making regarding the new missiles again and again. In June 1984 the center-right government of pragmatic Ruud Lubbers (CDA) finally forced a decision: the Netherlands would start deploying if the Soviet Union continued to deploy SS-20 missiles after November 1985. In the meantime, the influence of the leftist faction within the CDA had been reduced, and the Christian Democrats were able to close ranks and support their prime minister. The Dutch had finally been driven back to the NATO herd.

Emotions ran high between 1979 and 1985. The actions and demonstrations against the cruise missiles had been, above all, a moral outcry against the new American-Soviet nuclear arms race. Specific political circumstances, such as the divisions within the CDA, played an important role as well. But Laqueur's hypothesis of a renewed Dutch, or even European, neutralism, is highly questionable. According to opinion polls, most demonstrators continued to support Dutch NATO membership. The two parties in the Lubbers government that had pushed the cruise missiles ahead, the Christian-Democratic CDA and conservative-liberal VVD, were not punished for their behavior by the Dutch electorate, but even increased their parliamentary majority in the 1986 elections and therefore had no problem to form a second center-right Lubbers government.

In the end, the cruise missiles never arrived in the Netherlands. They were made redundant by the Intermediate-Range Nuclear Forces Treaty that Michael Gorbachev and Ronald Reagan signed in December 1987.

The Netherlands and Europe

As a crucial trading center with limited military resources, the Netherlands has – at least in principle – always favored free trade. In the 1920s and 1930s the Netherlands had pursued the cause of trade liberalization to no avail. During the Second World War, however, the governments-in-exile of the Netherlands, Belgium and Luxembourg had signed the Benelux treaty. After the war the Netherlands – together with the other Benelux countries, West Germany, France and Italy – became one of the founding members of the European communities. They were one of the original member states that founded the European Community for Coal and Steel (ECSC) in 1951, the ill-fated European Defense Community, and, of course, the European Economic Community (EEC) and the European Atomic Energy Community (Euratom) in 1957. The European Communities (ECCS, EEC and Euratom) merged in 1967 to become the European Community, which later in 1992 evolved into the European Union (EU).

As a trading nation and modern export-oriented economy the Netherlands had its own specific perspective on the process of European integration. To support its trading and exporting interests, the Dutch insisted that the EEC (and later the EC) should first of all realize a common market and abolish all trading barriers between the member states. Since the original number of six member states was considered to be too small, they also argued that the EEC should try to attract new members (not in the least the United Kingdom) in order to extend the scope of the common market. The realization of the common market, with all its implications, should be led by the "supranational" and technocratic institution of the EEC/EC, that is to say the European Commission, and controlled by a democratically elected European Parliament. There should be no room for power politics within the European communities, the Dutch propagated, which was a logical stand-point for one of the smaller EC member states. The Dutch, therefore, for a long time opposed the creation of a council of heads of governments, fearing that the heads of government of the European great powers would dominate such a council.

For the same reasons, the Dutch did not want the EEC to evolve into a political and military union. A European political and military union, led by the West-European great powers (France and West Germany) could only threaten the position and interests of the Netherlands. It would split NATO, reduce the influence of the smaller West-European states and could jeop-ardize the results that had been realized in the field of trade liberalization within the EEC. In the early 1960s, these standpoints led to a series of serious conflicts between the Netherlands and the French president Charles de Gaulle, who not only tried to turn the EEC into a political union, led by a council of heads of government, but also aimed to make Western Europe more independent of the United States.

The Dutch advocated a supranational, democratic, and non-military European community. This idealist and federalist view on European integration was, in fact, in some cases put forward in order to defend Dutch sovereignty. The Dutch especially balked when other EC member states moved to extend the scope of integration, starting with provisional, inter-governmental decision-making procedures. The Dutch reacted to such proposals by stating that it should be all (a supranational and democratic arrangement) or nothing (which the Dutch sometimes secretly preferred). Although this view was not without an element of hypocrisy, it also reflected a certain idealism and deliberate aversion to power politics on the Dutch side.

From the 1970s on, however, the Netherlands had to accept changes within the European Community that it had resisted before. The Dutch endorsed European Political Cooperation (EPC) in the field of foreign policy and the creation of the European Council (of heads of government). Step by step the EC developed in a direction the Dutch essentially rejected. In 1991 the Dutch, chairing the EC that year, for the last time tried to impose their supranational and Atlanticist views on the negotiations about the construction of the European Union. The majority did not agree with the Dutch proposals and decided that cooperation in the field of Foreign and Security Affairs (the "second pillar") and Justice and Internal Affairs (the "third pillar") would not be based upon supranational, but on majority-decision-making. In the 1990s the Dutch even went along with decisions to strengthen EU military cooperation (although most of these plans would not, or only partly, be realized). In the meantime, the EU had started to extend: in 1995 the number of member states reached fifteen, in 2004 twenty-three, and in 2007 even twenty-seven. This meant, among other things, that the position and influence of the Netherlands, once one of the proud founding members of the EEC, was in decline.

In the early years of the twenty-first century, the Dutch views on European integration seem to have become more cynical. Most of the original idealism, even if sometimes tainted by hypocrisy, seems to have vanished. The Dutch became more assertive in using their voting leverage within the European Union. They started to complain about the level of Dutch financial obligations and to criticize members of the Eurogroup (the states that had introduced the Euro) for their undisciplined budgetary behavior and their disrespect of the provisions of the financial Stability Pact. The Dutch government even publicly doubted the wisdom of accepting the new Central and East-European member states. Just like the French, in 2005 the Dutch electorate rejected the so-called "European Constitution," although it is not impossible that considerations other than the specific content of this "constitution" played a role in its decision.

Development Cooperation

The first Dutch activities in the field of development aid still had a strong colonialist background. In 1950 a committee within the Ministry of Foreign Affairs concluded, for instance, that Dutch aid activities had to fulfill several objectives: furthering Dutch economic interests and Dutch prestige, regaining influence in Indonesia, and employment for former colonial officials. In the same year Indonesia, in fact, received a loan of 280 million guilders, which was a considerable amount of money for the Netherlands, five years after the end of the devastating German occupation. Apart from the loan to Indonesia, the Netherlands would spend hundreds of millions on development projects in West New Guinea. For the time being, development aid to other non-Western countries remained limited, and consisted mostly of the deployment of experts, initially mostly former colonial civil servants.

In the 1950s, development aid was justified in the context of the Cold War as an important means to counter communist influences in the developing countries. However, at the same time, the issue of development and the necessity to end poverty were increasingly seen as important goals, even a moral duty in itself. From the early 1960s on, and especially after the end of Dutch sovereignty over West New Guinea, the budget for development aid began to rise. In 1965, for the first time, a minister for Development Cooperation was appointed, and a special Directorate-General for International Cooperation within the Ministry of Foreign Affairs was created, responsible for the spending of a growing amount of money. Throughout the 1960s, the Dutch activities in the field of development aid, now called "development cooperation," intensified and diversified. Since the end of the 1960s, the Netherlands, together with the Scandinavian countries, belonged to the four or five most generous aid donors worldwide.

During the Den Uyl government (1973-1977) the radical social-democrat Jan Pronk was minister for Development Cooperation. He advocated a new policy in development cooperation, directed at contributing to structural changes in the world economy (to a "New International Economic Order"). The developing countries should become more independent from the West and should enhance their "self-reliance." Pronk wanted to reduce the influence of Dutch economic interests on development aid. He preferred to provide aid to countries that had introduced socio-economic reforms, including communist states such as Cuba, the reunited Vietnam, and Mozambique. Pronk's approach aroused much controversy in The Hague, but had, in retrospect, only very limited results. Nonetheless, during Pronk's first tenure as minister the budget for development cooperation continued to increase considerably.

Although some of Pronk's decisions, such as aid to Cuba and Vietnam, were soon revoked by his successors, the level of Dutch aid in relation to the Dutch GDP remained high. During the 1980s and 1990s, Dutch development policy was more and more based upon liberal ideas. The days of a new international order and self-reliance were long gone. Doubts about the efficiency of development aid became stronger during the 1990s and at the start of the twenty-first century. The conservative parties began to plead for a drastic reduction of the budget for development cooperation. Although this budget is still high when compared to that of other Western countries and most Dutch citizens (according to opinion polls) still support development cooperation, the idealist zeal seems to be fading.

Idealism and Self-Interest

The constitution of the Netherlands stipulates that Dutch foreign and defense policy should be aimed at strengthening the international legal order. Is this an empty phrase or is Dutch foreign policy indeed driven by idealism and internationalism? One could argue that the Netherlands is indeed an idealist nation. The history of Dutch foreign relations seems to support that. For centuries, the Netherlands was a neutral and liberal power. After the Second World War, the Dutch have tried to further a supranational and democratic European Community and to counter power politics. They are a generous development aid donor and the Netherlands pursues, at least claims to pursue, an active human rights policy. Moreover, The Hague is an important center for international law, host town of, among others, the International Criminal Court and the Yugoslavia Tribunal.

In recent years, the Netherlands is often – more than other small Western countries – willing to contribute to international peace missions. The Dutch governments of the 1990s and the early years of the twenty-first century have deployed troops all over the world. In the 1990s, the Netherlands contributed to UN peace missions in Cambodia, in Bosnia, and in Kosovo. After the United States started a "War on Terror" as a response to the terrorist attacks of September 11, 2001, Dutch troops also participated in the stabilization missions in Iraq and Afghanistan. Although the Srebrenica tragedy of 1995 had a huge political and emotional impact in the Netherlands, the Dutch government continued its humanitarian activism in the following years, be it that the Dutch from then on preferred to participate in missions that were led by the United States or NATO instead of the United Nations.

On the other hand, the Dutch often did not hesitate to defend their own interests, even if this implied disregarding the above mentioned internationalist ideals. Human rights are an interesting example. If the Dutch government had to choose between human rights and economic interests, it often decided in favor of the latter. Within the European Union the Netherlands sometimes vigorously defended specific national or economic positions. Even the recent Dutch humanitarian activism can be explained in terms of opportunism, for instance as a means to please the United States or to strengthen the Dutch position within international organizations such as the UN or NATO. More in general, one could argue that the Netherlands has always been a rich country, home to several huge corporations such as Royal Dutch Shell, Unilever and Philips, and that it was inevitable that Dutch governments would take these vital economic interests into account. Even more social-democratic oriented governments had to live with these realities, as the actions of the Den Uyl government show, when faced with the oil crisis of 1973-1974: in spite of all the rhetoric about reforming the world economy, the Den Uyl government defended the status of the Dutch oil industry.

Dutch foreign policy is probably a mix of self-interest and idealism. As a traditional trading center with huge economic interests, but without a military tradition, the Dutch internationalist and idealist inclinations are understandable. It must be added, however, that these idealist tendencies have been weakening at the start of the twenty-first century. The social and cultural climate in the Netherlands has become harsher at the turn of the century. The rise of Pim Fortuyn's right-wing populist and anti-immigration party "List Pim Fortuyn" (LPF) during the election campaign of 2002 changed the Dutch political atmosphere. The successive coalitions led by Christian-Democrat Balkenende since 2002 have shelved many of the old idealist standpoints, and several politicians concluded that the Netherlands should – more than in the past – defend its own interests, not in the least within the European Union.

Srebrenica: A Catastrophic Peace Mission

All over the world, the massacre of some seven thousand Bosnian-Muslim men by Serb militias in July 1995 at the UN safe area of Srebrenica led to indignation. This widespread anger also affected the Netherlands. Dutch troops had been supposed to defend the safe area, yet had proved unable to prevent the atrocity. In fact, they had even decided not to confront the Serb invaders of the safe area at all. Some critics blamed the Dutch for their passivity. But a thorough and time-consuming historical investigation, conducted by the Dutch Institute for War Documentation (NIOD), concluded in 2002 that defense of the safe area had indeed been impossible. The Dutch troops were not to blame: they had been dispatched on an impossible, ill-conceived, and ill-prepared mission.

At first, the Dutch approach to the Yugoslavian crisis had been even-handed. The Dutch government, and especially Foreign Minister

Van den Broek, believed that the unity of Yugoslavia had to be preserved. When Serbian-led Yugoslavia went to war against the province of Croatia in June 1991 after it had declared independence, this standpoint proved unrealistic. Under German pressure, the Netherlands recognized the independence of Slovenia and Croatia in January 1992. When the UN Security Council established the United Nations Mission Protection Force (UNPROFOR), first to be deployed in Croatia and later also in Bosnia – where a bitter civil war had broken out after it, too, declared independence – the Dutch were prepared to send a liaison battalion. Despite UNPROFOR's efforts, the humanitarian situation in Bosnia became worse. In the meantime, the Dutch impartial approach to the Yugoslavian crisis had been replaced by a more morally inspired and explicit anti-Serbian point of view. So, when the Security Council decided to install six safe areas in Bosnia to protect Bosnian-Muslim refugees, the Dutch government agreed to contribute an infantry battalion, which became known as Dutchbat-II. It soon turned out that the Dutch troops were to be deployed in and around Srebrenica.

The Ministry of Defense and the military commanders had been reluctant to accept this assignment. Both the notion of a "safe area" and the role of UNPROFOR seemed complicated and contradictory. UNPROFOR was still a peace-keeping mission and the troops it deployed to protect the safe areas were lightly armed. It was, as the NIOD report concluded, a peace-keeping mission in an area without peace. Dutchbat-II left in February 1994 for Yugoslavia, driven by mixed motives, armed with insufficient weapons, and operating under an unclear mandate and insufficient rules of engagement. The situation in the safe area of Srebrenica, the "biggest open air prison in the world" as one commentator wrote, soon turned out to be unmanageable. Some forty thousand Muslims were living there under humiliating circumstances, completely surrounded by hostile Serbian troops. Both sides constantly violated the safe area rules.

When the Serbs attacked, Dutchbat, whose size had been reduced to some four hundred men due to Serbian restrictions, was in no position to effectively defend the compound. What followed has been characterized by the Yugoslavia Tribunal as genocide. It is a matter of controversy how far the Dutch were responsible for this horrible outcome of what had intended to be a humanitarian action. The NIOD commission in fact rehabilitated the men of Dutchbat, who at first were blamed for negligence and even cowardice. The memory of Srebrenica was to linger on for a long time. When the NIOD report was published in April 2002, the government, led by social-democrat Wim Kok, resigned as a whole. It was an unprecedented, but also unsatisfactory decision. Although the Netherlands was not guilty of the Srebrenica drama, someone had to take responsibility for it, Prime Minister Kok argued. The Dutch government nevertheless firmly rejected the obligation to compensate the Bosnian victims.

Growing Insecurity

At the start of the twenty-first century, the arguments and ideals that have determined Dutch foreign policy-making for decades increasingly lost their validity. In the field of European integration the pursuit of a supranational, democratic Europe was in fact dropped. As a consequence, the Netherlands to some extent lost its reputation as an idealistic, founding member of the EEC. In the policy field of security too, the certainties of the previous decades increasingly fell by the wayside. While it is true that the Netherlands often behaved in these years as a loyal lapdog of the United States, and accordingly sometimes voiced the usual Atlantic standpoints, the standpoints taken no longer seemed to reflect any consistent long-term vision of West-European or Dutch security. In the field of development cooperation, human rights and international law too, doubts seemed to sow themselves and grow. Increasingly, Dutch engagements abroad were justified by a pragmatic appeal to national self-interest; yet for the most part that appeared to be an expression of uncertainty about the long-term objectives of Dutch policy.

Moreover, it was not always clear what that self-interest exactly implied. In the case of the net contributions to the European Union it was, at least at first sight, still a clear directive for political action: the less the Netherlands paid, the better. But when one looked a little closer it was not that simple. After all, the Dutch interest lay above all in the development of a stable and decisive European Union and in good relations with the major European powers, a goal that perhaps justified a degree of financial sacrifice. In other areas too, the "national interest" seemed to be too vague a principle to be easily operationalized. Thus it was unclear precisely what the Netherlands had to gain by its frequently outspoken pro-American stance. And why did the Dutch armed forces have to be deployed in carrying out tasks everywhere in the world? Which interests were actually at stake?

Precisely because of major international changes occurring, it seemed necessary and unavoidable that the basic principles and objectives of Dutch policy should be subjected to a fundamental discussion. It was therefore all the more remarkable that the public political debate over international issues largely fell silent in these years. International political issues played only a marginal role during the elections of 2002 and 2003. It was significant that the "Strategic Accord," which laid the foundation for the successive Balkenende governments since 2002 hardly paid any attention to Europe or to international politics. In all this, one should not exclude the possibility that politicians in The Hague simply lost their bearings with the blurring of a clear and inspiring image of the Dutch position in the world. Within a few years, from being a progressive country that was respected for its pragmatic ability to achieve consensus despite differences, its tolerant and internationalist socio-cultural atmosphere, and its often idealistic and professedly humanitarian foreign policy, the Netherlands seemed to have lost most of this reputation.

Further Reading

Baehr, Peter, Monique Castermans-Holleman and Fred Grünfeld. *Human Rights in the Foreign Policy of the Netherlands.* Oxford: Intersentia, 2002.

Hellema, Duco. *Foreign Policy of the Netherlands: The Dutch Role in World Politics.* Dordrecht: Republic of Letters, 2009.

Krabbendam, Hans, Cornelis A. van Minnen and Giles Scott-Smith, eds. *Four Centuries of Dutch-American Relations.* Albany: State University of New York, 2009.

Nekkers, Jan, and Peter Malcontent, eds. *Fifty Years of Dutch Development Cooperation,* 1949-1999. The Hague: Sdu Publishers, 2000.

History

Chapter 6

From the Periphery to the Center

Marco Mostert

The story of the delta before the Dutch nation is somewhat different from the later history of the Netherlands. That later history, however, cannot be understood without knowledge of what went before. The Dutch Republic did not emerge in a single instant; it was made possible by earlier developments, and the culture and society of early modern times was heavily indebted to those of the Middle Ages. We have to start our story even further back, with the advent of the Romans. They came to the region where the rivers Rhine, Maas and Scheldt reached the sea during the first century BCE. They felt far away from home. To civilized Romans, the inhabitants of the delta, as this region can best be called, may have seemed to be like the mythological Tritons, who were half-man and half-fish. The land ran out here to make place for the sea, and with the land all that a Roman might call "civilization" came to an end. More than a thousand years later, when Hartbert, the bishop of Utrecht, came to the coastal abbey of Egmond in 1134 to dedicate its new church to saint Adalbert, he felt he had arrived "at the extreme margin of the earth."

In the long first millennium of our era the delta of the Rhine and its hinterland was a border region between the most important political spheres of influence of the day and their neighbors. Because it seems to be an almost universal human inclination to identify spheres of influence with the dominant civilizations of the people who live in them, the region may with some justification be thought to have been situated in the periphery of civilization. This did not mean, however, that the inhabitants of the delta experienced disadvantages due to their marginal situation. Quite the contrary. They participated in the Mediterranean civilization of Rome, and Batavian legionaries were thoroughly Romanized. Later, they shared in the civilization of the Franks, who, after the departure of the Romans, increased their sphere of influence in these parts. At the same time, they shared in the proceeds of Frisian trade. In the eighth and ninth centuries, when they definitively became part of Christian civilization, some continued to do things in their own ways. Later, it proved to be advantageous to live in a border region between the German and French spheres of influence. Contacts overseas, mainly with the Anglo-Saxon and Scandinavian areas, thrived.

At the end of the first millennium, things gradually began to change. The centers of Western civilization moved north. Especially after the year 1000 land reclamation laid the foundation for economic growth, and in the fifteenth century the development of towns, hesitant at first, resulted in a relatively urbanized region which was in constant contact with economic powerhouses such as the Rhineland and Flanders. Economically, the delta was now part of the center of Europe. After the initial missionary efforts in the seventh and eighth centuries, Christianity had become the dominant religion, and in the later Middle Ages urban forms of spiritual life developed here.

On the eve of the Reformation, the influence of the inhabitants had spread far beyond the delta, so that the region may be said to have become part of the center of Europe in religious matters as well. In the thirteenth century the culture of writing and literacy, too, had developed to levels similar to those elsewhere in Latin Christendom, making the delta part of the center in this respect as well. Printing with moveable type was invented in Mainz, in fifteenth-century Germany. Yet the persistent myth of its invention in Haarlem, in the county of Holland, is understandable against the background of the flourishing of manuscript culture and the subsequent role the delta was to play in the development of the culture of the printed word.

The Romans

The Conquest of Gaul by Julius Caesar in the first century BCE marked the initial contact of the inhabitants of the delta with the force of the Roman Empire. The country looked very different from today. The East and South consisted mainly of sand and loam, except where the rivers made their way to the sea. The western and northern parts of the country consisted of peat bogs and marshes. The coast was marked by sand dunes which were pierced by rivers and creeks, waterways which might shift their position from one year to the next.

Habitation was concentrated on the sandy deposits of the river banks and under the protection of the dunes. The soils were easier to plough there, and sweet water was readily available. In these low-lying areas wind, water, and land were in a delicate balance. A slight rise of the sea level could render large areas inhabitable, forcing the inhabitants to abandon their settlements.

It is improbable that Caesar himself ever set eyes on the coastal landscape. When he moved away in 49 BCE no troops were left behind. The Romans came back when Emperor Augustus (27 BCE-14 CE) decided that all of Germania, including the areas to the east and north of the Rhine, had to be conquered. From then onwards the area south of the Rhine was to form part of the Empire for some four centuries. The plans for conquest were soon abandoned, but contacts with people living there were maintained. Thus, we find Frisians trading with the Romans. They even drew up contracts according to Roman legal rules.

The delta was important as a border region. The Roman army could use it as a base of operations, and soon military camps were built on the banks of the Rhine. From the middle of the first century CE until the second half of the third century CE peace prevailed, under the protection of the Roman legions which developed their settlements along the Rhine into a permanent border (in Latin: *limes*). The rivers were crucial to the Romans from an economic point of view since they connected the Rhineland with its important cities and the cereal-growing province of Britain.

Forms of literacy were introduced. The traces of small cords found on many minuscule lumps of lead – discovered recently through the use of metal detectors – have been convincingly interpreted as the remains of the seals used to close wax tablets. Some 120 small boxes have been found that were used to protect the wax seals of letters. Interestingly, they were found also in civilian Batavian settlements. The language used when dealing with the Romans was Latin. The soldiers recruited to the Roman army managed to speak, and sometimes also write, this language.

During the time of the Roman presence, peace did not always prevail. Sometimes there were locally inspired revolts, such as that of the Batavi in 69 CE. Problems with maintaining order in the center of the Empire played a role too. In the third century the Romans temporarily abandoned the Rhine border, and in the fifth century the border was given up definitively. Thus the delta came to form part of the periphery of another sphere of influence, that, of the Franks.

The Roman *Limes*: A Cultural Meeting Place

In the center of Utrecht, a narrow canal marks what was once the border of the Roman Empire. The branch of the Rhine, which once was controlled by Roman soldiers, is now just one of the canals dissecting the city. Here, right at the foot of the present-day cathedral, is the location of the *limes*, the border between Roman and non-Roman controlled territories. In the second century the *limes* in the Low Countries continued across the North Sea to Hadrian's Wall in Britain, and to the east by the Rhine, upstream roughly to Coblenz, and hence overland to the upper reaches of the Danube. The territories controlled by the *limes* in the Low Countries belonged to the province of *Germania Inferior*, which had its capital at Cologne.

Where the *limes* lay was determined both by accidents of physical geography and the fortunes of the Roman Empire. The river Rhine, designated by Julius Caesar to be the border, branched out in the Low Countries; the branch flowing through the present-day towns of Utrecht and Leiden into the North Sea was chosen. Along the *limes*, military settlements were constructed of various sizes and forms. Nijmegen was the most important strategic settlement where legions were stationed. Along the Rhine itself, a series of *castella* (fortresses) was built, situated a few miles from one another. Some of the *castella* have subsequently been destroyed by the sea or by the rivers changing their courses; the ruins of some others have remained visible for long periods of time.

Excavations have shown that the *castellum* at Valkenburg (near Leiden) was rebuilt five or six times. It was built at a crossroads of the route along the Rhine and the route at the feet of the dunes. An earthen wall and palisade of 100 by 125 meters was erected around the fortress. A civilian settlement flourished next to the *castellum* and further along the Roman road granaries, a watchtower, a cemetery and possibly some shrines could be found. Around 180 CE the *castellum* was reconstructed once more: the walls and headquarters were rebuilt in stone, the other buildings in wood. In the fourth century at least part of the fortress was still functional. After the final departure of the Romans, it is quite possible that the deserted *castellum* became a quarry for the local inhabitants.

Although the *castellum* at Utrecht was a much smaller affair it nevertheless still symbolized the Roman presence centuries later. The Frankish king Dagobert I (†639) built his church within its walls to stress the perceived continuity between the Roman Empire and the kingdom of the Franks.

The *limes* formed the border of the Roman Empire, and Roman remains continued to inspire awe for centuries afterwards. But the *limes* was hardly impenetrable. It denoted an area where representatives of the "indigenous" cultures could meet with the Romans, an exchange took place, of foodstuffs such as cattle, but also of artifacts, and even of religious ideas. At times the *limes* was more of a meeting place than a border guarded by military force.

In the Periphery

The Roman border (*limes*) had never been impermeable. Warrior bands and other groups moved across the Rhine, and tried to settle in the Empire. Quite soon, they came to be known collectively as the Franks. They seem to have originated in the East of the present-day Netherlands, and to have moved south in several stages, first as allies of the Romans. At the end of the fifth century, Merovingian King Clovis (466-511) founded a durable Frankish kingdom in the north of present-day France, and in the course of the next centuries they tried to increase their territories. King Dagobert I (†639) managed to gain access to the delta. Further aspirations were thwarted by the Frisians, and the next centuries would see the advance and retreat of Franks and Frisians, trying to gain control of the mouths of Rhine and Maas, and thereby of the rich trade network centered on Dorestad, a few miles upstream from Utrecht.

The early medieval Frisians cannot decisively be identified with the Frisians of Roman times. The sea level seems to have risen, forcing the earlier coastal Frisians to abandon some, if not all, of their settlements. They may have played a role in the migrations to Britain which resulted in Anglo-Saxon England. In the seventh and eighth centuries, however, the areas under the dunes were once more densely settled, and their inhabitants were once again called Frisians. They took part in a trade network which connected Britain, Scandinavia, Germany and territories beyond. Dorestad, on the Rhine, was one of its most important trading centers. Because of the Frisian trade's importance, "Frisian" could in Old English become a synonym for "trader" or "sailor." As a corollary of these economic activities, the delta participated in a veritable "North Sea culture" in which goods, but also ideas and (oral) literary texts were exchanged. The Anglo-Saxons also took part in this economic and cultural network. After becoming Christians, their missionaries came across the North Sea to Frisia and to the Saxons who had settled to the east of them.

The missionary Willibrord (†739), who became "archbishop of the Frisians," chose Utrecht, where Dagobert I had already built a church within the old Roman fortress, to found his mission post. In time this city was to develop into the main diocese of the medieval northern Low Countries. Willibrord had Frankish support for his work, but had to abandon Utrecht whenever the Frisians took control of the area of Utrecht and Dorestad.

It was also in Utrecht that Willibrord taught the missionary skills to his pupil Boniface, who was to work mainly in Germany. This work included making the converts renounce their gods and making them pronounce the essentials of the Christian creed prior to baptism. To this end an English vernacular text was adapted in the dialect of the coastal areas where Willibrord worked. Boniface took this text with him to use in his work among the pagans in Germany. The absence of a serious language barrier between Anglo-Saxons, Frisians and Saxons, who were able to understand one another without too many problems, allowed the use of insular texts such as these in the conversion of Germanic-speaking pagans on the Continent.

The Frankish sphere of influence was to extend further northwards after Boniface was murdered by a group of Frisians at Dokkum, in the north of Frisia, in 754. After his death, the Franks retaliated and managed finally to subdue the western parts of Frisia. Missionary dioceses were instituted on the model of Willibrord's mission post at Utrecht. Münster became one of those posts, and in 805 Liudger, who had been born near Utrecht and had spent most of his time converting Frisians, became its first bishop.

For the first time, the delta had become part of a single political unit: the Carolingian empire of Charlemagne who had become king of the Franks in 768. It was a fragile unity at best. Under the Carolingian kings and emperors, the region came under threat from new contestants from the North. The demise of Frisian political rule over the Rhine had not meant the end of the trade network in which the Frisians participated. Its rich pickings continued to attract traders – and raiders. In 810 Frisia was attacked by "pirates" of Danish origin. This led Charlemagne to organize a navy. Under his son Louis the Pious the attacks resumed, and in 834 Dorestad was besieged. The Vikings – as the attackers came to be known – returned at least eight times. Rorik and his brother Heriold held Dorestad from Lothar I, the son of Louis the Pious. Another Dane, Godefrid, obtained Frisia in 882 on the condition that he be baptized.

Clearly, the Carolingians did not manage to keep the peace in these parts. Even Utrecht had to be abandoned by the bishop, who continued to reside for generations thereafter in Deventer on the IJssel, another branch of the Rhine. The local aristocracy, better placed to control violence, managed to increase its power bases in the delta. Gradually, the contours of the later county of Holland were taking shape. Elsewhere similar processes of power consolidation could be observed. They were helped by the position of the delta between the major political forces to come out of the Carolingian sphere of influence: the kingdoms of Germany and France.

Formally, almost all of the delta and its hinterland became part of what was to become the kingdom of Germany in 925. The counts of Holland and Zeeland, the dukes of Brabant and of Guelders, and the bishops of Utrecht emerged as the most powerful territorial princes. The bishops had been given their powers by the German kings and emperors, who tried in this way to extend their control over the principalities on the assumption that bishops ought not to father children, at least not leave legitimate heirs. By bestowing dioceses on the candidates of their own choice, the kings hoped to increase the numbers of their dedicated political supporters. The bishops of Rome came to object to this practice. With the Concordat of Worms of 1122, the turbulences between the king – who was supposed to be crowned emperor as well – and the pope came to a provisional conclusion, when it was decided that the pope was to invest bishops with their ecclesiastical dignity, whereas the king was to retain the right to invest them with their secular offices.

The bishops of Utrecht and Liège ended up in the camp of the pope, thereby effectively curtailing the influence of the German king in the Low Countries. From now on bishops, counts, and dukes might attend the ceremonial assemblies during which the Emperor showed himself in his regalia, thereby showing in a real sense the existence of the German Empire. Indeed, count William of Holland himself was chosen king in 1247 and was to rule until his death in 1256. But henceforth politics remained primarily a regional matter.

Land Reclamation, Urbanization, Literacy and Spirituality

Although politically on the sidelines, the delta began to escape the periphery of European medieval history in economic, social, cultural and spiritual respects. This was the result, first of all, of the work of land reclamation which had started already before the end of the first millennium, but was steadily increasing in importance. The peat areas in the western and northern parts of the region had never attracted many inhabitants. From Flanders to Denmark a wilderness extended, composed of half-consumed plant rests, almost without trees. Farmers could use this wilderness for pasture and fuel, or could hunt there and collect honey and wax. But the potential of these wastelands was only realized when they were turned into arable land through drainage. This slowly happened over the course of centuries. New settlements could be started either by a lord inviting farmers or on the initiative of peasant communities. The new reclamations realized by hand, using nothing more than wooden spades that were only reinforced with a strip of iron at the cutting edge, produced a surplus which enabled the population to grow. Once a settlement reached a certain number of inhabitants, it could acquire the status of parish and have a right to its own parish priest.

Experience in land reclamation was exported everywhere in Europe. Along the Baltic, for instance, there are traces of "Frisian," "Dutch" or "Flemish" settlements (the names seem interchangeable) on land reclaimed in the ways developed in the delta. The benefits were substantial, but there were also drawbacks. Because peat consists for eighty percent of water, draining the low-lying wilderness made the soil subside dramatically. The water level of a river might remain considerably higher than that of the drainage canals on the other side of its bank. Water management soon became a necessity. As rivers and creeks were directly connected with the sea and its tides, mistakes made could have repercussions many miles away. Cooperation on a local and regional level was called for and gradually water boards developed which had jurisdiction over dikes, drainage canals and rivers.

From the thirteenth century onwards, surplus agricultural produce enabled the development of more complex, multi-functional settlements. Towns began to develop with a distinctive urban infrastructure. Dordrecht was the first settlement in the county of Holland which was called a town (*oppidum*). It developed out of a village in a reclamation project, where it is mentioned for the first time shortly before 1050. It took the position of intermediary between England and the Rhineland over from Utrecht, which had been one of the successors of Dorestad when its harbor silted up. Other early towns are Maastricht and Nijmegen (which had been important already in Roman times) and Deventer, Zutphen and Arnhem, on or near the IJssel.

Trade and crafts provided specialized work for many. The profits were interesting enough for lords to offer town privileges to promising settlements, or to start towns literally from scratch. Although not all towns founded in this way prospered, at the end of the fifteenth century the delta had become one of the most urbanized regions in Europe. Towns had their own walls and militias, councils, trade and craft regulations, religious institutions and schools.

The first schools had been attached to ecclesiastical foundations such as monasteries and cathedrals. According to the Fourth Lateran Council, called by the pope in 1215, each parish church had to have its own school. Apparently, this injunction was taken seriously in the Low Countries. In the sixteenth century the Italian historian Guicciardini noticed that here even peasants could read. Latin schools were attached to an important church. Often, they also had a "lower school" or "writing school" teaching the rudiments of literacy. In the countryside, a sacristan or verger often doubled as schoolmaster.

Schools were too important, however, to leave to the Church. From the fourteenth century, the towns tended to take over the Latin schools, and to increase their fame by attracting renowned teachers. To keep their monopoly on learning, town councils discouraged "additional schools," founded on private initiative. In some of these latter schools, the curriculum was changed to allow for useful subjects such as French, arithmetic and bookkeeping. Some Latin schools taught at university level; their teachers had received a university education in Paris, Cologne, Louvain or elsewhere. Pupils from the Latin schools sometimes went on to university.

From the thirteenth century, as exemplified by the development of the schooling system, the culture of the written word differed in nothing from that available elsewhere. The uses of writing are wholly consistent with what is known from elsewhere in Europe. Whereas at the beginning of the twelfth century law was still predominantly oral, at the end of the thirteenth century the use of charters, legally valid documents, had become commonplace in securing acceptance for changes in ownership or other changes in rights. Bills of sale for relatively unimportant purchases were now drawn up. This development did not happen overnight, however. In the north, in Frisia, the thirteenth century saw the writing down of laws in the vernacular, so that a shift from the oral to the written can be said to have taken place here as elsewhere in the delta. Judging from the surviving charters, however, Frisia seems to have lagged behind in administrative literacy by a century at least. And it was only at the very end of the twentieth century that promises by word of mouth (for example to buy a house) were no longer to have any legal validity.

Written literary texts, too, were slowly becoming commonplace. From the early Middle Ages Latin texts had been imported, and Latin was to remain the most important written language because of its prestige as the language of the Word of God. Texts in the vernacular, even if some had been composed already in the mission post at Utrecht in the early eighth century, were to become current from the twelfth century onwards. As a language for written literature, Dutch developed first in the southern Low Countries; from there, it was gradually introduced in the delta. As for Frisian, the second vernacular spoken, the laws were the first written texts in that language. When printing was introduced in the delta, less than a generation after "writing without a pen" had been invented, the presses produced the Latin classics for readers old and new, but also texts in the vernacular. Many of these early vernacular texts were meant to further the spiritual life of their readers.

At the end of the Middle Ages, Christianity had developed many forms. The network of parishes and the official apparatus of the dioceses had been nearly perfected. Religiously inspired care for the poor, orphans and the infirm developed in the towns. The number of urban monastic foundations grew rapidly: in Amsterdam, more than one fifth of the town's surface belonged to the more than twenty monasteries in 1500. Lay people developed spiritual needs which were catered for by fraternities and other new institutions of religious life.

Individual Christians, helped by their growing reading skills, developed views which the Church deemed heretical. They had internalized the message of Christianity, and were willing to give their lives for their religious ideas. Others started movements with the aim of perfecting their personal spiritual lives. The Beguines, devout women who lived a spiritual life in separate dwellings loosely organized as a pseudo-monastic community, came from the Southern Netherlands. The Brethren and Sisters of the Common Life were an indigenous development. Their Modern Devotion inspired self-reflection and meditation on one's conscience. This movement was influential far beyond the delta. In the early sixteenth century, humanists such as Erasmus and reformers such as Martin Luther were, directly or indirectly, influenced by their ideas.

Hebban Olla Vogala: The Beginnings of Literature

Just before 1100, a Flemish monk in the Benedictine abbey of Rochester was trying his pen, and wrote on the flyleaf of his manuscript:

Hebban olla vogala nestas hagunnan,
hinase hic enda thu.
Wat unbidan we nu?

This roughly translates as "All birds have started making nests, except me and you. What are we waiting for?" It would take until 1932 before a scholar recognized these thirteen words in a manuscript – now in the Oxford Bodleian – for what they were: the first truly literary sentence in the Dutch language. Since then, they have been part of the staple diet of all literary histories taught to Dutch schoolchildren.

Strictly speaking this poetic effusion is a product of the southern Low Countries in exile, and there is no evidence that its words were ever heard in the delta. Had they been heard, however, they would have been understood, as they are written in a language which was

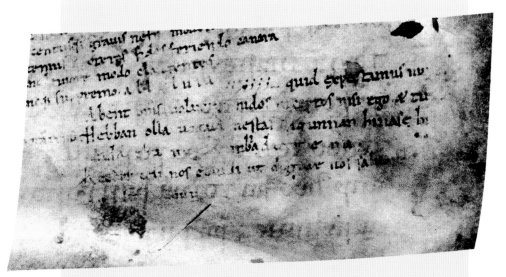

close enough to the dialects of Old Dutch spoken in the northern Low Countries. It would still take some time, however, before literary works in the vernacular would be written there.

It would be a mistake to reduce the history of literature to that of the authors writing in a particular language. We should also look at the reception of works written elsewhere, and when we do, we ought to look beyond the confines of the dominant vernacular. Indeed, we should look beyond written literature and take oral traditions into account as well. Word art is not confined to the written word, and the Middle Ages were always multilingual. Rather than studying "literature in Dutch" we should study "literature in predominantly Dutch-speaking areas," or more modestly phrased for instance as "literature in the delta." With such a perspective we would realize that, already in the eighth century, long before literary works were produced in Dutch, Latin literary texts were imported. In the mission at Utrecht the lives of saintly missionaries were written, and in or around Maastricht the story of Servatius, the first bishop, was written already in the early eighth century. In the monastery of Egmond, the abbey of the family of the counts of Holland, hagiography and historiography in Latin was practiced from the eleventh century onwards, a mere two generations after the abbey's foundation. Latin literature was followed by literature in French and German. Texts in these languages were read, heard and emulated in Dutch, once that vernacular had become an acceptable vehicle for written literature.

Many stories circulated orally before they were written down, such as the tenth-century "ghost story" of the priest of Deventer, who was killed when he stayed the night in his church while the noisy souls of the departed celebrated their Mass. This exciting story was written down by the German chronicler Thietmar of Merseburg. It suggests that many similar stories may have been told and sung, but did not find someone willing to preserve them for posterity, in Latin or in any other language.

Towards the Center of Western Civilization

Our survey started with developments in the delta after the arrival of the Romans. The region became an important border region, in which exchanges took place between the Mediterranean civilization of the Empire and the local populations. Literacy came in the wake of the Roman legions. After their departure, their place was taken by the Franks, the Carolingians, and the kingdom of Germany. "Frisians" traded across seas and along rivers. Christianity came in the seventh and eighth centuries to the mouths of the Rhine and the Maas, and the Church established itself. From the beginning of the second millennium, due to land reclamation and, later, urbanization, the delta could start to move towards the center of Western civilization. In the later Middle Ages we see growing prosperity, increased schooling and literacy, and new forms of spirituality. These major contributions to late medieval European Christianity eloquently show that the delta was now firmly at the center rather than at the periphery of Western civilization.

Politically, during the long period in which these shifts from the periphery to the center took place, the delta was never a clearly-defined, single entity. It formed part of larger entities, such as the Roman and Carolingian empires and the Christian Church. Several systems of law coexisted. The exercise of power, however, showed marked similarities with that of its neighbors. Daily life was not all that different from the way it was lived in neighboring areas, nor were beliefs, neither before nor after the introduction of Christianity. Maybe, because of the mobility of traders, knowledge of the world at large was slightly greater here than elsewhere, but we cannot be sure of that. The inhabitants of the delta did not consider it an entity, but identified with their relatives, region or religion. They did not even speak one single language, and it seems doubtful if someone from the Frisian islands in the North would have been able to sustain a conversation with an inhabitant of a town in the South East such as Maastricht about anything other than trade. There was as yet no Dutch state, and identification with "the Netherlands" was therefore a sentiment that could not yet develop.

Further Reading

Arblaster, Paul. *A History of the Low Countries.* New York: Palgrave Macmillan, 2006.

Blockmans, Wim, and Walter Prevenier. *The Promised Lands: The Low Countries under Burgundian Rule* 1369-1530. Philadelphia: University of Pennsylvania Press, 1999.

Blom, J.C.H., and E. Lamberts, eds. *History of the Low Countries*. New York: Berghahn, 1999.

Rietbergen, Peter. *A Short History of the Netherlands*. Amersfoort: Bekking, 2006.

There is no survey available of the early history of the Netherlands in English. Recent titles can be found through consulting the online *International Medieval Bibliography*, which can be accessed through www.brepolis.net.

Chapter 7

The Golden Age

Maarten Prak

During much of the seventeenth century the Dutch dominated European and indeed world trade. The Dutch guilder was the dollar of the seventeenth century, a currency accepted around the globe. During that same period, the Dutch army and navy were much-feared combatants. Scientists working in the Dutch Republic were prominent participants in the Scientific Revolution. Dutch artists from this period, like Rembrandt and Vermeer, are household names even today. The history of the Dutch Golden Age is therefore of much more than local importance.

That history is often told in terms of exceptionalism; the Dutch were the odd man out in early modern Europe. Many historians have analyzed this Dutch exceptionalism in terms of modernity. The trouble, of course, is that "modernity" is such an all-embracing and therefore slippery concept. Nonetheless, the concept can be used, if it is disaggregated, precise benchmarks are applied, and a comparative perspective is used. This chapter will do exactly that. Rather than assuming beforehand that a society will modernize across-the-board, it will look at a variety of aspects: the economy, social developments, political structures, religious identities, and science, to see what – if anything – was modern about the Dutch Golden Age.

The First Modern Economy

Perhaps the most straightforward indicator of the modernity of any pre-modern economy is the distribution of its workforce. Traditional economies are characterized by high percentages of their populations working in agriculture; higher numbers in non-agricultural sectors such as industry and trade, are a sign of economic modernization. Table I clearly shows how substantial numbers of Dutch workers had moved to the towns and in the process exchanged their rural jobs for urban ones. This process, which already started during the Middle Ages, was at the same time cause and consequence of the Golden Age. Estimates for various European economies between 1500 and 1800 suggest that the normal situation was one of stagnation. The Dutch economy, however, went through a spectacular phase of growth between circa 1580 and 1650; national income per capita increased by about fifty percent. All sectors of the economy – in Holland the economy grew by more than one percent per annum – contributed to these growth figures, albeit some more than others.[1]

The Dutch already had a very substantial share in the trade between Western and Northern Europe, but the volume of this trade further increased during the first half of the seventeenth century. Shortly before 1600 a new

	Rural agricultural	Urban	Rural non-agricultural
England	55	17	28
France	63	11	26
Dutch Republic	40	39	21

Source: E.A. Wrigley, "Urban Growth and Agricultural Change: England and the Continent in the Early Modern Period," in People, Cities and Wealth: The Transformation of Traditional Society (Oxford: Basil Blackwell, 1987), tables 4, 8, and 9.

series of commercial explorations was launched, most spectacularly direct voyages to the East Indies and the Americas. The former would lead to the creation of the Dutch East India Company (*Vereenigde Oost-Indische Compagnie*, VOC) in 1602. It was the world's first large-scale joint-stock company. By 1700 the VOC was employing around twenty-five thousand, of whom eighteen thousand were working in Asia. Almost four thousand were stationed in Batavia (now Jakarta), the town set up by the Dutch as their commercial headquarters in the Indonesian archipelago. Another four thousand were plying Asian waters, ferrying cargo between the numerous VOC trading posts set up in Japan, on Taiwan and Sri Lanka, on the Indian coast, as well as the various islands in the archipelago itself. To provision the shipping route between Europe and Asia, the VOC set up a station on the southern tip of Africa; the station eventually became Capetown.

Dutch merchants were less successful in the West. The Dutch West India Company, or WIC, was late to enter into the competition with Spain and Portugal. As a result, costs proved higher and revenues more difficult to come by in the American trade. Despite the windfall, in 1628, of the capture of the Spanish silver fleet, the WIC had a difficult time making a profit. Its colonies in North America (New Amsterdam, the future New York),[2] Brazil and the Caribbean, as well the slave stations on the African coast, required huge protection costs. Brazil was already lost in the 1640s, New Amsterdam was handed over to the English in 1667.

The booming trade helped launch various new industries, and revive older ones. Among the completely new industries were diamond cutting, sugar refining and tobacco spinning, none of which had existed in the Netherlands before, say, 1580. The same was true of the famous Delft blue pottery, which first emerged as a substitute for Chinese porcelain, when the supply of that coveted product was interrupted by the Ming-Qing transition during the middle decades of the seventeenth century. It was so successful that in the eighteenth century Chinese potteries were producing imitation Delftware!

The economic boom strongly stimulated consumer demand. There was a strong upsurge in the quantity and variety of products available to ordinary customers. In the sixteenth century farmers in the northern province of Friesland had no cupboards, no paintings, and no clocks. Books were only available in the wealthiest households. By the early eighteenth century all these items were present in even the poorest farming families. This was partly due to the availability of new products that appeared on the market for the first time in the course of the seventeenth century. These included tulips, which were grown commercially in Holland for the first time shortly after 1600, and as a spin-off also led to the production of Delft-blue tulip vases.[3] Also tobacco, which was not only imported, but grown on the sandy soils of the central Veluwe district in the Netherlands itself. And of course many colonial products, which by 1700 had become accessible to even the poorer social classes.

A distinguishing feature of the Dutch economy was its high level of integration. The relations between towns and countryside have been characterized as "symbiotic." During the middle decades of the seventeenth century an extensive network of new canals was created, along which towboats maintained a regular service, ensuring easy (and comfortable) connections between the towns of Holland. These towns were also in various other respects pivotal to Dutch society.

The Tulip Bubble: Horticultural Speculation

The tulip made its first impact on European history in 1389 in Kosovo, when the son of the Ottoman sultan rode into battle against the Serbs wearing a shirt embroidered with tulips. The tulip is a native plant of Turkey and much revered in that country, where it is known as *lale*. The Western name probably derives from a mispronunciation for turband (*tulband* in Turkish), which was reported back by early travelers as *tulipam*, and confused by them with the flower. In 1559 a Swiss physician and botanist, Conrad Gesner (1516-1565), published the first account and the first picture of tulips in Western Europe.

In those days tulips were cultivated in Europe by a mere handful of botanists. Most notable among them was Charles de l'Écluse, or Carolus Clusius (1526-1609), a native of Arras in the Habsburg Netherlands. Clusius helped establish the Imperial Botanical Garden at Vienna, at the behest of Emperor Maximilian II, and then created another botanical garden in Frankfurt, before his appointment as *Horti Praefectus* at the recently established university of Leiden in the Netherlands in 1592. Clusius had the largest collection of tulip bulbs in Europe and ensured that the university's botanical garden included numerous varieties of tulips.

By then the tulip had already become a fashionable item in aristocratic gardens; in the Dutch Republic it was to become a truly popular flower. Emanuel Sweerts from Amsterdam published his *Florilegium* in 1612, the first sales catalogue that included tulips. Dutch agriculture was already highly commercialized and quick to pick up this new product. As it was, the soil directly behind the dunes in the vicinity of Haarlem proved exceptionally suitable for the growing of bulbs. The interest in tulips reached fever pitch during the 1630s, when a single bulb could exchange hands for the price of a sizable house on one of Amsterdam's fashionable canals. Especially in demand were the so-called broken varieties, which displayed flamed patterns of many colors, instead of the more common solid coloring. Twentieth-century laboratory tests would reveal that breaking occurred as the result of a viral infection in the bulb. In the seventeenth century it was only understood that the broken varieties were rare, and therefore valuable. Of the Semper Augustus, perhaps the rarest of them all,  only twelve bulbs were known to exist, and at a certain point they were all owned by Adriaen Pauw (1581-1653), Amsterdam's, and later Holland's Pensionary, the country's most important civil servant.

In 1637 the tulip bubble burst, and it took the Dutch authorities years to sort out the financial mess, which left numerous people bankrupt. Although observers at home and abroad insisted it had taught the speculators a lesson, the tulip mania turned out to be a publicity scoop. It would establish in the public mind, for centuries to come, the closest possible connection between Holland and bulbs. Thanks to its flowers, Dutch agriculture is still one of the largest exporters in the world.

Towns and Their Immigrants

Early modern Europe was still a society overwhelmingly dominated by the countryside. Before 1800 less than ten percent of Europeans lived in a town, when we define a town as a community of ten thousand inhabitants and over. Of course there were variations around this European average, but in the seventeenth century the Dutch Republic was by far the most urbanized.[4] By 1700 one in every three Dutch men and women lived in a town; in Holland this had reached two in every three. Between 1560 and 1670 the towns of

Holland grew by an average of 250 percent. To a very large extent this growth was due to immigration. The first wave of migrants arrived in the 1580s and 1590s from the Spanish Netherlands. Amsterdam was the most popular destination. Its population shot up from 30,000 in 1580, to 105,000 in 1622, on to 240,000 in 1732. Immigrants made Amsterdam into Europe's third largest town, after London and Paris. Amsterdam's population was also boosted by Jews arriving from Portugal and Spain (Sephardim) and from Central Europe (Ashkenazim), by Huguenots from France who came over after the repeal of the Edict of Nantes in 1685, and especially by huge numbers of Scandinavians and Germans, who flocked to Amsterdam by the thousands throughout the seventeenth century.

Social change in the Dutch Golden Age consisted first and foremost of this combined process of immigration and urbanization. But this in turn entailed other changes. The economic boom benefited the wealthiest sections of society much more than the poorest. The sting was, however, taken out of this greater inequality, by the expansion of the urban system of poor relief. In the seventeenth century the social security systems of the Holland towns in particular were said to be among the most generous in Europe. No doubt this helps explain why the integration of such large numbers of immigrants into the urban social framework was realized with perhaps lots of minor frictions, but very few large-scale conflicts.

In Dutch society, and especially in the seaboard provinces, the towns were dominated in still another way. Whereas in most European countries the aristocracy – in other words: a rural elite – set the standard for social and cultural modes of behavior, in the Dutch Republic the urban bourgeoisie was at least as prominent. The famous Dutch canals were lined with their homes, and in the seventeenth century new canals were created to cater to the increased demand for bourgeois housing. The majority of these people had become rich in long-distance trade, but some were also industrial entrepreneurs. During the seventeenth century, however, some of these families started to specialize in political office and attendant careers. A new subsection of the urban elites emerged, the so-called regents. These were people who sat on the town councils, and through these positions influenced the course of Dutch politics.

Local Autonomy

The linchpin of the urban elites' dominance over society was their success in monopolizing municipal public offices. Due to the specific organization of the Dutch state, these municipal offices provided direct access to the most relevant channels of power in the Republic.

In the Middle Ages, the territories that were to form the Dutch Republic, were all part of the Holy Roman Empire, but in effect behaved like independent states. They were ruled by dukes (Gelderland), counts (Holland, Zeeland), bishops (Utrecht, Overijssel) or simply dozens of untitled nobles (Friesland, Groningen), none of whom accepted any superior authority apart from the Emperor – and him only because he was so distant. This began to change with the ascendance of the Burgundians in the Low Countries, but it was only under Charles V of Habsburg, during the first half of the sixteenth century, that the majority of these regions were included in the proto-state of the Seventeen Netherlands. The Dutch Revolt, which started in earnest in 1568, not only led to the break-up of this proto-state, but also restored much of the regions' former autonomy. As a result, the Dutch Republic became a state mainly for the purposes of international relations and more particularly its violent form. The main business of the States General, in which each of the seven provinces held one vote, was foreign affairs and the supervision of the army and the navy. Domestic politics was left to the provinces, which each had their own set of laws, their own political institutions and traditions, and so on.

Formally, all the provinces were equal. Holland, however, contributed almost sixty percent of the national budget. Holland could not dictate the country's policies, but its opinions were very important. Indeed, there were really only two circumstances that could provide a counterweight against this domination by Holland. Firstly, Holland was not always united in its opinion. Conflicting economic interests at times prevented Holland from taking the lead. The other factor helping to balance the role of the various provinces was the stadholder, who was the informal head of state as well as the commander-in-chief of the army and the navy.[5] Under the Habsburgs, the stadholder had been a provincial governor. The position was in the hands of the most important nobles of the land, like William of Orange, who was of German origin but owned extensive properties in the Low Countries. William had been the confidant of Charles V, but eventually emerged as leader of the Dutch Revolt, which he helped finance out of his own pocket.

The provinces, feeling they needed some sort of leader figure (and the money), decided to continue the stadholderate, albeit with a restricted mandate and under their own control. But time and again capable stadholders from the Orange dynasty managed to maneuver themselves into a dominating position, often with the help of the smaller provinces. And when persuasion failed, there was always the army to support them. In 1618 stadholder Maurice overthrew Holland's Grand Pensionary Oldenbarneveldt, and had him tried (and beheaded) for treason. In 1650 stadholder William II staged a coup against Amsterdam. And in 1672 William III returned to power after the lynching of John de Witt, another of Holland's Grand Pensionaries and the country's informal leader for almost twenty years.

This political violence was perhaps partly the result of the stadholders' double role as political and military leaders, but it definitely also had to do with their poorly defined job description. This was a problem more generally of the Republic's constitution: it was a hodgepodge of compromises. Politics in the Dutch Republic was essentially the art of squaring this particular circle.

According to the standards of political "modernization" the outcome was disappointing. Centralisation completely failed to gain a foothold. The central bureaucracy in The Hague, moreover, was understaffed and corrupt. And yet, if one looks at the results produced by this system, it all of a sudden does not look so bad at all. If we accept that the primary task of the state in the early modern period was to provide protection, the size of its army is an indicator of effectiveness. According to the most recent estimates the Dutch army in the 1630s and 1640s was about sixty thousand strong. France, with a

William of Orange: Founding Father

As leader of the Dutch Revolt against Spanish rule and founder of the House of Orange-Nassau, which rules the country until the present day, William of Orange has been called the father of the Dutch nation.

William was born in 1533 as heir to immense landed wealth. He was the eldest son of the Lutheran Count of Nassau in Germany who also owned large properties in the Dutch province of Brabant around Breda, and at age 11 inherited the sovereign principality of Orange in France. The Habsburg emperor Charles V, only allowed him to accept this inheritance and title on condition that he would be raised at the imperial court and convert to Catholicism. In Brussels, William learned French and colloquial Dutch, accepted many diplomatic and military responsibilities and quickly became an influential confidant of the emperor, earning the epithet "the Silent" for his ability to conceal his true intentions. When Charles V formally abdicated in 1555 he famously leaned on the shoulder of the young Prince of Orange. His son, King Philip II, admitted William to the influential Council of State and appointed him stadholder (governor) of the key provinces of Holland, Zeeland, and Utrecht when he departed for Spain, making him the most powerful nobleman in the Netherlands.

The relation between William and the absent king quickly soured, however. William and his fellow nobles felt that the autocratic directives from Spain trampled on their traditional liberties and privileges. Moreover, they also began to resent the religious persecution which the devoutly Catholic King Philip II imposed on the Netherlands to quell the spread of Protestantism. When the king sent a huge expeditionary army under the Duke of Alba to restore order and installed a special court which executed thousands of heretics and disloyal subjects, among whom two of William's closest allies, the prince of Orange fled to his estates in Germany to organize opposition. The failed military invasions which William launched against Alba in 1568 mark the beginning of a war that would last eighty years and resulted in Dutch independence.

Although William's plans for a union of seventeen Dutch provinces failed, ultimately his brother Jan the Elder managed to unite seven northern rebellious provinces in a Union of Utrecht in 1579, which two years later formally renounced its allegiance to the Spanish King. This declaration of independence left William of Orange the undisputed leader of the new nation, although his formal position was never properly settled. After King Philip put a price on his head, William of Orange was fatally shot in his headquarters in Delft by a French Catholic in 1584, at the zenith of his popularity. His son Prince Maurice succeeded him as stadholder of Holland and Zeeland, and later acquired that position in most other provinces as well, establishing the practice of a Republic with a hereditary stadholder.

population about ten times bigger, at the time had an army eighty thousand men strong. No wonder that the Dutch were by far the most heavily taxed nation in Europe. On top of that, the Dutch government accumulated a huge public debt, albeit against remarkably low interest rates.[6] All of this suggests an effective and efficient interaction between the authorities and their citizens. At a time when most European governments were fighting their citizens in civil wars revolving around the domestic balance of power and the degree of civil (religious) liberties, the ramshackle construction of the Dutch state, and its reliance on local political stand-offs, proved to be an advantage rather than a handicap.[7]

Religious Diversity

One of the hallmarks of modern societies is their capacity to accommodate religious diversity. During the early modern period, most rulers and their advisers felt that divergent opinions on fundamental issues were bound to undermine the unity of a country's population and were therefore a threat to any political regime. Against this background the Dutch Republic gained a reputation for tolerance, because it managed to create a society in which people of different persuasions lived peacefully side by side. As so often, the actual situation was much more complex.[8]

The Dutch Revolt had been, to some extent at least, a protest against the Inquisition. Therefore the Union of Utrecht of 1579, which bound the rebel provinces together in their struggle against Spain and later came to be seen as the Dutch constitution, famously granted freedom of conscience to all Dutch men and women. However, the Union also allowed each province to create its own religious order. The Calvinists had dominated the leadership of the Revolt, and they now stood to profit from its success. Despite their small membership – perhaps as little as ten percent of the Dutch had formally joined the Calvinist Church by 1600 – they were given the exclusive right to profess their faith in public. To that end, all existing Catholic church buildings were either handed over to the Calvinists, or confiscated by the local authorities and converted into hospitals, university lecture halls, or simply left to decay. The Calvinist Church was financially supported by the public authorities from the very start. Only those who were members of, or at least sympathized with, the Calvinist Church, could be appointed to public offices.

For a number of reasons, however, the Calvinists were never able to win the hearts and minds of all Dutch men and women. Clashes over issues of orthodoxy, and especially the problem of predestination, divided the church during the first two decades of the seventeenth century – and took the country to the brink of civil war. The Synod of Dordrecht in 1619 created a split in the church, and the establishment of a rival Calvinist church, the Remonstrant Brotherhood. When given the choice, the Calvinist leadership preferred a strict and therefore by definition small church, over an inclusive one. This in turn made them less popular with many politicians, who saw the Reformed ministers as a threat to civic peace. For this reason, the Church was placed under strict political supervision. Moreover, the town councils of Amsterdam and other mercantile centers in Holland were well aware that religious intolerance was "bad for business," and accepted religious diversity both as a boost to trade and at the same time a means to contain the influence of the Calvinist ministers.

Calvinism's failure provided space for the other religious communities to carve out a position for themselves. This was especially true for the Catholics, who comprised about one third of the Republic's population, but for a long time were tainted by their presumed association with the Spanish Habsburgs and the Pope. Given the size of their community, their religious needs could not be ignored. The authorities in many places therefore accepted their meetings (and the celebration of mass) in so-called hidden churches, buildings that looked like ordinary houses from the outside, but were converted into chapels on the inside. In Amsterdam alone almost thirty such churches were constructed during the seventeenth century. Their semi-clandestine existence was known to all – the police registered the arrival of new priests, and pocketed bribes to leave the Catholics alone. These bribes became even formally regulated during the eighteenth century. Catholic charities were allowed to collect money and buy property to support orphans and paupers of their own community.

Other religious communities could likewise obtain privileges. Jewish merchants, arriving in the Netherlands from Portugal around 1600, managed to negotiate significant liberties in Amsterdam, including access to the town's citizenship (albeit on restricted conditions). There was no Jewish ghetto in Amsterdam, even though most Jews preferred to live in close proximity of each other. During the seventeenth century both the Portuguese (Sephardim) and the Central European (Ashkenazim) Jewish communities were allowed to build huge synagogues in Amsterdam; the municipal authorities attended the opening ceremonies. In other parts of the country, however, religious policies were decidedly less tolerant. Around the middle of the seventeenth century towns like Utrecht, Deventer, Zwolle, and Arnhem, all introduced regulations preventing Catholic immigrants from obtaining rights of citizenship.

The image of religious tolerance, real enough in some parts of the country, thus needs to be circumscribed in two distinct ways. First, some regions were distinctly less tolerant than Holland's mercantile towns. And secondly, even in Holland tolerance was a way of life, rather than a principle. The idea of tolerance was accepted by very few people; in practice, surprisingly large numbers of people nonetheless accepted the implications of the fact that their neighbors, colleagues and even relatives were of a different persuasion.[9]

A Thirst for Knowledge

Religious diversity also helped create the intellectual space for the new philosophical and scientific developments of the period. Various indicators suggest that knowledge was highly valued in the Dutch Republic. Of the adult male population of seventeenth-century Amsterdam, sixty-four percent were able to sign their names; among females this was forty percent. The high literacy rates in turn created a solid domestic market for books and other printed documents, allowing the Dutch publishing industry to take over much of the European market as well. Many of these books were written by non-Dutch authors, and in languages other than Dutch.

Some of these authors, however, even though they were born abroad, had moved to the Netherlands in person. The most famous of these perhaps was René Descartes, who spent most of his adult life in the Dutch Republic. Descartes was one of many first or second generation immigrants helping to boost Dutch science in the period of the Scientific Revolution. Other examples include mathematician Simon Stevin, who came from the Spanish Netherlands, Christiaan Huygens, inventor of the pendulum clock, whose parents came from the same parts, and philosopher Baruch de Spinoza, who was born in a Jewish family that had recently migrated from Portugal to Amsterdam.[10] Thus, migration in its own right contributed to the dynamism of Dutch science.

But there were other factors stirring up intellectual ferment. Dutch artisans had been producing some remarkable instruments. In 1608 a spectacle-maker from Middelburg produced the first working telescope. Within a year Galilei was observing the stars' movements through his own. Probably less than a decade later another spectacle-maker produced the first microscope. Anthony van Leeuwenhoek was able to produce lenses that magnified 270 times – and observe the hitherto invisible world of micro-organisms through them. Due to the country's unusually wide and intense commercial networks, scholars working in the Dutch Republic had direct access to a wide range of data previously unavailable in Europe. Merchants and travelers brought home examples and pictures of plant and animal species unknown in these parts. These helped stimulate new research, especially in the life sciences.

Various Dutch authorities also made heavy investments in higher education. Before 1575 the area that became the Dutch Republic did not have a single university. In that year a university was founded in Leiden, primarily to train ministers for the newly established Calvinist Church. The university's board of governors bought talent from abroad. The number of students shot up; less than twenty students graduated annually from Dutch universities in the last quarter of the sixteenth century, by 1700 this had increased more than fivefold.

Outlook: The Modernity of the Dutch Republic

In many areas the Dutch Republic was ahead of the competition by the end of the seventeenth century. Its economic structure was more diversified and as a result more dynamic, as was demonstrated by the composition of the labor force and economic growth rates. Due to its economic performance the western areas in the country in particular attracted huge numbers of immigrants. This not only provided the country with a strong infusion of human capital, but also permitted further growth of the Dutch urban system. Bourgeois elites, already an important social force in earlier times, further tightened their grip on society. At the same time, urban forms of sociability, such as guilds and charities, provided stable structures for a rapidly changing social landscape. Through its citizenship arrangements the government was able to effectively tap the economic resources of the country. This in turn helped make the Republic into one of the Great Powers of its age, enabling the government to provide protection for the country's global trade network.

One element of these favorable citizenship arrangements was the religious freedoms available to non-Calvinists in the Netherlands. These freedoms were circumscribed in various ways, but they were significant nonetheless, as is demonstrated by the huge influx of religious minorities during the seventeenth century. Human and cultural capital formation were important aspects of the Dutch Golden Age. Investments in higher education gave Dutch students access to the most advanced knowledge of the age.

A specific interplay of long-term developments and short-term events helped to maneuver the Dutch into the distinguished line of relatively small, dynamic regions that propelled Europe forward during the late medieval and early modern periods. The fact that these regions were located in northern Italy and the Low Countries is no coincidence. Both areas displayed two crucial features: high levels of urbanization and low levels of political integration. These features were characteristic of the central urban belt (or "blue banana," as geographers call it) of Europe, that connected the two areas across Switzerland and Southern Germany. In the era before the Industrial Revolution this was economically the most dynamic part of Europe. The great political innovations, however, were pioneered in the territorial states, like England, France, and Prussia. Their advantages of scale would prove more successful in the nineteenth and twentieth centuries.

Further Reading

Davids, Karel, and Jan Lucassen, eds. *A Miracle Mirrored: The Dutch Republic in European Perspective.* Cambridge: Cambridge University Press, 1995.

Prak, Maarten. *The Dutch Republic in the Seventeenth Century: A Golden Age.* Cambridge: Cambridge University Press, 2005.

Price, J.L. *Holland and the Dutch Republic in the Seventeenth Century: The Politics of Particularism.* Oxford: Clarendon Press, 1994.

Vries, Jan de, and Ad van der Woude. *The First Modern Economy: Success, Failure, and Perseverance of the Dutch Economy, 1500-1815.* Cambridge: Cambridge University Press, 1997.

Chapter 8

A Tradition of Tolerance

Wijnand Mijnhardt

Today the Netherlands is known as one of the most permissive societies in the Western world. Yet the Dutch brand of permissiveness, which is readily associated with the acceptance of homosexuality, women's rights, abortion, same-sex marriage and the liberalization of soft drugs and euthanasia, originated from the cultural protests of the 1960s and 1970s that would dramatically transform the Dutch landscape.[1] As a result of that social revolution, many Dutch citizens consider permissiveness and tolerance as essential parts of their self-image and identity, even to the extent of creating a historical lineage that goes back to the early days of the nation. The seventeenth century, the Dutch Golden Age, is seen to supply a great deal of corroborative evidence for this belief. At that time, the Dutch Republic was the only country in which freedom of conscience was enshrined in the law, resulting in the influx of refugees of all possible religious backgrounds. Moreover, the Republic was the established Eldorado for authors and journalists who found the opportunity here to publish works that would elsewhere be put on the index of forbidden books immediately.

However, contrary to accepted wisdom, a continuous tradition of tolerance in the Netherlands is impossible to establish. True, the Netherlands experienced remarkable phases of tolerance in the seventeenth and early eighteenth centuries, as well as in the last decades of the twentieth century. Yet, these periods were exceptions rather than the rule and they resulted from very specific sets of circumstances. Moreover, both phases can hardly be characterized by hard-principled tolerance. Upon closer examination of that tradition, the Dutch practice of tolerance derived from a culture of lenient permissiveness and was rarely principled in character.

The Seventeenth-Century Tradition

Historians have found it difficult to understand Dutch seventeenth-century tolerance. On the one hand the Dutch state was exceptional in early modern Europe in that it had written the modern idea of freedom of conscience into its constitutional charter. Article 13 of the Union of Utrecht of 1579, which provided the framework for the United Provinces, explicitly stated that in the Dutch provinces "each person shall remain free in his religion and that no one shall be investigated or persecuted because of his religion." This provision was never questioned by any religious group in the Netherlands and the Republic experienced a practice of increasing tolerance. Yet, it still was some major conceptual leaps away from the modern liberal notions of tolerance that were developed in the later eighteenth century. Moreover, the

Dutch, with a few exceptions, never developed their own full body of theoretical literature on the subject.[2]

Dutch elites at the time simply were not engaged in a sophisticated philosophical debate. They had a state to govern, which from its inception at the end of the sixteenth century was fundamentally unstable, especially in matters of politics and religion. A few examples may illustrate this point. In the young Republic, of the approximately hundred towns with over 2,500 inhabitants, no fewer than fifty-seven directly participated in the national decision-making process through the assemblies of the Provincial Estates. This resulted in an extreme fragmentation of power. In this tough political school Dutch magistrates learned very early on to avoid the numerous bones of contention and seek compromises acceptable to an ever-changing majority without pushing matters to an extreme.[3]

The way in which the Reformation had been introduced into the Low Countries made religious diversity infinitely more problematic in the Dutch Republic than it did in England, France or Germany. Since no denomination had ever enjoyed open or tacit support from the secular authorities, none of the competing religions ever succeeded in reaching a strong majority. In the mid-seventeenth century Calvinism and Catholicism were still at loggerheads, with each about forty percent of the population, or even less, while dissenters of an almost unimaginable variety, including those who had not yet decided to join one of the competing religions, amounted to more than twenty percent of the inhabitants.[4]

As a result, quarrels over religion were endemic and took place against a background of – at least from a European perspective – unrivalled "public opinion." The Dutch Republic very quickly had developed into the most urbanized area of Europe. The 1550-1650 period saw unparalleled economic growth and unprecedented urbanization. A fundamental requirement for city-life was some degree of literacy. Almost from its infancy, the Republic was a very literate society, permeated with commercial values and skills, and quickly absorbing the flood of publications that issued from the many cheap presses. The Republic therefore boasted large and mobile audiences who were interested in politics and all questions of religion. The extensive literate audiences of the Republic throve on the production and distribution of large quantities of anonymous pamphlets covering internal and external politics and religious affairs, often garnished with biting political commentary.

Equally central to the atmosphere of instability was the breathtaking number of immigrants, which made for an exceptional level of diversity: social, geographic, linguistic (inhabitants of Dutch cities were used to hearing a dozen different languages), and most of all religious. Although many immigrants came from Calvinist territories, the majority were Lutherans and Catholics, but among them there also were many Jews, and adherents of a great variety of sects and other persecuted religions. This diversity produced a complicated system of crossed loyalties that made it extremely difficult to impose uniform standards of behavior.[5] These elements taken together made for fundamentally unstable political, social, and religious structures.

Certainly, the Dutch ruling classes would very much have preferred to force the population into joining a Unified Reformed Church. They dreamed of a manageable, broad, and popular established church that would supply a religious refuge to as many reformed varieties as possible. That the creation of such a broad and popular reformed church was a failure, however, was a result of the intractability of the Calvinist church leaders as much as of the prevalent ideals of tolerance. Calvinists were a large minority and that is exactly what they wanted to be. Most consistories, the congregation's governing body of elders, deacons and other elected officials, were by no means eager to receive the rank and file of the population into their midst. On the contrary, they applied strict rules for admission and laid a heavy emphasis on church discipline with expulsions as the ultimate penalty, a penalty that was frequently invoked. Governmental use of force in religious matters was equally impossible as it would have violated the basic provision of the Utrecht Union.

Owing to the fragmentation of sovereignty, the boundaries between the public and private spheres were not nearly as sharply drawn in the Republic as they were in the surrounding absolutist states where the authorities, as the carriers of an undivided sovereignty, tried to dominate public life by all available means. Freedom in the Republic was great indeed, and praised by many visitors. A considerable number of civic rights usually associated with those of the nineteenth-century citizen, already existed in a primitive form in the Republic. However, these rights were quite different from the *Rights of Man and of the Citizen* in French revolutionary times. At best they were realizable options within a fluid governmental practice dominated by compromise. The public sphere as the explicit domain in which the citizen proudly created a position for himself in relation to the state, was continuously being redefined in the Republic.

Most Dutchmen were townsmen. They were also citizens by want of any substantial aristocracy. Quite naturally the Republic knew great hierarchical and social differences, but city life meant that this inequality could – and at times had to – be lived and experienced in very different ways. In the towns, the various social classes lived in close vicinity. The upper classes along the canals, the craftsmen on the long, intersecting roads, the shopkeepers and the unschooled on the cross-streets, while the poorest of the poor huddled in the alleys and passageways that every street and canal concealed in abundance. These often underground passageways and alleys connected a large number of cellar-dwellings, and backyards crammed with yet another motley assembly of badly lit, ramshackle houses. This close physical proximity made social differences clearly perceptible, but at the same time demanded their bridging. The result was an impressive self-regulating system of contact and social control, teaching the townspeople to give and take. Within this framework, conspicuous consumption was unacceptable and unwise.

Religious as well as social tolerance in the Republic was both principled and pragmatic. The key to successful social interaction and religious cohabitation was relative tolerance, or rather a general culture of lenient permissiveness that aimed at the preservation of mutually good relations. Even the authorities were under this obligation. Not only did the administrative culture require a policy of compromise, city officials simply did not have the power, militarily nor politically, to enforce religious or social conformity, even if they wished to do so. As a result tolerance was much greater in the Netherlands than elsewhere. However, this freedom can only be understood within the unstable and complex political framework of compromising discussed above. Nobody could claim tolerance as a right and Dutch tolerance was contingent on a very peculiar social and political structure.

Hugo Grotius:
Founder of Enlightenment Thought

Hugo Grotius was a brilliant lawyer and an innovative philosopher who laid the foundations for international law. He was born as Huigh de Groot in 1583 in the Dutch city of Delft. A child prodigy, he entered university at the age of 11 and produced his first edition of a text from the classics three years later. Grotius became the chief legal advisor of Johan van Oldenbarneveldt, the leading politician in the early years of the Dutch Revolt. During his service, Grotius drafted the official position on the practice of religious tolerance that would eventually be adopted by most Dutch regents. He claimed that only the basic tenets necessary for maintaining civil order (for example the existence of God and Divine Providence) ought to be enforced, while all other differences on theological doctrines should be left to private conscience. Grotius' involvement in religious and political strife caused his arrest and his confinement for life in Loevestein castle. He succeeded to escape in 1621, with the help of his wife and a maid servant, in a bookcase. In the Netherlands today, he is chiefly famous for this daring escape.

Through his writings, Grotius, an exile for the rest of his life, became one of the founders of Enlightenment social thought. The Christian tradition assumed that human beings were incapable of living together peacefully. Only divine grace prevented the world from slipping into perpetual murder and mayhem. This constituted divine grace as the foundation of Christian society and gave human beings a clear choice between despair, death and destruction, or acceptance of their own sinful insignificance. Philosophers, however, began to wonder if one could conceive of a passably functional society without divine grace, based on human endeavor alone. The question became ever more pressing as Europeans learned more about the world beyond their continent, about civilized societies that were not based on Christian dogmas and traditions.

Hugo Grotius became a prominent ideologue in this debate. He asked whether it was possible to formulate universal principles of law based on self-love – the only principle of human action that would be left if God abandoned the world. Answering this question in the affirmative, he proceeded to devise a system of natural law (that is, one without any metaphysical foundations) based on the right of self-defense, from which logically derived an obligation, in his view, to avoid harming others. Grotius believed that this line of reasoning provided a legal basis for a human morality without any divine contribution. The consequences were immense. Grotius made it possible to conceive of a fully functional human society that sidestepped, as it were, the Christian dilemma. For rather than being faced with a stark choice between despair and divine grace, humans could achieve a livable society in which life and property could be safeguarded. On the basis of these principles society – as a human construct – could be analyzed, discussed, and even improved.

Grotius died in a shipwreck near Rostock in Germany in 1645.

Tolerance and the Dutch Origins of the European Enlightenment

The tradition of tolerance that the Dutch developed during the seventeenth century had far-reaching effects though. The most important result was the early Dutch Enlightenment that became one of the major sources of the European Enlightenment. Dutch intellectual culture was an intellectual battlefield on which three different groups were competing. The first were the radicals, headed by towering intellectuals such as theologian Balthasar Bekker (1634-1698), who claimed that theology and philosophy each had its separate realm and who launched a successful attack on the belief in witches and oracles. But the most important radical of all was the Dutch philosopher of Portuguese Jewish origin Baruch de Spinoza (1632-1677).[6] Not surprisingly, the intellectual skirmishes were triggered off by the intellectual system of French philosopher, mathematician, scientist and writer René Descartes (1598-1650) who trumpeted reason as the only reliable guide in the material world. After all, it was in Holland that Descartes published his major works and it was here that Europe's Cartesian struggles began, several decades before they took place in France. While Descartes himself still had entertained strict views on the number of subjects to which reason could be applied, his Dutch colleagues went much further and also employed Cartesianism, the rationalist assumption that all certain knowledge can be derived through reason from a number of innate ideas, to find solutions for all problems of religion and of the interpretation of the scriptures which in the Republic had become heavily politicized affairs.

The second competing group, the orthodox Calvinists, headed by the Utrecht professor of theology Gisbert Voetius (1589-1676), claimed that Cartesianism subverted all established religion and philosophy by its contention that large parts of the Scripture should be interpreted figuratively and in terms of their historical context. A third group that participated in the debate, composed of moderate theologians, tried to steer a middle course. Their ideas can be traced back to the Dutch humanist Hugo Grotius (1583-1645).

Initially, the radical Cartesians succeeded in dominating the debate. Lodewijk Meijer (1629-1681), for instance, an Amsterdam lay philosopher, applied Cartesian methods to theology in his *Philosophia Sacrae Scripturae Interpres*, published in 1666. In his view the Scripture was so full of contradictions and discrepancies, that it would be a disgrace to God to attribute its authorship to Him. Spinoza, equally setting out from Cartesian premises in his *Tractatus Theologico-Politicus* (1670) reached even more outrageous positions. He claimed to liberate the individual and society from "superstition" fostered by fear and, by freeing society from superstition and accepted religion alike, to liberate the individual from intellectual servitude. The only means towards this end was bringing the light of reason to biblical studies and undermining the "principle that it is in every passage divine and true."[7]

By the mid-1670s the heyday of radicals was over, however. Surprisingly, the ultimately successful campaign against the Cartesian radicals was organized not by the orthodox Voetians, but by the moderates who let themselves be inspired by Descartes as well. By attacking Spinoza and his friends, these leading intellectuals of the Republic hoped to fend off the attack of the orthodox Voetians on themselves, show that the new rational philosophy did not lead to atheism and to pose as the defenders of the religious and moral order.

A crucial role in the framing of a new consensus in the field of theology and philosophy was played by Herman Alexander Röell (1635-1718), a professor of philosophy at Franeker University. Röell defended the divinity of Christ and argued against Spinozism alike, but exploited Cartesianism to the full and went further than any previous Calvinist theologian. He forged a theology linked to reason and produced a synthesis of the new philosophy and reformed theology, in which Christianity was portrayed as the most reasonable of all religions.

Dutch radicalism and its moderate reaction originated from religious and political issues that were typical of the Republic. Although they were initially only fit for indigenous consumption, in the decades around 1700 these ideas were disseminated throughout Europe. Crucial in this respect was the extended series of wars that Louis XIV imposed on Europe after 1672 in his aspiration to achieve a universal monarchy. It turned the Republic into the heart of a European-wide coalition against French imperial adventures and The Hague into the centre of European diplomatic intelligence. In this period the city band in the heart of Holland, consisting of Amsterdam, The Hague, Leiden, Rotterdam, and Utrecht – which would later develop into the *Randstad* – became the undisputed focus of the European Republic of Letters and the center of an emerging European knowledge society. In this cosmopolitan milieu the Dutch urban Enlightenment – both in its radical and its moderate forms – that had profited so immensely from the Dutch brand of tolerance, found its European reception.[8]

Baruch de Spinoza: Philosopher of Liberty

Bento – as he was called by his friends and family – was born in 1632 in the large Portuguese-Jewish immigrant community in Amsterdam. He was the second son in a prominent family of modest means. Though he must have been one of the star pupils in the Talmud School, at the age of seventeen his formal studies there came to an end as he was forced to help run the family's importing business. In 1656 Spinoza was served the most radical sentence available to his religious community: he was excommunicated for "monstrous deeds"

and "abominable heresies." Though the documents never made clear what these heresies exactly contained, it is very likely that he already had explored ideas that would become part of his legacy later: the rejection of the idea of a providential God, the denial of the immortality of the soul and the claim that the Law did not come from God and therefore could not be binding for Jews or anybody else.

Spinoza left the Jewish community and soon would leave Amsterdam as well. After a few years in the small village of Rijnsburg near Leiden (the small house in which he rented a room is now a museum) he moved to Voorburg near The Hague in 1663, where he supported himself by grinding lenses until his death in 1677. In Voorburg he composed his most influential treatises, the *Ethics* and the *Theological-Political Treatise* that was published anonymously in 1670 and caused a great stir. His *Political Treatise* remained unfinished, but it was published by his friends, along with other works and unpublished manuscripts.

Spinoza no doubt was the most creative and original disciple of René Descartes, the French philosopher who coined the phrase *Cogito Ergo Sum* ("I think, therefore I am") and who claimed that the physical world around us could best be understood by rational means without any divine intervention. However, whereas Descartes made a sharp distinction between the mind and the body, Spinoza asserted that everything that exists in the universe is only one reality. There is only one set of rules governing the whole of the reality which surrounds us and of which we are part. For Spinoza God and Nature were just two names for the same reality. As a result, Spinoza's God is not a personal God. He cannot be revered nor is he a Creator. No human attributes can be attributed to him – as was usual in the Jewish and Christian tradition that saw God as almighty, as a revenging God who nevertheless can also present himself as a father to his children.

Because of his naturalistic views on God, the world, human beings and on the ways human beings arrive at knowledge, Spinoza was able to develop a moral philosophy that centered around the control of the passions leading to virtue and happiness and that became the basis of a very important strand in Enlightenment thought. It laid the foundations for a strongly democratic political philosophy and a penetrating critique of the Scriptures.

The Contingency of Golden Age Tolerance

Dutch supremacy on the intellectual world market was not destined to last. The relative peace in Europe after 1715 and the growing practice of tolerance elsewhere made the Republic serve less often as a refuge for intellectuals and their publishers alike. England, Scotland and Germany would become important cultural centers in their own right and in France the new intellectual elite personified by famous philosophers such as Montesquieu and Voltaire saw the Republic still as an essential European print shop, but they did not need it anymore as a place of exile. Soon the position of the Republic as a European clearinghouse for French books and journals began to suffer as well, mostly as a result of the same sort of structural changes that affected the Republic's economy as a whole: the emergence of cheaper and much more conveniently located production centers elsewhere. In the second half of the century the Dutch book trade only succeeded in maintaining its international reputation as a production center of classical and oriental scholarship. Dutch tolerance practices for a very long time had been far more modern than anywhere in Europe. After 1750, however, the Dutch were surpassed by a host of philosophers all over Europe who no longer contented themselves with the ideal of freedom of conscience, but developed the concept of tolerance as a basic right of the individual.

Even more detrimental to the Dutch version of tolerance was the dramatic reduction in immigration numbers. At the end of the seventeenth century contemporaries began to see economic decline. The inability to compete with much more resourceful countries, such as England and France, forced the Republic to retire to those markets where it remained competitive, such as the money market. This change in the economic structure led to a decline in shipping and industry, which in turn caused a slow polarization of the division of income. Beginning in industrial regions around Haarlem and Leiden, the polarization drove considerable numbers of the ordinary towns-people into poverty and pauperism, and even began to threaten the economic security of the middle classes.

As demand for workers continued to fall, immigration came to a virtual standstill. While in the seventeenth century immigrants made up about eight percent of the Dutch population – albeit with heavy concentrations in the Holland towns where foreigners could count for between thirty and forty percent – in the eighteenth century most cities went into decline. Leiden and Haarlem lost more than a third of their populations and peripheral cities such as Enkhuizen and Zierikzee even lost more than half. Dutch cities not only became smaller and more self-centered, they also became much more homogeneous. Whereas in the seventeenth century uniformity had become almost impossible to implement, creating a thriving and innovative culture, in the eighteenth century uniformity and cultural homogeneity became the norm. This prepared the ground for an inward-looking nationalism that would engulf the Netherlands from the revolutionary period of the 1800s onwards.[9]

Central to Dutch cultural homogeneity was a peculiar mixture of visions of decline, religion, and Enlightenment, as developed by Dutch intellectuals. They began to interpret Dutch society as a moral community in which religion, patriotism, and good citizenship were expected to enhance one another. Together they would enable citizens to overcome the country's decline and to restore the nation to its former glory. What mattered to the Dutch was the degree to which someone had acquired knowledge and civil virtue supported by religion. This image of the country's future dramatically changed the role of ministers of religion. They had to concern themselves more than before with the cognitive and moral as well as with the religious education of their congregation. As a result, religion was very far from being marginalized around 1800. On the contrary, religion rather became a prerequisite instead for the undisturbed spread of enlightenment and civilization. Precisely the preponderance of Christian religion of whatever persuasion would provide Dutch culture of the nineteenth and early twentieth centuries with an inward-looking, unadventurous and conventional quality that abhorred intellectuals of stature.

It is therefore hardly surprising that quite a few eminent authors and intellectuals chose to leave the country: the brilliant literary critic and Utrecht professor of Greek Rijklof Michael van Goens (1748-1810) wandered through the German lands, never to return. The most influential literary critic and historian of the nineteenth century Conrad Busken Huet (1826-1886) emigrated to Paris where he died. The famous Dutch author Multatuli (1820-1887) moved to Germany from where he continued to castigate Dutch society and politics. Throughout most of the twentieth century the Netherlands would continue to be the most religious nation in Europe. Church membership and church attendance were invariably high and Christian parties, who since the introduction of universal suffrage in 1917 dominated national politics, had used their monopoly to ensure the public funding of religious education out of public means and to enshrine Christian morality in the laws of the land.[10]

Tolerance and Permissiveness in the Later Twentieth Century

The sudden collapse of Dutch religion in the 1960s stood at the basis of a new phase of permissiveness and tolerance. Church membership declined and attendance dropped dramatically. At the beginning of the twenty-first century less than forty percent of the population is recorded as belonging to any congregation, and those who still do are much less involved with church life than ever before. Within one generation religion, that had been the pillar of society for centuries, was transformed into a ghettoized minority.

It is too simple to explain this radical collapse by reference to processes of secularization and modernization. In the Netherlands modern mass politics had fully integrated politics, social change, and religious fervor in the powerful mix of pillarization – that is the segregation within society according to church membership and social status – which had made Dutch religion almost impervious to traditional secularizing trends. The disintegration of Dutch Christianity had a different background.

From the 1950s onwards the Netherlands once again went through a rapid process of urbanization and industrialization that would transform the country. The *Randstad*, in particular, could rapidly compete with city states such as Singapore and Hong Kong as the most densely populated region of the globe. These changes produced a novel world view that encouraged individual entrepreneurship and individual creativity. Most of all, it favored the introduction into mass culture of the full idea of the self, that up to then had been confined to a small elite.[11]

This cultural revolution exemplified by values such as authenticity, expressivity, reflexivity, culminating in individual self-fulfillment clashed radically with the inflexible and authoritarian character of Dutch Christianity. It is here that we find the causes of the rapid demise of the hold of organized Christian religion over society. Dutch churches continued to offer a conformist identity that allowed no individual variety, whereas increasingly the general public perceived the Netherlands as a society of individuals, who needed to be tolerant of each other's religious preferences. Soon these new-born individuals would claim autonomy in establishing their personal life-styles and their modes of consumption as well. Society needed to provide space for these new forms of self expression. The state was expected to step back and to discontinue, first of all, the traditional Christian morality regimentation, but also to go easy on the enforcing of all laws limiting the opportunities for individual self-fulfillment. It is hardly surprising that the new ideals of tolerance and permissiveness fuelled by conceptions of the expressive self, focused on questions of sex and gender, especially the acceptance of homosexuality and female emancipation.

The rapid acceptance of the new models of self-expression and tolerance, especially when compared to other European states, can be partly explained by the fact that this cultural revolution took place in a homogeneous society. The Dutch were predominantly white, all inhabitants had received a comparable education and cultural styles did not differ fundamentally from region to region nor from class to class. Dutch social homogeneity was so overwhelming that for decades the ever-growing immigration of guest laborers and their families from Europe's Islamic fringes, with their totally different religious and cultural backgrounds, did not impair the prevalent policies of permissiveness and tolerance. As the sojourn of the Islamic workers was supposed to be only temporary, for a very long time they could remain an invisible and irrelevant category. In the meantime many Muslims found attractive legal opportunities to organize themselves on a religious basis – as the legal framework that had made early twentieth-century "pillarization" so successful was still in place. As a result, this seemingly easy integration of Muslims into the Dutch nation through the traditional pillarization framework could easily be interpreted as another success of tolerance and permissiveness Dutch style.

However, Dutch tolerance would turn out to be a contingent affair once again. Though some adverse opinions could be heard in the late twentieth century, the new millennium put an end to the atmosphere of optimism, tolerance and permissiveness. After 9/11, Muslims soon came to serve chiefly as the image of the "Other," as the opposite of the favored Dutch self-image of a nation of tolerant individuals, as a representation of a past that the Dutch were now glad to have shaken off and even as a danger as they might function as the Dutch base for a world-wide Islamic revival.

As a result, Dutch tolerance and permissiveness today seem to be in a quandary. Muslims now are seriously advised to adopt Dutch tolerance and to restyle their Muslim religion accordingly. A counter revolution urging the return to more traditional values seems to be gathering momentum and citizens increasingly ask for non-permissive and strict governance again. Even though the outcome of the debates is by no means certain, the tolerant and permissive policies of the last quarter of the twentieth century are very unlikely to return. Dutch culture has entered a new unadventurous phase that reminds one of earlier periods and certainly will serve as a new impetus to question the myth of the permanency of Dutch tolerance so dear to Dutch intellectual elites.

Further Reading

Israel, Jonathan. *The Radical Enlightenment: Philosophy and the Making of Modernity,* 1650-1750. Oxford: Oxford University Press, 2001.

Kaplan, Benjamin J. *Divided by Faith: Religious Conflict and the Practice of Toleration in Early Modern Europe.* Cambridge: Harvard University Press, 2007.

Kloek, Joost and Wijnand Mijnhardt. *1800: Blueprints for a Society.* London: Palgrave/ MacMillan, 2004.

Mijnhardt, Wijnand W. "The Construction of Silence: Religious and Political Radicalism in Dutch History," in *The Early Enlightenment in the Dutch Republic,* edited by Wiep van Bunge, 231-262. Leiden: Brill, 2002.

Chapter 9

Politics between Accommodation and Commotion

Ido de Haan

On May 6, 2002, Pim Fortuyn was killed. He was the leader of a new populist party, simply called List Pim Fortuyn (LPF), which was leading the polls for the national elections that were to take place nine days later. Dutch prime minister Wim Kok told the *New York Times* that day: "I feel devastated by this. … What went through my head was, 'This is the Netherlands, the Netherlands, a nation of tolerance.'" While his reaction testified of the in-clination towards – or at least the self-image of – a politics of peaceful accom-modation, the murder of Fortuyn was a symptom of a broader tendency. Dutch politics in fact appeared to move away from time-tested models of conflict resolution, towards a much more eventful and antagonistic political climate. The nation known for its tolerance suddenly seemed to have turned into an intolerant nation, where ethnic minorities were targeted by populist politicians. Progressive parties in turn were accused of muffling the debate on the drawbacks of the multicultural society under a blanket of political correctness. Adding to the confusion was the fact that the fear of "Islam-ization" of Dutch society was voiced by the manifestly gay Fortuyn, and that progressive values of gender equality and sexual liberty were suddenly presented as the core of Dutch identity. That identity was considered to be endangered by the overly tolerant attitude towards the more traditional attitudes among Moroccan and Turkish minorities. Careful accommodation was thus replaced by constant commotion.

This unexpected reassessment of Dutch political culture can only be understood against the historical background of Dutch politics. What was the nature of the politics of accommodation? What are the causes and conse-quences of its transformation? How did Dutch political elites respond to these changes?

Politics of Accommodation

The American political scientist Robert Dahl once argued that the Nether-lands were a theoretical impossibility. How was political stability feasible in a society where social divisions were so strongly institutionalized, and where the leadership of the pillars mobilized its members on the basis of strict inter-nal discipline, negative mutual stereotyping, and social exclusion of those

Pillarization: Segregation and Consensus

One of the most distinctive characteristics of the Netherlands is the religious, social and cultural segregation the Dutch call *verzuiling*, which is most commonly translated as "pillarization." This societal structure dominated Dutch society from the beginning of the twentieth century until the late 1960s and left remnants well into the twenty-first century.

Pillarization originated in the late nineteenth century from the desire of Catholics, conservative Calvinists, and socialists to emphasize and preserve their identity within a society dominated by a liberal political elite and the Dutch Reformed Church. Whereas the process of pillarization has been interpreted as a process of emancipation of minorities, it was also a strategy of the religious elite to insulate members in their congregation from an increasingly secularized world. Since each compartment comprised both lower classes and elites the vertical metaphor of a separate "pillar" was used.

Each of the groups created their own social and political institutions. An orthodox Protestant, for instance, would vote for the Anti-Revolutionary Party (ARP), belong to a Protestant labor union and read a Protestant newspaper such as *Trouw,* whereas a Catholic would vote for the Roman Catholic State Party (RKSP), join a Catholic labor union and read a Catholic newspaper. It went without saying that one could only shop at a grocer, baker or butcher of one's own pillar. Pillars also had their own hospitals, insurance companies, housing corporations, youth clubs, sports clubs, marching bands and other social organizations – a practice which turned the Roman Catholic Pigeon Fancier's Club into a proverbial example of pillarization in popular culture. The number of "mixed marriages" between partners of different pillars *declined* between 1945 and 1960, indicating a

reinforcement of the social aspects of pillarization in the immediate postwar period.

The legacy of pillarization was probably most prominent in media and education. With the introduction of radio and television each pillar created its own broadcasting association, each of which would survive the end of pillarization and continued to characterize the Dutch public media landscape in spite of the competition from commercial networks. More importantly, each denomination founded its own schools. The ensuing political battle over governmental funding for education was solved in a famous agreement in 1917 that guaranteed all schools equal financial support, regardless of their religious identity. This pragmatic arrangement, which was formalized in article 23 of the Dutch constitution, is often described as the high-water mark of pillarization.

Pillarization declined after the 1960s when secularization and democratization undermined the denominational and ideological identity of each pillar and as increased prosperity allowed for more mobility, education and the availability of television that offered people a glimpse across the boundaries of their own group. The Catholic and socialist labor unions merged into one union (FNV) in 1975 and the three mainstream religious political parties united into one Christian Democratic Alliance (CDA) five years later.

Some argue that the influx of Muslim immigrants since the 1970s, who initially were not particularly encouraged to integrate but left to their own resources, created a new form of "pillarization."

who refused to conform to the pattern of pillarization? Dutch-American political scientist Arend Lijphart answered this question in his classical formulation of the pillarization theory, in which he presented the "politics of accommodation" as the essence of the Dutch political system.[1] While political elites stirred up their constituencies with their manifest political rhetoric, he argued, they showed prudent constraint in their dealings in the backrooms of politics. Dutch political elites aimed for practical compromises, in which mutually acceptable outcomes were guaranteed by the rule of proportionality between pillars and the secrecy of negotiations. When a compromise was not feasible, elites were able to depoliticize the issue by referring it to technocratic advisory boards, or by postponing a decision by turning it over to committees of wise men.

According to Lijphart's colleague Hans Daalder, this mode of conflict resolution had a long pedigree in the "consociational" tradition that stood at the basis of the Dutch Republic, and even before that time had developed out of the common struggle against the sea and the shared interest in building and guarding the dykes to protect the country against flooding.[2] From this perspective, the elite's "rules of engagement" that emerged at the end of the nineteenth century were an adaptation of older elite practices. These rules were now applied to the new problems of emerging social groups such as the orthodox Protestants and socialists, who claimed cultural recognition and a fair share of the national wealth. The politics of accommodation became a way of peacefully integrating new groups into the Dutch state.

Yet, from another perspective, the politics of accommodation can be seen as a new invention, aimed not at emancipating and integrating, but at mobilizing and disciplining a constituency, which could function as the storm troopers in the struggle between political elites. This point of view also affected the perspective on the famous Pacification of 1917 by which the elites reached an agreement on two issues that had been fiercely contested in the years before – the position of confessional schools and the introduction of universal suffrage. This agreement was now no longer seen as the moment when political disagreements were solved, but on the contrary, as the institutionalization of the conflicts between pillars that only then developed into full-blown social networks.

The system of pillarization had been remarkably stable between 1917 and the middle of the 1960s. It survived severe criticism from intellectuals outside and even inside the pillars, as well as the German occupation between 1940 and 1945. After 1945, all major parties returned to the scene, be it for some under another name: the Protestant parties ARP (*Anti Revolutionaire Partij*) and CHU (*Christelijk Historische Unie*) returned unaltered, yet the Catholic party was re-established as the Catholic People's Party (*Katholieke Volkspartij*; KVP), the social-democrats merged with progressives from all sides of the political spectrum into the Labor Party (*Partij van de Arbeid*; PvdA), while the more conservative oriented liberals formed the People's Party for Freedom and Democracy (*Volkspartij voor Vrijheid en Democratie*; VVD). More importantly, the pillars were able to impose their pattern of organization on all aspects of society, by controlling life from the cradle to the grave, just like the emerging welfare state in which the pillarization became deeply entrenched.

The "pillarized" division of society constituted a pervasive, structuring force in Dutch society, even though some groups stayed clear of the grip of the pillars, such as for example intellectuals, writers and artists, substantial parts of the world of business and industry, and also large groups of urban youngsters. During elections in the 1950s, at the highpoint of pillarization, the five main political parties received ninety-five percent of the vote, while the electoral support for each of the parties was remarkably stable. The stability of the system was strengthened by putting divisive political issues on ice. This turned the "pillarized" civil order as a whole into a "frozen party system" in which parties and groups inside the political system had an insuperable advantage over interests not represented by the cooperating elites.[3]

Shifting Involvements

The 1950s were not just the highpoint of pillarization, however, but also the period when the system began to show its first cracks. Indicative of these fissures was the official warning (*Mandement*) the Dutch bishops issued in 1954, in which they threatened to excommunicate all Catholics who had sympathized, or even just interacted with social-democrats. Was this a sign of ultimate assertiveness, or of increasing uncertainty of the Catholics? Although historians are still undecided on the issue, it is clear that it signaled the beginning of deteriorating relations between political elites, in 1958 finally resulting in the end of twelve years of political cooperation between Catholic and socialist parties.

Political interaction became much less predictable in the following decade, leading to a major political crisis and a landslide defeat of the Catholic party KVP in 1967. This inaugurated a long period of restructuring of the party system, which initially hurt the confessional parties the most. After prolonged and difficult negotiations, the Catholic and Protestant parties agreed in 1980 to merge into the Christian Democratic Appeal (*Christen Democratisch Appèl*; CDA). The social democratic party initially profited from the problems of the confessional parties, reaching its apogee in the middle of the 1970s, when its leader Joop den Uyl led a progressive coalition. The party scored an all-time high of thirty-five percent in the elections of 1977, crowding out the other small left-wing parties of communists, pacifists and radicals, which finally merged in 1990 becoming Green Left (*Groen Links*). However, the success of the social democratic party was only short-lived, since it fell into a deep electoral and ideological crisis in the 1980s, only to re-emerge in the middle of the 1990s under the leadership of Wim Kok, who aimed to liberate the party of most of its socialist inheritance.

The Dutch politics of accommodation lost its resilience in the mid-1990s, however. In 1994 the conservative coalition of liberals and Christian Democrats, which had formed three consecutive governments under prime minister and CDA party leader Ruud Lubbers that lasted a total of twelve years, finally came to an end. The CDA, which was out of power for the first time, fell into a deep crisis, losing almost half of its votes and even more of its self-confidence. Just like the Christian Democrats had done in the late 1990s, the PvdA lost half of its electoral support in 2002. The party of Pim Fortuyn, which had profited the most from the defeat of the PvdA, in turn imploded almost completely already in 2003, making room for a series of other political newcomers to experience their fifteen minutes of political fame. As pollsters and political scientists have acknowledged, the very radical swings in voters' preference have made it much more difficult to give an accurate prediction of electoral results.

Underneath these political changes lie social and cultural processes that are often summarized by catchy phrases like individualization, fragmentation, secularization, and the most popular *ontzuiling* (depillarization). Since these concepts do not tell us much, it is more useful to point to three major developments: in the composition of society, in the functioning of the state, and in the political mediation between the two.

Social and Cultural Changes

To begin with, the social composition and cultural perspective of Dutch society has changed dramatically since the 1960s. Until that time, the Netherlands had a substantial agricultural sector and an industrial working class. The latter formed a reservoir of political mobilization that quickly disappeared after the rise of wealth and the transition to a service and knowledge economy since the end of the 1950s. At the start of the twenty-first century, most people belonged to the middle class and lived in suburban areas or even in newly developed cities in the polders, such as Almere – established in 1976 and already the seventh largest city in the Netherlands.[4]

A remarkable convergence of cultural values has taken place within this very large middle class. While the 1960s are often depicted as the era of radical experimentation – exemplified by relatively marginal social groups, such as students and intellectuals – the more decisive transformation might actually be the sudden and widespread acceptance of progressive cultural values among the majority of the Dutch population.[5] Yet, while the cultural homogeneity of the majority of the population increased since the 1960s, ethnic diversity also increased due to the immigration of people from the former colonies, labor migrants from the Mediterranean region, and refugees from all over the world. At the beginning of the twenty-first century the population of the Netherlands reached sixteen million, three million of whom originated from elsewhere – almost half from Western countries such as Germany, Belgium, the United Kingdom and the United States, and the other half from non-Western countries. In the Netherlands these non-Western immigrants are called _allochtonen_, "those who come from elsewhere."[6] The combination of a massive shift to progressive values among the native Dutch middle class and the influx of ethnic minorities has resulted in a country where the progressive values receive wide support, while at the same time an increasingly intolerant attitude has emerged towards the new minorities that deviate from this progressive consensus.

Pillarization and the Welfare State

These changes are not unique to the Netherlands, but characteristic of all Western countries. Yet in the Netherlands, these developments were reinforced by two additional factors. The first is the scope of the welfare state. Together with the Scandinavian countries, the Netherlands has one of the strongest welfare states, which has taken care of people from the cradle to the grave. This development was strongly promoted by the pillars. Welfare state programs often were carried out by "pillarized" institutions such as hospitals and organizations for social work. Welfare provisions also indirectly contributed to the legitimacy of political parties and trade unions, which were able to guarantee their constituency's social security and a high standard of living.

Secondly, the leadership of the pillars had always been concerned about the moral effects of the welfare state, fearing that its materialism would undermine the normative foundations of society. They also believed that true human development consisted of individual mental or even spiritual growth, or – as it was called in the 1950s – "freedom in connectedness." As a result, Dutch political elites were committed to a kind of pre-emptive progressivism, in other words they aimed at stimulating the development of individual autonomy as a precondition of responsible citizenship and social stability. For example, the Department of Social Work, established in 1952 as a bulwark of Catholic organizations for social work, changed in the 1960s into a Department of Culture, Recreation and Social Work, which presented itself as the vanguard of a society on its way to a more relaxed and playful social well-being. In this way, Dutch elites strongly contributed to the culture shift of the 1960s and 1970s that undermined the pillarized social network their authority was built on.

The erosion of elite authority was exacerbated by the development of the state. As a result of the disintegration of pillarized networks, it became ever more difficult to channel and aggregate the demands of citizens. The American neoliberal political science of the 1980s described this as the mechanism of rising expectations, provoked by the tendency of the bureaucratic state to provide an increasingly wide range of services. Again, this more general development had a specific Dutch twist. In response to the erosion of pillarized authority, many of its organizations started to look for alternative sources of legitimacy, which they generally found in a more service-oriented mission: they argued that they deserved a role in the execution of the welfare state because they were actually able to deliver the goods. Many of the formerly pillarized organizations now formulated new "mission statements," presented in colorful brochures, and tried to represent the modern, cost-efficient and market-oriented version of the public sector as was promoted in the management theories that became known as New Public Management.

The rising – and increasingly varied – expectations of citizens were met – and even stimulated – by the former networks of pillarization. It created a welfare state in which ever more detailed and specific legislation was introduced for an increasing number of handicaps and setbacks. This in turn contributed to the emergence of a managerial and technocratic style of governance. The highpoint of this development were the two consecutive "purple" coalitions of social democrats (red party colors) and liberals (blue) that governed between 1994 and 2002. These were not only the first coalitions without participation of any of the confessional parties since 1917, but also coalitions that presented themselves as explicitly non-ideological, in which the social democratic party in particular "had shaken off its ideological feathers," as its leader Wim Kok argued. The coalition was to be held accountable for its practical results, not for its ideological intentions.

And so it was: the purple coalition lost thirty-six of its eighty-three parliamentary seats in the election of 2002. Ironically, the coalition had led the country through a period of unprecedented prosperity, yet was held accountable for a series of unfortunate events and policy failures: in the years leading up to 2002 public scandals erupted over disastrous fires, continuously delayed trains, waiting lists at the hospitals, but most importantly over the apparent failure to adequately address the problems of second- and third-generation immigrants. According to the populist leader Fortuyn, the social democrats in particular had evaded these complex issues by promoting a soft multiculturalism, while abandoning the concerns of the "true Netherlanders" and the poor "autochtonous" people in the older districts of the major Dutch cities. *natives*

The Disconnection of State and Society

The rise and fall of Fortuyn's populist movement LPF points to a third development, which is the transformation of the relations between state and society. During the period of pillarization, an almost seamless network of institutions existed by which the demands of citizens were channeled to the state and – vice versa – policy measures were implemented in society. Political parties played a central role in this network. Party leaders were often also the editor-in-chief of the newspapers of their own pillar, and parties had a strong grip on their own public broadcast companies. Connections were also strong with the pillarized trade unions. Even Wim Kok started his career within the social democratic trade union NVV, and was its president before he was tapped as party leader of the PvdA.

Yet the role of parties eroded in the course of the 1980s. Membership declined, from almost 500,000 for the confessional parties and around 150,000 members of the PvdA in the 1950s, to respectively 70,000 and 58,000 in 2008 – while the population grew by fifty percent. Political parties remained the main channel for recruitment of political personnel, yet the pool from which people were selected had diminished. Moreover, the media became independent from the pillars. The national newspaper *de Volkskrant* lost its Catholic identity and turned into a bulwark of progressivism, while the social democratic newspaper *Het Vrije Volk* lost many of its subscribers before its last issue appeared on March 30, 1991.

The public broadcast companies kept their identity for a longer time, mainly because their broadcast license was based on the idea that they represented a relevant group in society. But their ratings suffered from the competition of commercial private broadcast companies, which tried to gain access to the broadcast system since the 1960s, until they finally succeeded in 1989. As a result, the media became much more independent from political parties and powers, and thus developed into an alternative channel for the articulation of social interests.

Consequently, political parties and their representatives in parliament and government lost much of their legitimacy, a tendency that was exacerbated by the technocratic style of government of the 1990s. Citizens did not lose their trust in the democratic system as such, nor was there a decline in voter turn-out – this has been invariably high, around eighty percent since mandatory voting was abolished in 1970. Yet the politicians themselves became increasingly worried about the relationship with their constituency. When Fortuyn voiced the populist cliché that the "political class" had lost its connection with the "real people," especially those who were said to suffer from the burdens of multiculturalism, he was expressing a concern that was already widespread among mainstream politicians. This both helps to explain the success of Fortuyn, as well as the lack of a reply to his populist challenge.[7]

Pim Fortuyn: Libertarian Populist

Pim Fortuyn was the colorful populist who is credited with exploding the political consensus system in the Netherlands by mobilizing resentment against immigration and the political elites.

W.S.P. (Pim) Fortuyn (1948-2002) was born into a Catholic family. He studied sociology in Amsterdam, where he submerged in Critical Theory and Marxism, and explored the gay scene. He became a charismatic lecturer of radical sociology at Groningen University, where he received a PhD for a well-researched and balanced dissertation on the policies of economic reconstruction in the Netherlands between 1945 and 1949.

His academic career stagnated in the late 1970s, perhaps due to his quarrelsome character. He left the university to become a professional policy consultant and acquired some fame by his efficient management of the introduction of the national public transportation card for students. Increasingly convinced of the inefficiency of many government organizations, the former Marxist embraced privatization and the rolling back of the state. His inaugural lecture as professor of Labor Relations at the Erasmus University of Rotterdam in 1991 was pointedly entitled "Without Civil Servants" – a theme that consistently returned in all his later work, for which he found a wider audience after he became a columnist for the rightist weekly *Elseviers Weekblad*. In several books he addressed issues of bureaucracy, the educational system and the healthcare system.

In the mid-1990s, Fortuyn was a well-known speaker for disaffected entrepreneurs who resented the "soft" policies of the nanny state. After several attempts to become prominent within a number of parties, Fortuyn began to present himself as "politician without a party," and as a savior who would be able to lead the country back to prosperity. He also began to criticize immigration and multiculturalism, and warn against the "Islamization of the Netherlands." After 9/11, increased media attention for these issues helped his voice to gain momentum.

Late 2001 he was invited by a platform of disenchanted former social democrats to become the leader of a new national party: Livable Netherlands (*Leefbaar Nederland*). He made a spectacular impression in the media with his acceptance speech, ending by saluting the audience, shouting, in English, "At your service!" Notwithstanding the remarkable rise of the party in the polls, Fortuyn managed to anger his party by his anti-immigration rhetoric and resigned as party leader in February 2002. Two days later he presented a new List Pim Fortuyn (LPF). After winning a landslide victory with "Liveable Rotterdam" in the local elections in Rotterdam on March 6, 2002, Fortuyn became a media hype, irresistible to politicians and journalists alike, none of whom were able to cope with his inflammatory rhetoric. The polls for the national elections on May 15 predicted a huge success for the LPF: "Mark my words, I will become the next Prime Minister of this country," Fortuyn prophesied. On May 6, however, he was shot dead by an animal-rights' activist who later declared he considered Fortuyn to be a danger to society. The life of the political dandy had ended, yet his death marked the beginning of a calamitous period in Dutch politics.

The Politics of Fear

In response to the rise of populism, a significant part of the Dutch political elite has adopted its politics of fear, based on the evocation of dangers only they would be able to ward off. Again, the rise of populism is not a strictly Dutch phenomenon. There is a remarkable resemblance between Fortuyn and later populist leaders such as Rita Verdonk and Geert Wilders, and Austria's *Freiheitliche Partei Österreich* (FPÖ) of the late Jörg Haider, the Flemish *Vlaams Blok* of Filip Dewinter, the *Schweizerische Volkspartei* of Christoph Blocher, and even in Italy with the *Lega Nord* and Berlusconi's *Forza Italia*. All of these parties had a strong impact on the political system by mobilizing an anti-political and anti-establishment sentiment, as well as by an attack against foreigners within the country. In each country, these populist basics were amplified by more specific issues such as the language conflict in Belgium, the division of North and South in Italy, or the anti-European sentiment in Switzerland. Moreover, the traditional parties have also reacted differently in the various countries. While the Flemish Block has been isolated within a cordon sanitaire, the Austrian confessional ÖVP collaborated with the FPÖ in a coalition between 1999 and 2005. In the Netherlands, even though its leader was murdered, the List Pim Fortuyn (LPF) won 17.3 percent of the votes in the elections of 2002, becoming the second largest party with 26 seats in Dutch parliament. The LPF was then invited by the Christian Democrats and liberals to form a coalition government. After only eighty-six days the coalition collapsed, due to internal struggles within the LPF, leading to their electoral defeat in the intermediate elections in 2003.

Despite the short-lived success of the LPF, many of the populist themes have found other outlets. The LPF has been succeeded by the anti-Islam radical Geert Wilders, who gained international attention with his internet video-pamphlet *Fitna* in 2008. After he left the liberal VVD, Wilders won six percent (nine seats) in the parliamentary elections of 2006. A year later, another liberal renegade, Rita Verdonk, created the movement *Trots op Neder-land* (Proud of the Netherlands), which for a while also scored high in the polls. Even more remarkable is the adoption of populist themes in other, more mainstream parties. Especially after the murder of controversial filmmaker Theo van Gogh by a radical Muslim on November 2, 2004, there has been a strong tendency to adopt a much more negative stance against foreigners and a widespread call to reinforce the Dutch national identity. For instance, the Christian Democratic politician Maxime Verhagen called for a renewal of the awareness of a Dutch *Leitkultur* (leading culture), while Jan Marijnissen, the leader of the Socialist Party (a formerly Maoist splinter that became the voice of the disenchanted underclass) argued in favor of the belonging to a *Heimat* (native region) – in both cases the adoption of German words indicated they said something new for which their vocabulary was insufficient. Prime Minister Jan Peter Balkenende on various occasions also stressed that "the minorities profited from a more demanding approach ... A society should be demanding and conscious of the values of the community, the mastery of the language, and the meaning of its history." Also the social democratic PvdA – which was accused by Fortuyn of having become a multiculturalist "leftist church" – began to stress the need to listen to the "autochtonous" Nether-landers, and to impose stricter norms on "allochtonous" – that is, especially second and third generations immigrants from Morocco and Turkey.

The result of all this has been a long series of heated debates on potential dangers of Islam, threats posed by Moroccan youngsters and the nature of Dutch identity. For instance, the refusal of some imams to shake hands with women and the wearing of a head scarf were discussed as signs of a rejection of Dutch society. After a number of politicians of Moroccan descent were installed in parliament, a debate ensued whether their double nationality and the possession of the Moroccan passport (Morocco does not acknowledge the right to denaturalization) were an indication of their insufficient integration in Dutch society. And the social democratic minister for Housing, Neigh-borhoods and Integration, Ella Vogelaar was criticized as "weak on Islam" for suggesting that in the course of the next *centuries* it might become another cultural influence in Dutch society. In 2008 she was forced to resign, not by the populist opposition but by her own party, PvdA, because of her lenient stance towards minorities.

In response to these changes, historians have begun to question the self-image of the Dutch nation and to look for the more rebellious and violent aspect of Dutch history. Yet, as the Dutch-American historian James Kennedy has argued, it is not so much the violent nature of Dutch political transformation, as its sudden and also massive character that is striking. The Netherlands is a country of consensus, yet there are moments this consensus undergoes a rapid and collective transformation, as a result of the pro-active attitude of Dutch elites.[8] In the 1960s this contributed to a dramatic shift to progressive values. In the first decade of the new century, the pendulum has swung to the other side, creating a political commotion that hinders the peaceful accommodation of the conflicts of the twenty-first century.

Further Reading

Daalder, Hans. "Consociationalism, Centre and Periphery in the Netherlands." *Politiek en Historie: Opstellen over de Nederlandse Politiek en de Vergelijkende Politieke Wetenschap*, 21-63. 1981; Amsterdam: Bert Bakker, 1990.

Hendriks, Frank, and Theo A.J. Toonen, eds. *Polder Politics: The Re-Invention of Consensus Democracy in the Netherlands*. Aldershot: Ashgate, 2001.

Lijphart, Arend. *The Politics of Accommodation: Pluralism and Democracy in the Netherlands*. Second Revised Edition. Berkeley: University of California Press, 1975.

Schuyt, Kees, and Ed Taverne. 1950: *Prosperity and Welfare*. Dutch Culture in European Perspective, Volume 4. Basingstoke: MacMillan Palgrave, 2004.

Visser, Jelle, and Anton Hemerijck. *A Dutch Miracle: Job Growth, Welfare Reform and Corporatism in the Netherlands*. Amsterdam: Amsterdam University Press, 1997.

Chapter 10

The Second World War: Dilemmas of Occupation

Christ Klep

On May 4, National Memorial Day, the Dutch commemorate all civilians and members of the armed forces who died in wars and peacekeeping operations since the outbreak of the Second World War. The Dutch flag is flown at half-mast and two minutes of silence are observed at eight o'clock in the evening, during which time public transportation comes to a stand-still. In most cities and villages people gather around monuments, listen to speeches and lay down flowers to remember the dead. The official commemoration, which is attended by the Royal Family, members of the government, military author-ities and representatives of the resistance movement and survivors of perse-cution, is held at the National Monument on Dam Square in the city center of Amsterdam and is broadcasted on public television. Similar events are organized at other locations such as the Waalsdorpervlakte in the dunes near The Hague, where many Dutch resistance fighters were executed during the war.

The following day, on May 5, Liberation Day is celebrated with a wide variety of festivals, concerts, fairs and other lively events. It can be argued that these two days, perhaps together with the Queen's Birthday on April 30, belong to the few truly national holidays during which the Dutch display and ponder their national identity, as is witnessed by the traditional playing of the national anthem and the general display of the tricolored flag, both rare occurrences in the Netherlands.

Although the commemorative festivities aim to address wider themes of freedom and liberation from all kinds of war, persecution and hatred, the dates are anchored in the more specific memory of the Second World War in the Netherlands. The dates were chosen because on May 5, 1945 the com-mander of the German army in the Netherlands, General Johannes Blaskowitz, surrendered to his Allied opponent, Canadian Lieutenant-general Charles Foulkes in the small town of Wageningen.

The yearly commemoration of what for most people is still "The War" illustrates the huge impact the Second World War had – and still has – on Dutch society. In common parlance the twentieth century is divided into prewar and postwar generations. Even more than half a century later refer-ences to the war can be found daily in Dutch newspapers and media. For much of the discussion about a variety of topics such as the requirement to carry identification documents, official registration of minority groups, Dutch membership of NATO, participation in international peacekeeping operations, abidance to international law and taking a stance against genocide, the experience of the Dutch during five years of German occupation is still an essential frame of reference.

The German Invasion

When England and France declared war on Germany after its invasion of Poland on September 1, 1939, the Dutch government still hoped to be able to stay out of the conflict. After all, when the First World War broke out, the German army had passed by the Netherlands in its massive attack, and the belligerents had respected Dutch neutrality, which was considered of mutual interest to all. Partly with that experience in mind, Dutch foreign policy remained strictly neutral. Politicians and the population at large alike tended to believe that war would not reach the Netherlands.

The Dutch Army was mobilized at the beginning of the hostilities, but consisted of no more than a quarter of a million troops, most of whom were young recruits and poorly equipped. Since the Eighty Year War in the seventeenth century, Dutch defensive strategy was mainly based on the so-called "waterlinie," a defense line that consisted of land that could be flooded in case an enemy attacked. This line, which had been perfected and expanded during the nineteenth century, mainly protected "Fortress Holland," the western part of the country where the major economic and political centers were located. Although newer defense lines were prepared to the east, the last line of defense remained the relatively small area behind inundated land and the great rivers in the West. But this static "waterlinie" was obsolete and not able to withstand the new warfare from the air, with bombers and paratroopers.

The German attack in the early morning of May 10, 1940 came almost as a complete surprise. The German invasion was supported by airborne troops, some of which immediately occupied strategic points in the center of Rotterdam and landed near the governmental city of The Hague, although they failed to capture the Queen or the government. German troops succeeded in conquering the southern and eastern parts of the Netherlands within no more than two days. Only "Fortress Holland" and the isolated province of Zeeland in the south held out against the German forces when on the early afternoon of May 14 the German *Luftwaffe* bombed the city of Rotterdam, completely destroying the city center and killing eight hundred civilians. After the Germans threatened to attack other major cities the next day, Commanding General Henri Winkelman was forced to capitulate on May 15, 1940. Dutch military defenses had withstood the German attack for no more than a mere five days, a defeat that would linger in the Dutch mind for many years to come.

Meanwhile, Queen Wilhelmina, her daughter Princess Juliana, and other members of the royal family, together with the prime minister and his cabinet had all fled to England in a controversial decision that would be debated throughout the war, and long after. In London the government-in-exile continued to govern over the overseas territories. Especially the Netherlands

East Indies remained an important source of raw materials and money until the Japanese invaded and occupied the colony in March 1942.

Despite Dutch neutrality Germany had decided to invade and occupy the Netherlands. The first reason for this decision was strategic. From a military perspective, the Netherlands was of vital importance for the plan of the German regime to invade England. The Dutch coast and harbors were an essential spring board in the German military plans for this *Operation See-löwe*. But occupation of the Netherlands was equally appealing to the German regime from an economic perspective. Occupied Netherlands would become a vitally important economic center during the war and contribute to the German war effort.

The German Administration of the Occupied Territory

National-socialist Germany had two aims for the occupied territories in the Netherlands, one mainly economic, the other ideological. First of all, the Netherlands presented a rich source of economic wealth because of its industrial capacity, agricultural riches and educated work force. It was in the interest of the German authorities that citizens in occupied territories would continue their daily lives.

Until well into 1943 the Germans were quite successful in maintaining continuity and normalcy. They installed a civil authority in the Netherlands that was headed by the Austrian politician Arthur Seyss-Inquart. This civil administration initially tried to portray itself as friendly, bound the German military to strict rules and – most importantly – made full use of the Dutch national bureaucracy, local civil servants and mayors, almost all of whom stayed in office. For most citizens in occupied territory life continued more or less as usual, in spite of war-time limitations such as curfew, black-out and the obligation to carry identity cards. As a result, Germany largely succeeded in the economic exploitation of the Netherlands.

A second German aim was the "nazification" of the Dutch population. The occupation authorities hoped to win the Dutch over for the ideology of national-socialism that had brought Adolf Hitler to power. The Germans tried to convince the conquered Dutch that the German political system was superior, especially in fighting communism (bolshevism) and Judaism. Propaganda emphasized that the Dutch and the Germans were "blood brothers" since they belonged to the same "Aryan race," the term the Nazi's used to describe the master race of people of Northern European descent. After the German invasion of the Soviet Union they argued that the Dutch should join their fight against the "red barbarism."

However, the "nazification" of the Dutch population was not very success-ful because it was hindered by several factors. First of all, the Dutch generally tended too much towards individualism and parliamentary democracy to feel attracted to a centralist and collective ideology such as Nazism. Denomi-national and political segregation, or "pillarization," as a form of institut-ionalized tolerance, was a further strength in Dutch society and largely contradictory to the centralism as embraced by Nazism. Furthermore the churches, to which eighty percent of the population belonged, provided an ideological alternative. And, finally, Queen Wilhelmina in London, after the first disappointment of her departure had subsided, presented a very powerful rallying point for patriotic feelings, symbolizing the unity of the nation. The powerful speeches in which she regularly addressed the people in the occupied Netherlands through Radio Orange, a service provided in London with the support of the BBC, turned her into a strong and beloved figure.

Ausweis: The Dangers of Identity Registration

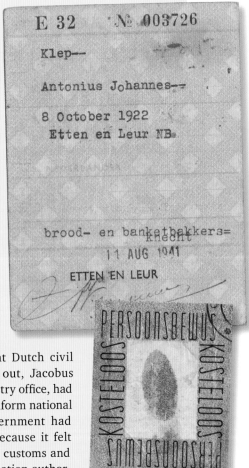

One of the deadliest instruments the German occupation administration used to control the Dutch population was the introduction of a new identity card. In April 1941 all citizens older than fourteen years were required to carry a newly issued identity card (*persoonsbewijs*). The new identity card was almost impossible to forge and also meticulously registered in a central file system. This handed the Germans a highly efficient and inescapable registration system, which they soon put to use in the persecution of the Jews.

Tragically, the new identification card that was to cost thousands of people their lives, was the brain child of a dedicated but ruthlessly efficient Dutch civil servant. Long before the war broke out, Jacobus Lentz, the inspector of the national registry office, had been obsessed with the creation of a uniform national registration of all citizens. The government had declined implementation, however, because it felt such registration conflicted with Dutch customs and traditions. But once the German occupation authorities had expressed the wish to register all citizens Lenz set to work to develop the most perfect identity card in Europe. The card, which contained name, address, place and date of birth, a photo and a finger print, was printed on specially produced carton with small lettering that was impossible to erase, made use of special ink and glue, and carried a seal that was attached to the photo and carried a copy of the finger print. The document also contained a serial number and date of issue that made it easy to track in the central register.

The card was so perfect that the Dutch resistance movement would never be able to produce a passable forgery. In April 1944 allied bombers attacked the central registrar's office in The Hague at the request of the resistance.

With equal dedication Lentz started to implement the registration of all Jewish citizens in a separate file system or *Judenkartei*. He even compiled a list of all last names that could possibly indicate a Jewish origin to catch people who failed to register. In September 1940 exactly 140,552 Jews and 20,268 citizens of partial Jewish decent were registered in his file system. The files would be used one year later when the Germans started the large razzias with which they rounded up Jews in Amsterdam. In January 1942 all Jews were identified with a large capital J printed on both sides of their identity card and in the file system. Thus, the Dutch registration system was turned into the most lethal administrative tool for the identification, segregation and deportation of Jews in the Netherlands.

The memory of the dangers connected with a centrally controlled identity card lingered long after the war. When the Netherlands introduced the requirement to carry an identification document in 2005, many protested and cited the war years to warn against central registration, as it could be used to exclude unwanted persons and could constitute an intrusion of privacy by the government.

Coping with the German Occupation

It is customary to distinguish three fundamental alternatives in the way the Dutch population reacted to the policies of the occupation authorities: those of accommodation, collaboration and resistance. Although these are useful categories in understanding the behavior of the population, one should keep in mind that reality often was much more confusing and people reacted differently under various circumstances, changed positions over time and were sometimes ambivalent.

The first and most common strategy was that of accommodation. Most Dutch civil servants such as teachers, police officers, and mayors stayed at their posts, some for formal reasons since a government directive from 1937 ordered them to obey any authority, others arguing that their resignation would only mean replacement by willing henchmen of the Germans. This grueling dilemma of the "wartime mayor" became something of a trope in later discussions on civil authority during occupation.[1] As the war progressed, especially from 1942 onwards, the attitudes sharpened on both sides. When the German authorities felt they were slowly losing control over the war, they reacted with stricter rules and regulations, and acted with increasing violence. This slowly undermined the willingness to accommodate throughout all layers of society.

A small part of the population, however, opted for the second alternative of active collaboration, some in the hope of personal gain, others for ideological reasons. The Dutch National-Socialist Movement (NSB) had never managed to receive strong support. Since it was founded in 1931, the anti-parliamentary and authoritarian "movement" won about eight percent of the vote in provincial elections, but was already in decline when war broke out. Even during the occupation, when it was the only legal party, its membership never exceeded 75,000. The NSB always remained rather isolated within Dutch society because it had to balance support for Hitler, who was widely hated in the Netherlands, and Dutch nationalism, which was unacceptable for the Germans who saw the Netherlands as a province rather than an ally. The leader of the NSB, the uncharismatic civil engineer Anton Mussert who was neither a convincing demagogue nor a strong personality, faced the problem of always being "in between" since he was not trusted by anyone: not by the Dutch, and even less by the Germans.

A similar fate was destined for the 25,000 Dutch who joined the SS, the elite of the German military, for ideological or more pragmatic reasons. They were obviously not liked by the Dutch, but despised by the Germans as well: after all, they were traitors to their own country, non-patriots. As a consequence, they were always given inferior tasks, and most were sent to the Eastern front, where many of them died.

The third and most courageous alternative was that of resistance. During the five years of occupation, probably not more than between ten and twenty thousand people participated in any form of armed resistance. The small size of militant resistance can partly be explained by the geographic circum-stances providing few places to hide because of the absence of mountains and forests. Also the geographical position of the Netherlands between Nazi-Germany on the one side, occupied Belgium to the south and the North Sea to the north and west, made resistance difficult to organize. Only a few dozen of the some 1,700 resistance fighters who tried to reach England (*Engelandvaarders*) succeeded in completing the difficult journey over sea or over land through neutral territory. Also, the absence of a strong military tradition of armed resistance, the short duration of actual fighting in May 1940 and the prevalence of a cautious, pragmatic attitude, limited the incentive for armed resistance in the Netherlands.

Some armed resistance movements executed individual activities, such as sabotage of military installations and the execution of German officers or known collaborators. But the Germans often reacted with heavy reprisals against the civilian population, sometimes summarily executing innocent bystanders. These reprisals fuelled moral objections to armed resistance for which innocent people paid with their lives. Some raised the question whether it was morally worthwhile to pay that price. Such moral debates dominated the political and moral discussions at the time, in which for instance questions were raised whether or not it can ever be ethically "right" for a civilian resistance fighter to kill a German. The fact that the Germans, at first, seemed to behave quite civilized added to such considerations.

Most resistance was unarmed and ideologically motivated. Some acts of resistance erupted as a direct response to the increasing limitations and restrictions dictated against the Jewish population. When in the fall of 1940 all professors at Dutch universities had to sign a "non-Jew" declaration, Professor Rudolph Cleveringa, the dean of the Law School at Leiden University, publicly spoke out against it in what was to become a famous speech. In February 1941, Amsterdam dock workers initiated the first and only strike in protest against the increasing persecution of the Jewish population. At the statue of the symbolic "Dock Worker," which was erected in Amsterdam directly after the war, this strike is commemorated annually on February 25.

One of the main resistance activities, often carried out in the greatest secrecy by individual citizens but sometimes organized in informal networks, was to help people to go into hiding to avoid German arrest. These persons in hiding, or "divers" (*onderduikers*), were not only Jews, but also for instance Dutch men refusing to participate in forced labor (*Arbeitseinsatz*) in Germany. Official documents were forged on a large scale to provide individuals with new identities, and food-ration cards were produced to supply people in hiding. It is estimated that about 350,000 people were in hiding at one point, assisted by 15,000 members of the resistance.

Another major activity of the resistance was the production and distribution of an underground press, which was extremely important since Germans controlled all Dutch newspapers and radio networks. At one point, there were twelve hundred different newspapers and periodicals, one printed in no less than a hundred thousand copies a week. Some of the newspapers that were started during the occupation still exist today, such as *Vrij Nederland* (Free Netherlands) and *Trouw* (Loyalty). Looking back, it is amazing how such a large scale operation could have been established. People had to show great resourcefulness, for instance, to find the necessary paper, lead and ink – at times even producing ink themselves.

The Holocaust in the Netherlands

An important part of the German administration's goal to achieve complete nazification of the Netherlands was the elimination of Jews, gypsies, homosexuals and other groups it considered undesirable or inferior. The prosecution of the Jewish population is one of the darkest periods in Dutch history. Less than thirty percent of the total Jewish population of about 140,000 Jews that lived in the Netherlands in 1939 survived the war. This bleak statistic gives the Netherlands the worst record after Poland. In Belgium, for instance, about seventy percent of the sixty thousand Jews survived the war; in Denmark all but one hundred of the 7,500 Jews survived. The contrast between the image of the Netherlands as a nation of tolerance without a strong tradition of anti-Semitism, and this grim historical reality has been called the "Dutch Paradox."

Historians have offered a number of explanations for the dismal Dutch record, such as the concentration of Jews in Amsterdam and other cities and the lack of hiding places in the crowded Dutch cities, as well as the thoroughness of the Dutch system of civilian registration and the cooperation of mostly law-abiding civil servants and the Jewish organizations themselves. Some also point at latent anti-Semitism in Dutch society and the absence of the Queen as leader of symbolic resistance. But Dutch Jews also faced a ruthless and ideologically motivated German civil administration that carefully paced the registration, persecution, internment and deportation of the

Jewish population in various stages and proved remarkably efficient and radical.[2]

Within months of the start of the occupation the German administration announced a series of restrictions and prohibitions which aimed to separate Jewish citizens from the rest of the population. In 1940 Jews were banned from the civil service and universities. Early 1941 the German occupation authorities initiated the next step of registration and concentration. One of the most insidious and far-reaching preparatory measures was to require all Jews to register in a central file system, which was followed early 1942 by the requirement to stamp a capital letter J in their identification papers and a few months later by the order to wear a yellow Star of David at all times. Jewish store-owners had to place signs in their shop windows.

After completing the administrative segregation the Germans ordered all Jews in the country to move to Amsterdam, where they were concentrated in the Jewish Quarter with the about eighty thousand Jews already living in the capital. Jews were banned from restaurants, cinemas, and other public places. This operation of administrative and physical concentration was executed with the assistance of the Dutch police, public transportation, and citizens.

Things would rapidly get worse. Foreign and stateless Jews had already been transported to Westerbork, a former refugee camp in the north-east of the country. In July 1942 the Germans and their Dutch collaborators started the fateful mass deportation of other Jews from Amsterdam to Westerbork, which now served as a transit camp from where trains left for camps in Germany and Poland each Tuesday. Immaculate records were kept: until September 1944 exactly 103 transports left Westerbork, deporting 97,776 people, most of them to the extermination camps of Auschwitz and Sobibor. From Westerbork and other camps in the Netherlands 107,000 people were deported. Only 5,200 returned. At the end of the war an astounding seventy percent of Dutch Jews had perished.

Anne Frank: Icon of the Holocaust

Anne Frank was born in 1929 in Germany, the daughter of Otto, a Jewish businessman, and his wife Edith. Immediately after Hitler came to power in 1933 Otto decided to move the family to Amsterdam, where he had business connections. Anne went to school, learned Dutch and lived the life of any other girl. When the German occupation brought persecution of the Jews to the Netherlands, however, she was forced to move to a segregated Jewish school and had to wear a yellow Star of David. When the Germans started the deportation of Dutch Jews in July 1942, Otto moved the family into a secret hiding place that he had prepared in a house behind his firm at Prinsengracht 263. The entrance to the *Achterhuis*, or annex, was hidden behind a bookcase and only known to four trusted employees who provided the family with food and other necessities.

Aug. 1942

The narrow three-storied house became the hiding place for Otto and Edith, their daughters Margot and Anne, the befriended family Van Pels with their son Peter, and later the dentist Fritz Pfeffer. They lived together in a confined space, sometimes under unbearable tension, for more than two years, until they were betrayed and arrested by the German police. In August 1944 the group of eight was deported to transit camp Westerbork, and from there on to extermination camp Auschwitz. Anne and Margot were transported to camp Bergen-Belsen where both died of typhus in March 1945, several weeks before the camp would be liberated. Only Otto would survive.

Inspired by an appeal from Radio Orange to record the memory of the war for later generations, Anne, who developed ambitions to become a writer, had kept a diary. In her notes she confided her daily experiences, reflections on what she knew happened in the outside world, and the feelings of a young girl coming-of-age in a slightly fictionalized form to her imagined friend Kitty. After the war Otto learned that Anne's diaries had been rescued from the hideaway by a friend. It took him until 1947 to get the manuscript published, but the diary soon became world famous after the English translation was published in the United States in 1952 as *The Diary of a Young Girl.* The book was turned into a successful play in New York three years later and in 1959 was adapted for the screen as *The Diary of Anne Frank,* which won three Oscars.

Anne Frank, probably more than anyone else, gave a face to the six million victims of the Holocaust. Her diary became one of the canonical texts of the twentieth century, because of the literary quality that brought the hiding to life, but also because it was felt to address the universal drama of human dignity in the face of persecution. The *Achterhuis* itself, rescued from neglect by international interest, was turned into a museum in 1960.

A Balance Sheet

Within a few months after the landing of the Allied Forces in Normandy on D-day, June 6, 1944, Belgium and the southern provinces of the Netherlands were liberated. The Allied attempt to cross the rivers at Arnhem in September 1944 infamously proved "a bridge too far," however. Whereas the south of the country was liberated, the north faced another winter under occupation. For the population in the northern provinces this was to become the worst period of the war: it was a bitterly cold winter and because transportation had come to a stand-still and large quantities of food were confiscated by the Germans, little food supplies remained. This led to the starvation of an estimated twenty-five thousand people, especially in urban areas. During this "Hunger Winter" many city dwellers tried to survive by skimming the countryside for food, or by eating flower bulbs. These last months of the war colored the memory of the occupation as a period of suffering, even though most Dutchmen had enough to eat until the last winter.[3]

The allied forces finally resumed their advance in March 1945; the capitulation of the German Army in the Netherlands followed on May 5. Parts of the country were left devastated, large areas in Zeeland were flooded and forty percent of industry was removed to Germany or destroyed. After the war, the economic damage was regarded as something that could be repaired, but the psychological damage was far greater. After all, the Netherlands had not been occupied since its start as a modern state in 1814/1815 and had suffered a severe blow in realizing that the trusted neutrality policy had proved completely ineffective.

The war did not present a very proud story, which helps to explain why at first emotions were dominated by a thirst for vengeance: to expose, humiliate and convict collaborators, and to take revenge on Germany. No less than 150,000 people were accused of collaborating in some form or another, sixty thousand of these accusations resulted in court cases. Finally, four hundred convicted collaborators faced long prison terms, and forty were executed. In comparison to Belgium or France, however, the period of revenge and retribution did not last very long.

Research of the war years formally started exactly three days after the liberation by the founding of the National Institute for War Documentation (now Netherlands Institute for War Documentation, NIOD), headed by Lou de Jong, a historian who had worked for Radio Orange in London during the war. De Jong started the public discussion by presenting a popular television documentary series on the Occupation in the 1960s and authored *The Kingdom of the Netherlands during the Second World War*, the officially commissioned history of the war that was published in no less than twenty-seven tomes of about fifteen thousand pages between 1969 and 1988. This study turned De Jong into the most visible representative of the first generation of historians who described the Dutch occupation and holocaust for a broader readership.[4]

During the first postwar years, public discussion tended to look back on the war in rather black and white moral terms of "right" and "wrong." But from the 1980s on a new generation of historians started to question the heroic story of mass resistance and suffering. Those historians began to ask new questions concerning the invasion and the mobilization of the Dutch army, which looked at military leadership and refuted many popular preconceptions, such as the myth that the Dutch Army was stabbed in the back, that is to say betrayed by a "Fifth Column." Most historians now point at the many continuities in the developments of the mid-twentieth century, such as pillarization, that were left unchanged by the occupation. Other publications have analyzed the many differences between various resistance groups who sometimes fought among themselves, and the size of collaboration in relation to the comparatively modest number of resistance fighters.[5] In short, this kind of research led to a more balanced picture in which shades of grey became visible between the black-and-white dichotomy of "right" and "wrong" that dominated in the first postwar years.

Looking back at "the" war years is also a way to explore the more general messages to be learned from the Second World War. The perspective is much wider than that of fascism and national-socialism, as the historical events of this period are now evaluated in the broader context of issues such as racism, nativism and exclusion, versus tolerance, human rights, and democracy.

Further Reading

Dwork, Debórah, and Robert Jan van Pelt. *The Holocaust: A History.* New York: Norton, 2002.

Fuykschot, Cornelia. *Hunger in Holland: Life During the Nazi Occupation.* Amherst: Prometheus, 1995.

Jong, Louis de. *The Netherlands and Nazi Germany.* Cambridge: Harvard University Press, 1990.

Lee, Carol Ann. *Roses from the Earth: The Biography of Anne Frank.* London: Penguin, 2000.

Maass, Walter B. *The Netherlands at War, 1940-1945.* London: Abelard-Schuman, 1970.

Moore, Bob. *Victims and Survivors: The Nazi Persecution of the Jews in the Netherlands, 1940-1945.* London: Arnold, 1997.

Wolf, Diane L. *Beyond Anne Frank: Hidden Children and Postwar Families in Holland.* Berkeley: University of California Press, 2006.

Art & Culture

Chapter 11

The Making of Rembrandt and Van Gogh

Ghislain Kieft & Quirine van der Steen

Rembrandt and Van Gogh are names every reader and every visitor of museums knows – their names are so familiar that even the illiterate and the blind will recognize them. In every history of Dutch art substantial and deserved attention is given to their paintings; sometimes even beyond the point of being reasonable. By far the most expensive study in art history was the "Rembrandt Research Project," which tried to establish once and for all the exact size and boundaries of Rembrandt's oeuvre. The project was so big, that it was said it could be seen from the moon. However, it failed to achieve its aim: art historians continue to quibble over Rembrandt. A former director of the Amsterdam Stedelijk Museum used to say that every Dutch student of art history should write his or her doctoral thesis on Rembrandt (although he failed to do so himself). A considerable amount of money is spent on research-ing Van Gogh's legacy as well. In the most ambitious project ever initiated by the Van Gogh Museum in Amsterdam – the museum which boasts the most visitors of all Dutch museums – more than fifteen years of research have recently been invested in newly publishing the complete correspondence of Vincent Van Gogh, including images of all the works mentioned in the letters.

Both painters are worldwide known to be "Dutch artists." That the Dutch public proudly considers them to be Dutch as well, was illustrated when in a public poll in 2004 television viewers were invited to elect "The Greatest Dutchman of all Time": both Rembrandt and Van Gogh ended in the top ten. Interestingly though, both artists were an exception rather than exemplary when compared to other Dutch painters of their time, which could raise questions as to the nature of their "Dutch" character.

Rembrandt: A Dutch National Artist?

Dutch history is rich in many very good painters, and in the history of the geo-graphically broader defined "Low Countries" even more so. However, Rem-brandt (1606-1669) was just "one of the boys," both in his own time and later on in the eighteenth century when Dutch paintings attracted the attention of foreign collectors. When glancing through the list of auctions of that era, other Dutch painters stand out. First and foremost there is the name of Gerrit

Dou (1613-1675), a former pupil of Rembrandt, and in his wake that of other painters of a similar bent, like Frans van Mieris (1635-1681) or Adriaan van der Werff (1659-1722), names hardly familiar to the public nowadays.

Dou, Van Mieris and Van der Werff were considered typical Dutch painters of the genre. "Genre" is a term used for the depictions of seemingly everyday life, like snap-shots. Such – often small-sized – paintings, depicting scenes of the decent, bourgeois, Dutch interiors, but also the scenes of taverns and brothels or sometimes odder topics, were produced in considerable quantities during the seventeenth century. Gerrit Dou's "Dropsical Woman" (right, *Louvre*, Paris) is a good example of such a painting, typical of his painstakingly precise style. It also attests of Dou's international fame in former times: it was said that this very Dutch painting, then in Turin, was given to a French general during the siege of that Italian city in 1799, in order to avoid its ransacking by the French.

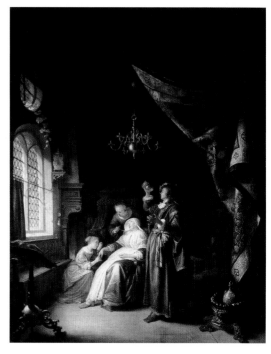

Yet, the subject of the painting could raise questions. Who would want to paint a girl suffering from dropsy? On closer inspection, however, one learns the girl has another kind of "illness:" she is lovesick. The man standing next to her, in his fanciful dress, is inspecting her urine in a urinal, and concludes that the young maiden unknowingly must be pregnant, much to the tearful distress of the others, for she is not married. This interpretation is confirmed by the fact that the subject was painted time and again in the seventeenth century. A snapshot it is not, but more the theme of a comedy or a dubious farce. Certainly not the kind of good, clean family-life the Dutch obviously wanted to be known for.

Other Dutch painters, whose work fetched high prices in the eighteenth century, were for example Jan van Huysum (1687-1749) or Maria van Oosterwijck (1630-1693), virtually forgotten nowadays. They were painters of still life, another very Dutch kind of painting, depicting flowers or food, for instance. Van Huysum and Van Oosterwijck were specialists in painting flowers, often in very precise arrangements. Today, they look very normal, even commonplace, but those flowers were precious – tulips came from Turkey – and never bloomed at the same time. The food in still life paintings is luscious, exotic and luxurious: lobsters from Norway, citrus fruits from Spain, grapes from France. In the seventeenth century this was a kind of culinary pornography. Similar things can be said about landscapes: although the genre is very Dutch, the subjects often were not. The Dutch loved mountainous scenery set in sunny Italy, or Germany, or even Sweden or Brazil;

it was only for the foreigners to later prefer the cliché of flat grasslands, windmills and cows.

In this array of Dutch specialties – genre, still life, landscape – the work of Rembrandt does not fit. He rather seems an exotic Dutch painter, who was not "made in Holland." He approached his trade far more dramatically than other Dutch painters, as he competed on an international level. It is true that a large part of his oeuvre consists of portraits, with a special fondness for self portraiture, but even there he often tried to be a narrator. Most representative of that affinity is perhaps the self-portrait that he made in 1640, after seeing Titian's portrait of Ariosto, copying the exact pose of the Italian poet in his own painting (left, *National Gallery*, London).

Rembrandt's famous "Nightwatch" (*Nachtwacht*) is in itself just a group portrait of one of the Amsterdam civic guards. As such this was a fairly common commission, but Rembrandt carried it out in his own way: it looks like an episode in a theatrical drama, not of people posing, but of playing out a role. What the scene is all about we do not know, but it decidedly has all the looks of a history painting. Similarly, in his later "Staalmeesters" – a group portrait commissioned by the Syndics of the Draper's Guild, a rather prosaic office – it looks as if a grand, ominous or heroic decision has just been made.

Rembrandt was a painter of history pieces, a genre never considered to be particularly Dutch, and rightly so, because it was an international genre of painting, developed in Italy. Although the young Rembrandt once proudly professed that there was no need for him to go to Italy, that was just a way to stress his ambitious "Italianate" outlook. For he added that what one could see scattered around in Italy, could be seen in Holland in a concise way, since Amsterdam in the seventeenth century was rapidly becoming the transit port of all kinds of goods, including Italian art. And indeed this interest is everywhere to be seen in Rembrandt's work; his "Blinding of Samson" (page 152, *Städelsches Museum*, Frankfurt) is both in size and cruel sublimity comparable to works of such artists as Titian or Michelangelo.

Rembrandt indisputably was interested in dramatic painters like Caravaggio, whose chiaroscuro he did not know firsthand, but definitely through Dutch followers such as Gerrit Honthorst (1592-1656) and Hendrick Terbrugghen (1588-1629). These very competent, Dutch painters of the early seventeenth century, originating from Utrecht, are known as the Utrecht Caravaggists. They were not very Dutch, and hence they are practically forgotten. Yet Rembrandt was their heir.

The fate of the Utrecht Caravaggists in later times, being forgotten or rather being denied their Dutch birthright, is emblematic of what happened in the early historiography of Dutch art. In the nineteenth century art history was written in a nationalistic register of thinking. It was the age of expressions of nationalism such as national anthems, flags, passports and capitals –

things both romantic and bureaucratic. Dutch artistic inventions, therefore, such as landscapes, still lifes or genre painting – the sort of artwork foreigners initially thought interesting and were willing to pay for – suddenly seemed somehow to represent the pure, unadulterated face of the Netherlands. Anything else, obviously coming from abroad, was to be reproached at best as "import" or as a form of "decline" of the Dutch character or words to that effect.

Yet, in that cult of patriotism, it was precisely the odd-one-out, Rembrandt, who became the true, national artist. It is difficult to say exactly why: maybe it was the very un-Dutch grand manner of his work that made him fit to become a hero. Of course, the country had many untold heroes, but few romantic, stirring heroes. Only Admiral Michiel Adriaensz de Ruyter (1607-1676) readily comes to mind: the sort of man, in other words, fit to be honored with an oversized bronze statue in a square – another custom from the nineteenth century.

But in terms of this retrospective typecasting, history could not find much of a heroic scale in that purified canon of Dutch artists, painters as they were of tulips, cows, brothels and dropsical girls, to put it negatively. At best, though, Dutch seventeenth-century art has offered the pictorial equivalents of Japanese haikus – think of Vermeer – in that it forces the viewer to concentrate on the beauty of practically nothing. Zen-like maybe, but not epic. Perhaps with the exception of Rembrandt.

Remarkably the fame of Rembrandt as a painter in the Dutch national tradition only took off in the course of the nineteenth century, as royal and aristocratic collections were moved to museums that were accessible to the public. Such democratization of art was initiated under the French occupation in the early 1800s, when the art collections of the stadholder became the nucleus of a truly national museum, which moved to Amsterdam in 1808.

Rembrandt's "Nightwatch" became the undisputed masterpiece in what would be called the "Rijksmuseum Amsterdam." Rembrandt's fame as "the" national artist was established when he became the first painter to be honored with a statue, which was unveiled in 1852 on the Rembrandtplein in Amsterdam. When the Rijksmuseum moved to the present location in 1885, architect P.J.H. Cuypers designed a special hall for the "Nightwatch," at the end of a gallery of fame, and in 1906 a separate extension was built for the painting, even further emphasizing its canonical status. Thus Rembrandt entered the consciousness of the wider public.[1]

Vermeer: Interior Fantasies

Johannes Vermeer (1632-1675) is definitely famous. His name often appears second to Rembrandt's as one of the great Dutch painters of the seventeenth century. In contrast to Rembrandt, who was already a well-known painter during his life, Vermeer's name was not really made until a good 200 years after his death, when his works reappeared in the late nineteenth century.

Compared to Rembrandt, Vermeer was a different kind of painter. Scholars still discuss the actual size of Rembrandt's oeuvre, which consists of about three hundred paintings. Scholars agree that the oeuvre of paintings by Vermeer is thirty-four – with further discussion about two more. This relatively small oeuvre is sometimes explained by the fact that he did not have a large studio with many pupils. Yet, one cannot be certain, since very little is known about his life. During his lifetime, Vermeer was not completely unknown; his name and descriptions of his works appear in some contemporary journals and books. However, very few people knew his paintings, and in the years after his death, many works were attributed to other painters and disappeared into private collections.

It was not until the late nineteenth century that scholars and art lovers rediscovered Vermeer and his paintings. Instantly, his paintings became famous, for obvious reasons. "Girl with a Pearl Earring" is special, even in reproduction. A young girl looks over her shoulder directly at the observer. Her headdress and one of her earrings, a beautiful pearl, dominate the image. Her mouth is slightly opened as if she is expecting something, which gives the painting an almost sensual atmosphere. The luminous quality of Vermeer's paintings, combined with a very serene, Zen-like tranquility makes them unique.

The paintings by Vermeer fit the period they were made in: they almost always depict interior scenes with one or a few people engaged in something. It is not always obvious in what exactly, which gives rise to all kinds of speculation, also among scholars. In a way, that makes Vermeer's paintings even more interesting: we have no idea what stories he wanted to tell the viewer, or if there are any. Consequently, we like to fantasize about them, try to figure out what a character is doing and why, as if it is a stage we look at. True or not, those fantasies can (and have) lead to novels and movies, such as "Girl with a Pearl Earring." In a novel with the same title, Tracy Chevalier tried to find an answer to the question about the identity of the girl. The novel was made into a movie by Peter Webber in 2003. Is there truth in the book or movie? Not very likely, but the fantasy is wonderful.

As a result of the movie and the world-wide distribution of reproductions her image has become familiar to many. But believe us, the mass media reproductions by no means come close to experiencing the real painting as it can be admired in the Mauritshuis Museum.

Van Gogh: The Invention of an Artist

In contrast to Rembrandt, it would be surprising if anybody ever thought of Vincent van Gogh (1853-1890) as a "typical" Dutch artist. The fact that he was born in the Netherlands seems just as coincidental as, say, the fact that the Eiffel Tower was built in Paris: it might as well have been elsewhere. His work does not look Dutch; as a matter of fact, it does not look like anything familiar. Yet, Van Gogh himself aspired to be a painter in the canonical art tradition. Throughout his short life he was full of breathless admiration for other "true" painters and desperately tried to become or to be an artist. However, his contacts with the professional painters, whose help or instruction he solicited, were always to remain very short and somehow uncomfortable.

It was not until he was around the age of 27 that Van Gogh decided to become an artist, after having failed at a religious career. In that year, 1880, he worked for a few weeks in the studio of Anton Mauve (1838-1888), a fairly typical painter of the so-called "Hague School." He painted by and large in the idiom of the Dutch landscape painters of the seventeenth century. Yet, contrary to the Dutch landscape paintings of that period – when Italianate and mountainous scenery was often preferred – the painters of the Hague School specialized in a picturesque genre of beaches, heaths and woods. This fondness for the "typical" Dutch landscapes decidedly originated in the nineteenth century, and these painters contributed, probably more so than anyone else, to establishing the image of Holland as made up of grass, milk and speckled cows (page 155, Anton Mauve, *Sheperdess with sheep* (1885-1886), *Rijksmuseum*, Amsterdam).

Van Gogh did not stay more than a few weeks with Mauve. In the winter of 1885-1886, Van Gogh entered the Antwerp Academy of Art, but again his stay did not last much longer than a few months. He left for Paris, where he studied for a while in the atelier of the French painter Fernand Cormon. Notwithstanding such rather short-lived and unsuccessful attempts to work within an established artistic context, Van Gogh would never be short of connections with the art world. He always stayed in contact with Dutch and later also with French artists, many of whom he met while staying in Paris.

Yet, by no means did Van Gogh lack the desire to become a normal artist in the traditional sense of the word and to establish a name for himself in the world of art. He just did not have the character for it. Incidentally, he did not seem to have the right mind for anything. He was restless, overempathic and oversensitive, more or less patiently supported by his family, especially his younger brother Theo, who was an art dealer. It was to this brother that Van Gogh directed many of the hundreds of letters he wrote. About eight hundred of his letters have been preserved and selections of them are still widely published in many languages, providing an invaluable source of information. They give insight not just into his life, but also into his thinking about art and being an artist – as if, rather than only to Theo, he was writing them for posterity also. Although Van Gogh wrote with staggering honesty, it should not mislead us in thinking that he was naïve: those letters are very much a careful picture of what he liked us to think about him, ear and all (page 156, *Courtauld Institute Galleries*, London). Inadvertently, he was thus creating his own persona, portraying himself as an artist with an oeuvre to leave to later generations.

The letters, as well as many of his self-portraits, attest to the fact that Van Gogh was evidently convinced about one thing: that he was truly an artist. From among the almost nine hundred paintings and eleven hundred drawings he created in just ten years time, Van Gogh was consciously fashioning a personal, coherent oeuvre, as if he wanted to leave a legacy of his paintings for posterity (and to make things easy for later curators and art historians). The concept of creating a personal oeuvre, to reveal one's artistic personality to the world, was not completely new in the nineteenth century. Yet, Van Gogh considered it an almost religiously inspired life's commitment to leave a "legacy to humanity."[2]

Rather critical about his own work, he considered a large part of his work as just studies, created for use in the studio only. Clearly distinguishing between "studies" and "paintings," his true oeuvre – the artistic essence of his work – was only to consist of the "finished" paintings he worked on and corrected in his studio. In his letters he mentions this oeuvre to consist of fifty (or later he mentions thirty) paintings. Among the paintings that he considered being part of it are the "Potato Eaters," – the first work he was to name "a painting" – made in Nuenen, in the south of the Netherlands, in 1885. Most of his oeuvre however consists of paintings he made in the south of France – where he lived and worked from 1888 onwards – among which "the Bridge at Langlois" (1888) and the "Nightcafé" (1888).

Painting in the nineteenth century was subject to change. Two developments proved instrumental in the artists' search for new directions and means of expression. Although painters still had studios, they were no longer restricted to only painting there, because of what might seem a simple invention: the tube. Combined with mass produced paint, it now became possible for the artist to simply take tubes of paint in all sorts of colors outside and paint *en plein air* – although the outdoor circumstances were not necessarily ideal. In his letters Van Gogh described that he was working in such a strong wind that sand was blown into the wet paint, or that the sun was almost too hot to bear. Remarking on the weather while painting in this way is very characteristic of the nineteenth century.

Being able to paint outside allowed for more spontaneity in the creative process. This was related to another important development, caused by the invention of photography. For centuries, creating realistic images had been an important function of art and artists. Because of photography, "realism" in visual art was slowly given another meaning or interpretation. Painting as realistically as possible was no longer that important: for a realistic image, a photograph could be taken. Instead, painters increasingly attempted to show the reality of the artist himself. Not copying or imitating nature, but presenting the artist's perception of it – a process in which spontaneity was considered an important factor. This intention of showing the personal way in which he experienced the world around him was certainly what Van Gogh did and aimed for, and this intention became all the more obvious in the work he painted in France.

Van Gogh did not lack knowledge of art history – in fact, he knew a fair bit about it, as he often admired and studied the masters of the past. He appreciated the seemingly spontaneous way in which Rembrandt, and also Frans Hals (ca. 1582-1666), used paints and brushes. Time and again he sets the admirable examples before his mind's eye in his letters:

> Hammer into your head that master Frans Hals, that painter of all kinds of portraits, of a whole, gallant, live, immortal republic. Hammer into your head the no less great and universal master painter of portraits of the Dutch republic: Rembrandt, that broad-minded naturalistic man, as healthy as Hals himself. I am just trying to make you see the great simple thing: the painting of humanity, or rather of a whole republic, by the simple means of portraiture.[3]

Yet, Rembrandt's gestures are always controlled and choreographed. Van Gogh does not dance: he often rages. Even the paintings he made in France – or perhaps especially these – with their sunny, bright and yellow glare, are at the same time uncomfortable, even agonizing, dark gestures of throwing paint on a canvass. "Style" is a word that can no longer be used here. Van Gogh devoted his artistic life to searching his own style.

Sadly, in the appreciation of his work, his intentions and the essence of his quest were after his death soon to be overshadowed by biographical data about his short artistic career. Although a great deal is known about the personal life of Rembrandt, this hardly compares to the extensive and detailed knowledge about Van Gogh. Facts about his life are widely known among the general public: he was poor, he lived in France (the last five years of his life, that is), he cut off his own ear, he never sold a painting during his life (well: just one) and he committed suicide. The idea that an artist should suffer for his talent, that life should not be easy, that there is a price to be paid for this talent, that the true artist is poor and successful only after death: this romantic cliché of an artist was not an invention of Van Gogh. But what he accidentally invented is what kind of painting should go with it. During his life, Van Gogh was an oddity; after his death he set the standard.

When he died in 1890, Van Gogh left an incomplete oeuvre. His brother Theo was stuck with his brother's innumerable, unsold paintings and drawings. In the subsequent twenty years, the family managed to sell some of them, but eventually they donated the largest part of the collection to the Dutch state. This Van Gogh collection, the largest in the world, is now on display in the Van Gogh Museum in Amsterdam. Thus Vincent van Gogh became a Dutch painter.[4]

Afterthought

The rest, as they say, is history. Both Rembrandt and Van Gogh somehow – and sadly – became legends, made into the two most famous Dutch painters. In a sense, Rembrandt and Van Gogh are indisputably Dutch painters. Yet, they are the false emblems of Dutch art history – a history which is much more diverse, complex and interesting.

The fact that the most extensive collections of works by Rembrandt and Van Gogh are to be admired in the Netherlands is not a result of a deliberate policy of the Dutch government, but is owed to the generosity of private donors. The fact that the finest works by Rembrandt are to be seen in the Rijksmuseum in Amsterdam and the Mauritshuis in The Hague is the felicitous product of the struggles of some art lovers who persuaded the rich middle classes to pay for them. The donation of the Van Gogh family led to the founding of the Van Gogh Museum in Amsterdam. In addition, the wealthy private collector Hélène Kröller-Müller (1869-1939), wife of the shipping magnate Anton Kröller, formed the basis for the Kröller-Müller Museum in Otterlo, which possesses another substantial number of Van Gogh's paintings and drawings.

The fame of Rembrandt and Van Gogh has placed them in the same league as mass fantasies such as Napoleon, Sisi (Empress Elisabeth of the Austrian-Hungarian Empire), Marilyn Monroe, or Elvis, and made them into Dutch brands for the tourist industry. Their works are reproduced to serve as souvenirs "from Holland," albeit that these are not necessarily "made in Holland."

Mondrian: Is this Art?

A rectangular painting with a white background that is divided by black lines, with some colored panes in red and yellow. That is what one observes when looking at this painting by Piet Mondriaan (1872-1944), or "Mondrian" as he wrote his own name. To be honest: it would appear to some that they could have been made by a four-year-old. Yet, easy and simple as they may seem at first sight, the paintings by Mondrian are decidedly not.

Mondrian had a very long career and painted in many different styles, which was not uncommon for an artist around the end of the nineteenth century. However, Mondrian is particularly famous for the kind of paintings he created in the second half of his career. It is obvious that this kind of painting is in so many ways different from the work made by Rembrandt, Vermeer or even Van Gogh, as there is no recognizable image. Art in the nineteenth century changed and realism was slowly given a different meaning. To Van Gogh, realism already meant something different than it did to Rembrandt. But to Mondrian, realism was an entirely new concept altogether. Mondrian asked himself what a painting really was. To him, it was an object of

its own, a flat, two-dimensional piece of wood, covered with canvas on which things can be drawn or painted. He considered it remarkable that for years and years, through the image they tried to paint on it, artists made that canvas look like something it is not: a three-dimensional object. For someone who believed in the laws of nature and respected them, this was something he no longer wanted to do.

Mondrian did not come to this idea overnight. Nor was he the only one, as other painters were dealing with similar questions. Yet, they found different answers. To Mondrian a canvas was also a natural object and should be part of the larger nature it was an element of. In his view, the entire world around him was nature: not only the trees and the fields, but also man-made objects such as the house one lives in. Nature he considered to be dominated by two directions: vertical and horizontal, and by the primary colors: red, yellow and blue. In his paintings, Mondrian wanted to express those natural elements. After some time, he no longer used realistic objects as examples, but only the natural rhythm of nature: panes of primary colors, divided by vertical and horizontal lines in their own rhythm, emphasizing the flatness of the painting.

Because all reference to objects have gone, observers sometimes tend to see abstract paintings as simple and easy, but they are everything but that. The attention and thought given to these works leave the observer a concept to be discovered, and a rhythm to be felt.

Further Reading

Fuchs, Rudolf Herman. *Dutch Painting*. London: Thames and Hudson, 1996.

Luijten, Hans, Leo Jansen and Nienke Bakker, eds. *Vincent van Gogh: The Letters; The Complete, Illustrated and Annotated Edition.* 6 vols. London: Thames & Hudson, 2009; Dutch edition: *Vincent van Gogh: De Brieven; De volledige, geïllustreerde en geannoteerde uitgave.* 6 vols. Amsterdam: Amsterdam University Press, 2009.

Schwartz, Gary. *The Rembrandt Book*. New York: Harry N. Abrams, 2006.

Slive, Seymour. *Dutch Painting, 1600-1800*. New Haven: Yale University Press, 1995.

Wetering, Ernst van de. *Rembrandt: The Painter at Work.* Berkeley: University of California Press, 2009.

Chapter 12

Style and Lifestyle in Architecture

Rob Dettingmeijer

Architecture today offers a paradox: on the one hand it is more popular than ever, on the other hand it is losing all the aspects that once defined this art and craft. More full-color magazines, websites, books and tourist destinations with a great emphasis on, or totally devoted to, architecture are published than ever. But this architecture is more about images than about objects. In contemporary architecture, tastes are changing even faster than fashion. Ben van Berkel of architect's firm UN-studio proudly claimed that "the architect is the fashion designer of the future." [1] Is this the result of the fact that the production of buildings is increasingly seen in terms of materialistic real estate development rather than a functionalist approach to provide shelter or as a meaningful reflection of social values? In this process the idea of architecture as a slow art, meant to survive the centuries and taking place in landscapes or townscapes loaded with memories and artifacts of distant times, seems to be almost lost.

In Utrecht both faces of architecture can be found. In the "Brainpark" of the Utrecht University (and other institutions for research and higher education) an open-air museum of the latest trends in architecture with star-architects has been built and is still under construction. The renowned architect Rem Koolhaas and his Office of Metropolitan Architecture – who have designed the master plan for the Utrecht University campus – but also UN-studio, Mecanoo, Wiel Arets, Neutelings and Riedijk, Jan Hoogstad and many more famous architects or young architects on their way to become famous, all seem to be engaged in a competition to show the most impressive, colorful, weird or funny designs.

Battle Between Gothic and Renaissance

It is also telling, however, that the ceremonial center of Utrecht University is still located in the heart of the old city: the *Academiegebouw* (University Hall), touching the limits of the Roman *castellum*, which was built to defend the northern border of the empire, formed by what was then the main stream of the river Rhine. It was within the remains of this *castellum* that some of the first Christian churches in the Netherlands were constructed and a diocese was founded. The oldest part of the *Academiegebouw*, the Auditorium, dates back to 1462. It was built as a chapter house of the Cathedral. The Union of Utrecht, regarded as the foundation of the Dutch Republic, was signed in

this room in 1579. This spiritual and historic center was the obvious choice as first seat of learning in 1636.

Two hundred and fifty years later the citizens and the Province of Utrecht offered to incorporate this hall into a new building satisfying the growing demand in the university for space. Academic education was considered the responsibility of the national government, which also owned large parts of the grounds and buildings that were to be incorporated in the new building. So the government offered help in the person of J. van Lokhorst, national architect for buildings of education. However, the local government and the university preferred Eugen Gugel, professor of Architectural Design at the Polytechnic in Delft. Gugel designed a monumental neo-renaissance building directly next to the former cathedral and connected to the cloister. This was met with heavy criticism by Van Lokhorst, who even felt obliged to make a new design in the neo-gothic style. It became a national issue and only after more than four years a compromise was found. The building kept the Renaissance facades but found a new location. The "new" plan folded itself around the monumental staircase so that it fitted into the corner of the square. Buildings had to be bought and demolished for this solution, but the government paid the extra costs. As a kind of revenge Victor de Stuers, the indefatigable leader of governmental-sponsored cultural conservation who had fuelled the conflict, ordered the placement of a new monumental entrance to the cloister in the gothic style as close as possible to the new building (above).

This story clearly illustrates that the difference of opinion was not about the function, but about the meaning of the building. The choice of style implicated a choice of vision on what the best moral civilization in the past and for the future was. In Europe in general the choice for neo-renaissance meant the choice for humanism or even for materialism, as in the case of the famous architect and theorist Gottfried Semper. Gothic was considered by many as the true Christian style or even the most rational style, as E.E. Viollet-Le-Duc stated. In the Netherlands this ideological watershed was even stronger. The emancipation of the Roman Catholics in the last quarter of the nineteenth century found expression in the building of a large number of Catholic, neo-gothic churches.[2] At the same time the national identity was clearly constructed around the Dutch Revolt by the seven Protestant provinces against Catholic Spain. Consequently, the "Dutch Renaissance" or "Old Dutch" architecture of this period and most of the Golden Age was seen as the national style.

The architect of most of the Catholic churches was Pierre Cuypers.[3] He became the architect of the Roman Catholic circle that gained power in the governmental circles and in the capital Amsterdam. Grouped around a free-style gothic church near the Vondelpark in Amsterdam they built their ideal picturesque village of villas and even a beerhouse. It was this Roman Catholic circle that enabled Cuypers to realize two of the most monumental profane buildings in Amsterdam: the *Rijksmuseum* (1876-1885, above) and the Central Station (1882-1889, with A.L. van Gendt). Both buildings were built in a mixed style but many, including the king, still considered them too gothic and "church-like."

Building with "Community Art"

Upon leaving the Central Station in Amsterdam one can already see the Amsterdam Stock Exchange (1884-1903, page 166 top), although this north side of the building intentionally blends into the old cityscape. Seen from this angle it is hard to believe this is considered by most historians and architects as the start of modern architecture. The vast brick wall at the Damrak screening two large halls covered with iron and glass roofs caused almost everybody to think it was a modern ugly building. This "bourgeois opinion" helped the architect, H.P. Berlage, to become the father of modern Dutch architecture.[4] Comparing the first designs of Berlage and Th. Sanders, more or less in a renaissance-style, to the way the second series of designs of Berlage evolved, in which he incorporated the examples and theories provided by architects Semper and Viollet-Le-Duc (see above) who pioneered in neo-styles, it is clear that an architecture for the twentieth century was born, but with its roots in the previous age. In the iconographical program of the sculptures, tiles and texts, a utopian socialist vision was clearly expressed, which

was rather strange for a "palace for trade." This Dutch version of the *Gesamt-kunstwerk* was called *Gemeenschapskunst* (Community Art). It was the ideal of many in the first half of the last century, so many sculptures, reliefs, stained-glass windows, and other applied arts are still visible even in social housing.

It is not surprising that Berlage liked his design for the Dutch union of diamond industry workers (*Algemeene Nederlandsche Diamantbewerkersbond*, ANDB) much better, because the Community Art was much more appropriate there. In the Stock Exchange, the brokers felt so ill at ease that they commissioned a new exchange building (1909-1912) on the same square (above, building to the right). They chose Eduard Cuypers, a nephew of Pierre, and partly trained at his office. The building is in the restrained fin de siècle style, *De Nieuwe Kunst,* that was popular at that time. The firm of Eduard Cuypers

was so successful among the Dutch elite and in the Dutch East Indies that it served as a school for nearly every Amsterdam architect of the next generation. So one could consider Eduard Cuypers the true father of the Amsterdam School, rather than Berlage who often has been given that tribute.

Without doubt the most famous products of the Amsterdam School can be found in the Spaarndam-merbuurt (left).[5] Michel de Klerk composed three blocks (1913-1915; 1915-1916; 1917-1920) in a flamboyant way, making him internationally famous overnight. No side of a building block looks the same and the sometimes complicated combinations of different types of dwellings, a school and even a post-office in the last block astonished everybody. In other parts of the city a large number of houses in this style were built as well. Many foreigners visited these examples of modern architecture and the social democrats even used these visits in their propaganda during the elections. This masked the fact that the first social-democratic alderman, F.M. Wibaut, hoped (like most other political parties) to provide shelter for the working class in one-family houses and not in large building blocks. But even under the new Housing Act of 1901 this proved to be impossible in almost all cases. Socialists still longed for the "Garden City," although only occasionally sections could be realized, mostly at the fringes of the city (for example in B.T. Boeyinga's Tuindorp Oostzaan, 1922-1924).

The Rietveld Schröder House: Icon of Architecture for the Modern Age

The Rietveld Schröder house is on the UNESCO-World Heritage List as "an outstanding expression of human creative genius in its purity of ideas and concepts as developed by the De Stijl movement," the modernist art movement that flourished in the 1920s. Incidentally, architects connected with *De Stijl* at the time did not consider it the best example of *De Stijl* architecture, a recognition which only came later.

The house is revolutionary in at least three aspects: the translation of the way a widow with children wanted to express her modernity; the way a building is no longer about walls, but about spaces in the inside connected as directly as possible with space outside; and the way the house is best appreciated by moving, because there is not one ideal observation point.

Rietveld was already well-known for his modern furniture and interior designs among a small circle of people who wanted to propagate modern living. One of his admirers was Truus Schröder. When her husband died in 1923 she decided to move into a smaller and new house with a view over the meadows. She liked the open skies so much she chose to live on the first floor. She and Rietveld held the opinion that every function of a dwelling should require an active decision to perform it. In this way one space could be used for different functions at different times. So by moving panels to a different position the kitchen can turn into a dining room; a bathroom is created by folding surfaces out of the wall. Most spectacular is the way sliding walls can divide the first floor into small bedrooms, or make it part of the continuous space of the living room.

Rietveld started the design process with a simple cubic form. He had already created a large wooden model of a design by architect Cornelis van Eesteren and artist Theo van Doesburg for Léon Rosenberg, the owner of the *Galerié de l'Effort Modèrne* in which the first *De Stijl* exposition in Paris was held. It deconstructed one solid into an abstract composition of horizontal and vertical planes. Rietveld did the same with his cube: first by applying colors and shades of gray to suggest depth; second by subdividing the planes of the cube and almost taking them apart. At first glance this just looks like an abstract play, but the horizontal protruding planes give shelter from the sun and the vertical planes give shelter against too much light and openness for the sleeping areas. The living and dining room area can be opened up so far that even the corner disappears. Rietveld himself said that the small poles in the primary colors were meant to create the suggestion of a scaffolding with only glass and no walls behind it.

In later designs Rietveld was less sculptural and fitted more into the mainstream of modern architecture. He designed his own version for the *Existenzminimum*, the *Kernhuis*, but could never realize it. Only near the end of his life he was asked to build social housing projects and more prestigious buildings.

Striving for a New Way of Life

The Housing Act of 1901 had opened the possibilities of subsidies for building low-cost housing. Mostly such low-cost housing was realized by housing associations, with low or even interest-free loans from the government. But from the middle of the 1920s onward private capital invested as much as – or even more than – the successive governments did.

The Housing Act also proscribed that every city of more than ten thousand inhabitants and cities with a sudden increase of the population by more than one fifth should design an extension plan. In this way housing became the most important tool in urban planning in the Netherlands.[6] The most famous example of this new urban planning is Amsterdam South. In the first plan (1900-1904) Berlage designed a picturesque cityscape, under the influence of foreign city planners and theoreticians, such as the noted Austrian architect Camillo Sitte. His second plan shows a more dramatic, almost baroque monumental style that was adapted to the view from modern transportation – such as car or tram – rather than that of a pedestrian (1915-1917). Berlage was also involved, mostly as aesthetic advisor, in other cities such as The Hague, Groningen, Utrecht, and Rotterdam. At the core of his designs was his belief that, as the cathedrals were the expression of the Middle Ages and palaces and castles the expression of the totalitarian civilization, the well-composed building blocks of social housing would be the expression of the coming civilization of socialism.

Modern architecture therefore was not so much about creating a different style, but about providing elements for a new way of life. Rotterdam succeeded in building the most social housing projects, although they hardly looked like "palaces for the workers." In the meadows, many kilometers away from the southern outskirts of the city, an initiative of the local elite succeeded in building one of the few examples of social housing that could be compared with the "garden cities" in England. The initial plan of Vreewijk (literally: "Neighborhood of Peace") was designed by Berlage (1915-1916), but other architects built far more pragmatic, traditional one-family houses on a larger scale, amidst well-composed streets, canals, small squares, and around common greens.

But to the northwest, bordering on the old city of Rotterdam, the dream of the small family dwellings proved to be as impossible as in Amsterdam. J.J.P. Oud designed his building blocks in these neighborhoods, Spangen (1918-1920) and Tusschendijken (1920-1922).[7] Although they all looked beautiful in pictures and provided considerably better living conditions than the inner city, they were still too crowded to the liking of social democrats and progressive liberals, and far too luxurious for the conservatives. How important the idea was for every family to have at least a front door and a window facing the street is demonstrated in the design by Michiel Brinkman for Spangen (page 169). At considerable expense an elevated street ("luchtstraat") was created, running along the entire inner courtyard of the large building block.

Oud had one chance to design a real alternative to Vreewijk: Kiefhoek (1927-1928), also situated at the southern border of the town. But most of the inhabitants and even Oud himself thought it was a failure. The design was meant to be realized in concrete, and not with second quality brick and with hardly any fundaments. However, it did not alter the international reputation of Oud as one of the best designers of the *Existenz-Minimum* dwelling as the *Congres Internationaux d'Architecture Moderne* (CIAM) presented in Frankfurt in 1928. In the rhetoric of the avant-garde, the houses in Kiefhoek formed an alternative for the "farmhand sheds," as they called the houses in Vreewijk. The architectural innovations of Oud could not prevent more conservative buildings being built in far greater quantities than in the Kiefhoek model. The only clear exception is the city of Hilversum, where W.M. Dudok built almost a new town with the town hall, many schools, and even a cemetery in a moderate modern architectural language, which was nationally and internationally much appreciated.[8]

Modern architecture – in what later would be called the International Style – was even more an exception in more prestigious buildings such as government buildings, banks, offices, museums, and not to mention churches, although technical innovations were as much or even more used than in the modern-looking buildings. A good example of the average taste is the Museum Boymans (1935, Rotterdam), designed by A. van der Steur. One of

the most outspoken exceptions to this case are the buildings commissioned by the tobacco, coffee and tea firm Van Nelle, also in Rotterdam.[9]

Most famous is the Van Nelle factory and offices, designed by J.A. Brinkman and L.C. van der Vlugt (page 170), although the success is almost as much the result of the manager of the company, C.H. van de Leeuw. The first element of the design is the office block, which curves alongside the access way and is crowned with a circular tearoom, looking like the bridge of a modern steamer. The tobacco-, coffee- and tea-buildings follow with decreasing heights, as there are fewer stages in the preparation of tea in comparison with the tobacco. The raw material is transported from the warehouses and boiler house-block near the river Schie on glazed transport belts into the buildings. The construction consists of slender armed concrete floors supported by mushroom pillars; a curtain wall envelops the buildings. The staircases and the access to the washrooms, strictly separated for men and women, stood tower-like against the main buildings. At night the effect of the transparency was even more dramatic. This architecture was meant to make the employees healthier and happier. Three managers of this firm, Van der Leeuw included, believed so firmly this architecture could be a vehicle for new men, that they let Van der Vlugt design their own new villas at almost the same time.

Reconstruction and Dreams Turning into Nightmares

The Dutch could stay neutral in the First World War, but in 1940 the Germans invaded the country. Rotterdam and Middelburg were bombed to force the nation to surrender. The rebuilding of Rotterdam and Middelburg showed more or less to the extreme the two possibilities that were open to all planners in all the devastated cities.[10] Middelburg restored its great monuments and rebuilt the rest of the town almost with the same typology as before the disaster, but the city-plan was cleverly adjusted to foreseen future developments, especially the increase of traffic. Rotterdam started as blank as possible by tearing down all ruins and clearing the way for a far more rationalized city-plan, with new bridges, great parkways, and boulevards and creating newer and larger building blocks. But the original plan by Witteveen was still considered to prescribe too much the form of the future city. In secret meetings – sometimes in the tearoom on top of the Van Nelle building – the leading industrialists and bankers decided that a modern city center almost without dwellings should be kept open to future developments and traffic would be given total supremacy. In doing so they acted as if they had read the Charter of Athens, which stated that working, living, and recreating must be separated, with traffic as the structure connecting them. The outline sketched by C. van Traa, grouping only functions, was even more formless than the General Extension Plan for Amsterdam (the famous *Amsterdams Uitbreidingsplan*, 1935) outlined by C. van Eesteren, president of CIAM. It was exactly this formlessness that paved the way for new building types, such as the Wholesale Building (*Groothandelsgebouw*) by W. van Tijen and H.A. Maaskant (1951), with a street for lorries running through the building, and the more internationally influential Lijnbaan, by the firm of Van den Broek and

Bakema, consisting of shops, offices and flats, with one of the first absolute divisions of the different forms of transport.

In the meetings of CIAM after the war, the Dutch were still much admired for their bold compositions of new dwellings at the outskirts of Rotterdam, like Pendrecht and Alexanderpolder, or the new village, Nagele, in the new polder. But this was only a very small part of the production of dwellings, theaters, schools, and churches. Most of this production used the lay-out and even the product development as was presented for the first time in the "competition for inexpensive dwellings" in 1934. In and after the war this was developed into a set of suggestions and regulations ("*wenken en voorschriften*"), which were used as a guideline for all the building of houses. What was defined as *Existenzminimum* (minimum for existence) became the maximum allowed. Younger architects cried out that the dream of avant-gardist and elegant designers like Rietveld, Van der Vlugt, and Duiker was lost. Aldo van Eyck stated that the profession had never had so many opportunities, yet had failed so deeply.

From New Forms of Dwelling to New Forms for Roofs

The young architects, like Van Eyck and Bakema, concluded the wrong persons and institutions profited from the manifestos of CIAM and decided to liquidate the organization in Otterlo in 1959. As Van der Leeuw stated at the opening of the meeting: Van Nelle in Rotterdam and Bauhaus in Dessau, which before the war had been seen as beginnings, proved after the war to be the highlights of a discipline deep in crisis. Bakema tried to keep the big scale and fast production for large companies and organizations under control with his "story of the family." Van Eyck tried to combine the tradition of the modern avant-garde, classical and vernacular architecture, and used institutions, such as an orphanage (1960) or a house for single mothers with child (1981), as testing grounds. But when the orphanage opened it had only one orphan in addition to a lot of problem children who had to be kept under surveillance. The pill changed single mothers from victims into proud independent women, and very soon the house for single mothers with children was changed into a refuge for battered and exhausted housewives. Society was changing much too fast for architecture.

Mainstream building had little to do with an individual architect designing buildings, let alone demonstrating possibilities for a more social world. It was the time that the Bijlmermeer – an extension of Amsterdam in a polder to the south-east of the city (page 173) – was built with mega-blocks that were even larger than Le Corbusier ever built for dwelling. At the heart was a belief in modern, flexible and mobile mankind living in spacious flats in endless parks. Instead the "Bijlmer" became housing for new immigrants: people from Surinam fleeing their new independent state and opting for the Dutch nationality, and families of the working class imported from Mediterranean countries. Although these circumstances were at the root of the failure of the Bijlmer, the architecture was blamed and people even became nostalgic about their dwellings in the noisy and dark old city.

Almost the same thing happened with the shopping mall Hoog Catharijne in Utrecht. The initial idea was to create a greater and more compact version

of the successful Lijnbaan in Rotterdam – floating above the ground and directly at the intersection of railways and freeways with abundant room for parking. But after tests in the wind tunnel, it was decided to opt for a closed and air-conditioned shopping mall with added offices and some expensive flats. However, not only consumers flocked into the new environment, but also drug addicts and the homeless.

The inhabitants of the old neighborhoods that had to be demolished to make way for highways, freeways, and renovations protested and sometimes won their cases against the government. This countermovement cleared the way for architects to design in wilder and happier forms and formats. Even the politicians agreed it was time for a change, now the housing shortage was becoming less pressing. The most favored elements – such as small individual rooftops and decorative elements, suggesting individual dwellings in large scale renovations – were taken from Aldo van Eyck's projects, first for the city of Deventer and later for Zwolle. Architects such as Herman Hertzberger or Piet Blom tried to provoke people to live more sociably by providing them with only the framework to finish according to their own liking, or with a very exuberant form such as the houses in the form of tilted cubes (*kubuswoningen*). Lesser talents created mazes of small houses which all wanted to be original and became boring. Especially in Germany, but increasingly all over the world, this escape from boring modernism (before post-modernism was even named) was much admired. This success of the small-scale maze of buildings in every reconstructed neighborhood or outskirt of every city and in many new neighborhoods or new towns was so considerable that in the beginning postmodern architecture had hardly any influence.

Neomodern and neotraditional critique came almost at the same time. Young architects and students looked back at the heroic days in-between the two World Wars. In many museums exhibitions opened about the architecture of this period. Rem Koolhaas, who founded his O.M.A. in New York and showed his admiration for the aspirations and congestions in Manhattan,

returned home to the Netherlands to save modernism and hoped in vain to play an important role in introducing Manhattanism in Rotterdam, The Hague, and Amsterdam. He chose a mix of international models from the tradition of modernism to sketch the new neighborhood of the IJ-plein area near Amsterdam. In Maastricht Jo Coenen made almost the same statement with his plan for the former industrial area of the Sfinx factories (1987-2004), but his inspiration was more oriented at the boulevards and vistas of the European cities in general.

In the 1980s and 1990s "architecture as culture" became official government policy and the best expression of this is seen in the Dutch Architecture Institute, designed by Jo Coenen (1988-1993).

In the meantime things were changing rapidly. Housing was now considered a commercial product, just as everything else by nearly everybody. New neighborhoods were built in direct connection to the old. New cities were created for a growing market of young urban professionals, most of whom had loved to live in the old cities as students. They did not want to part with the old city, but also wanted the neatness of almost gated communities. The best translation of this desire is Brandevoort near Helmond (above), built under the supervision of Krier & Kohl. It poses as a historically developed town, but is in fact an almost cartoon-like collage of most beloved building types, varying from canal-houses to bourgeois-family row houses from the 1930s. The development of Brandevoort is not yet finished, but the Netherlands is already flooded with copied fragments of it.

But the best example of the change between the 1970s and the present situation can be seen in the history of Hertzberger's *Muziekcentrum* (Music Center) in Utrecht. It was built as a center hiding between everyday shops. It took the nineteenth-century "passages" as a model and presented a critique of the shopping mall Hoog Catharijne with which it was connected. In 2007 a grand-scale reconstruction started, in which everything except the concert-hall was demolished. Hertzberger himself supervised the building of a new superstructure, a "Music Palace," above his hall, incorporating different architectures by different architects for different styles of music. The aim was to make it the focal point for all possible lifestyles in the heart of the city, turning Utrecht into a favorite for future investments. Thus, within half a century, the Vredenburg square once again was to change its appearance profoundly – although the new palace was based on the remains of the old castle and the former canal would reappear.

174

The Royal Tropical Institute: Architectural Symbol of Colonialism

The Royal Tropical Institute (*Koninklijk Instituut voor de Tropen*, KIT) was founded in 1910 as a "Colonial Institute" to study the tropics and to promote trade with and industry in the Dutch colonies. The collection of ethnological artifacts from the colonies of the Colonial Museum, founded in 1864 in Haarlem, had proved increasingly useful in the training of civil servants and future leaders of plantations and estates in the Dutch East Indies. In 1910 the geographer, entrepreneur and former Minister of the Colonies Henri Hubrecht, honorary chair of the museum in Haarlem, decided to move the collection and staff to a large new building on the Mauritskade in Amsterdam. Together with a number of large companies and the government, he provided much of the funding, making it an early example of public-private partnership.

The design of J.J. van Nieukerken looked more like a small town of the Golden Age rather than one building, but the board loved the "plastic expression of the intentions of the Colonial Society." The governmental architectural "esthetics committee" (*schoonheidscommissie*), however, fiercely opposed the design as "a mixture of styles and a strange combination of different building elements," and instead favored a unity of expression in large buildings. This protest illustrated that the statement of the Stock Exchange of Berlage was finally accepted in the world of architecture. The committee resigned in protest upon learning that the local government followed the advice of Victor de Stuers, former head of the Department of Arts and Sciences, who praised the design of Van Nieukerken as "good and sensible."

The "KIT" finally opened its doors in 1926, ten years after the first stone was laid, and more than two years after the Rietveld-Schröder house was completed. Visitors who had climbed the large outside staircase were welcomed in a large hall before entering the auditorium. The museum had an almost as monumental entrance which gave access to an even larger hall with a glazed ceiling upon aisles three stories high, which could be accessed by a monumental staircase. The most expensive marbles from Europe and from the colonies were used. Walls were decorated with majolica and paintings celebrating the exploits around the world and the many battles fought since the start of the Dutch Revolt. Even in the capitals of the columns and pilasters aspects of colonial life are illustrated.

Although the institute at first glance looked old-fashioned, it was in fact a modern building in its construction, machinery and other technical aspects. It became a tool in modernizing and intensifying colonialism and imperialism of the Dutch state and private initiative. In 1950, a year after the independence of Indonesia, the institute was renamed the Royal Tropical Institute. Reconstructions since then have tried to hide or remove the most obvious signs and symbols of imperialism, such as the monumental staircase, which was demolished because it was considered undemocratic.

Today, the KIT is a center of knowledge and expertise in the areas of international and intercultural cooperation, and contributes to sustainable development, poverty alleviation, and cultural preservation and exchange.

Further Reading

Dijk, Hans van. *Architecture in the Netherlands in the Twentieth Century*. Rotterdam: 010, 1999.

Groenendijk, Paul, and Piet Vollaard. *Architectuurgids Nederland /Architectural Guide to the Netherlands, 1900-2000*. Rotterdam: 010, 2006.

Ibelings, Hans, and Ton Verstegen. *The Artificial Landscape: Contemporary Architecture, Urbanism and Landscape Architecture in the Netherlands*. Rotterdam: NAi, 2000.

Ibelings, Hans, Francis Strauven and Jozelf Deleu, eds. *Contemporay Architects of the Low Countries*. Rekkem: Ons Erfdeel, 2000.

Kuper, Marijke, and Ida van Zijl. *Gerrit Th. Rietveld: The Complete Works*. Utrecht: Centraal Museum, 1992.

Longmead, Donald. *Dutch Modernism: Architectural Resources in the English Language*. London: Greenwood, 1996.

Woudsma, J. *The Royal Tropical Institute: An Amsterdam Landmark*. Amsterdam: KIT Press, 1990.

Zijl, Ida van, ed. *60 + 20: The History of the Rietveld Schröder House*. Utrecht: Centraal Museum, 2005.

Zijl, Ida van, and Bertus Mulders. *The Rietveld Schröder House*. Utrecht: Matrijs, 2009.

The Dutch Architectural Institute (NAi) offers the best library and the most extensive website for information on Dutch Architecture of the nineteenth and twentieth century, http://en.nai.nl. Especially interesting is the link to BONAS, a project about biographies and bibliographies of less famous Dutch architects of the nineteenth and twentieth century.

Chapter 13

Literature, Authors and Public Debate

Frans Ruiter & Wilbert Smulders

Dutch is spoken by some twenty-five million people living in the Netherlands and Flanders (the Dutch-speaking part of Belgium). Before decolonization it was also spoken in the East Indies (now Indonesia). South African, with its rich literary tradition, directly developed from Dutch. The famous Dutch historian Johan Huizinga once described the Netherlands as a transit port, both in a literal as well as in an intellectual sense. Neighboring cultures from England, France and Germany met and were connected in the Netherlands. This has led to a cosmopolitan and outward looking literary tradition, which produced great writers such as the romantic Multatuli in the late nineteenth century, the naturalist Louis Couperus at the fin de siècle, and, more recently, rather postmodern authors such as Harry Mulisch and Cees Nooteboom, who also appeal to an international audience. Somewhat lesser known abroad are Willem Frederik Hermans and Gerard Reve. Yet, precisely these two writers are considered to be the most influential authors in modern Dutch literature. This chapter takes their work as a starting point for reflecting on some essential developments of Dutch culture.

Modernist Friends

Early in their careers, Willem Frederik Hermans (1921-1995) and Gerard Reve (1923-2006) maintained a rather ambiguous friendship. In the 1950s, Hermans relentlessly criticized his literary colleagues in his merciless polemical writings; the only writer he spared was Reve. "You are the only real literary talent I met in all these years among my acquaintances, and that's enough, whatever may be your faults and errors," he wrote to Reve. Conversely, when Hermans was prosecuted because of his controversial novel *Ik heb altijd gelijk* (I Am Always Right, 1951), Reve was willing to hide the complete stock of this novel in his attic ("under a tarpaulin"), although he was not even rewarded a free copy for this noble deed. Their friendship was seriously compromised later on, when Reve professed to the Catholic Church and Hermans – whose worldview was strongly inspired by the natural sciences – could view Reve as nothing but a buffoon. Later still, when Reve was himself indicted because of his theological idiosyncrasies, it would have been unimaginable to Hermans to hide Reve's writings in his attic. Yet, because of their literary affinity and their continuous clashes with the Dutch establishment, both authors represent an excellent point of departure to characterize Dutch literature in the nineteenth and twentieth century in more general terms.

Hermans and Reve made their debut shortly after the Second World War, a war that left the Netherlands ransacked, with a heavily damaged infrastructure and an economy that had virtually come to a standstill. Thus it was in the wake of a long period of postwar reconstruction that Hermans and Reve started their impressive careers. This period was characterized by a climate of "work not play," leaving no room for frivolity or pursuing personal interests. A paternalistic morality, in which austerity and economy were predominant, called for solidarity.

The literary power and significance of both writers in this period was to be found – quite similar to that of the then emerging poetic movement of the *Vijftigers* – in what had been the major thrust of the modernist literature after the First World War: moral subversiveness. Hermans and Reve considered it a mission to antagonize the bourgeoisie. As shortly after the exaltation of the liberation in 1945 the pressure of common decency and morality increased, and everyone was again supposed to stay in line with dulled ideals, Hermans' and Reve's provoking novels produced a wave of indignation.

Hermans' work expresses a feeling which thus far had been unfamiliar in Dutch culture. It evokes a mentality which intends to undermine every belief, and which leaves no room for solidarity. The sources of his imagination are on the one hand the gloomy worlds of De Sade and surrealism, and on the other hand the stern world of science and technology. His poetics is a harsh plea against a psychological version of modernist literature, which generated novels evoking infinitely subtle reflections of a particular sensitive mind, preferably that of the author himself. As opposed to this, Hermans was strongly in favor of unadulterated fiction. He was convinced that it was through the internal logic of literary fiction that literature allows us to experience, however indirectly, something about reality. The profoundness of fiction cannot be surpassed by confessional prose.

Similarly, Reve's work in the 1940s and 1950s is characterized by an atmosphere of melancholic nihilism, surrealistic dreamlike leanings and a subtle absurdist idiom. Sobering as the work of both authors may be because of its bleak outlook, it emanates a vital humor. Both were *Einzelgänger* ("loners"), who, because of their common literary destiny, became friends and brothers in arms.[1] Their forceful expression of human loneliness broke the taboos of an oppressive confessional-bourgeois cultural climate, in which the fear of judgment passed by one's neighbor in the church benches suffocated all non-conformist inclinations. Both demanded "total authorship:" rather than a regular profession, writing is to be considered a calling. A calling, which very regularly conflicted with the narrow-minded social conventions of the time. As in the 1960s these conventions loosened, the nature of their conflicts changed as well, and their friendship would not last.

Summoned

The antagonistic character of their work brought both authors into trouble with the law.[2] In the beginning of the 1950s, a prepublication of sections of Hermans' novel *Ik heb altijd gelijk* (I Am Always Right) stirred up serious commotion. The immediate cause was a paragraph in which the main character of the novel, Lodewijk Stegman – a demoted sergeant, just returned from the colonial war in the East Indies – had a go at the Catholics:

> The Catholics! That's the most shabby, lousy, scabby, crummy part of our nation! Screwing from one day to the next, that's all they do! They do propagate! Like rabbits, rats, fleas, lice. They won't emigrate! They sit on their asses in Brabant and Limburg, with pimples on their cheeks and rotten molars from stuffing wafers!

The Catholic and the conservative press cried out for legal prosecution. According to these critics, it was not just in this particular passage that Hermans overstepped the mark. In the 1950s, the dead-end nihilism of his work was generally considered a stumbling block. Legal proceedings were instituted, charging him with insult of a community. It is significant that Hermans, in addressing the court during the trial, chose not to base his defense on proving the superiority of his world-view over that of his plaintiffs. On the contrary, he rather stressed the autonomous and fictional character of literature. According to Hermans, one could not blame an author for a character in his novel doing something illegal. To ignore this simple distinction would be tantamount to "mistake a policeman who writes a report for the driver who committed an offense." The charge against Hermans itself shows that the concept of an autonomous literature was still not completely accepted in the "pillarized" Netherlands, where society was segregated along denominational lines, and literature supposed to support the ethics of the respective denominations. Yet, ultimately, Hermans was cleared of the charge.

Some fifteen years later, it was Reve's turn to collide with the law, once again because of religious feelings being hurt. However, this time the social situation was rather different, as was the strategy of defense Reve opted for. With his publicly avowed homosexuality, Reve had already purposely antagonized the Christian community years earlier. He completely succeeded in doing so by indulging in fantasies about having sexual intercourse with God, who had returned to earth, not as a young man but as a donkey.

> And God Himself would drop by disguised as a one year old, mouse-gray donkey, and he would stand in front of my door, ring the bell and say: "Gerard, that book of yours – do you know I cried reading some of the passages?" [I would] start kissing Him en pull Him inside and after a tremendous climb up the stairs to the little bedroom, I would possess Him three times prolongedly in His Secret Opening, where after I would offer him a complimentary copy, not sewed, but hardcover – not that miserly and narrowly – with the inscription: For the Infinite. Without Words.

In his court case, Reve – unlike Hermans – did not rely on using the fictional aspect of literary communication as an argument. Incidentally, this would have been rather difficult, since Reve had made autobiographical confession his literary trademark. Reve mimicked pillarized discourse in basing his defense on a denominational argument by stating that he too had every right to his own image of God.

> Everybody has a right to his own conception of God, and everybody has the right to testify to it, if he wants to. For example, I imagine our Savior just as I see and experience Him, and not as the blasphemous images on mission calendars. Many people wish to imagine Him with hair much too long, parted down the middle, dressed in a white dress with embroidered little neck, and, preferably, without genitals, or, at least, without sexual intercourse. That is their image and they have a right to testify to this. To me, however, the Son of God had rather well-proportioned genitals, which he definitely did not allow to get rusty. I imagine Him as a bisexual, albeit with a dominant homosexual preference, slightly neurotic, but without hate towards any creature, because God is Love, incapable of excluding any creature from Him. That is my image of the Son of God, which I will not impose on anybody, but neither am I prepared to be robbed of it, by nobody whomever.

Ultimately, in an appeal to a higher court, acquittal from blasphemy followed. A year later, Reve acceded to the Roman Catholic Church, just at the time that large numbers of people were leaving it and the Netherlands witnessed an irreversible process of secularization, which marked a sudden end to the segregation of Dutch society along denominational lines.

Multatuli: Anti-Colonial Literature

In 1860 Multatuli published the famous novel *Max Havelaar* which successfully criticized the Dutch colonial exploitation of the Dutch East Indies.

Multatuli is regarded as the first exponent of romanticism in the Netherlands. When in the first half of the nineteenth century romanticism flourished in England, France and Germany, Dutch culture was dominated by a calm, if not indeed sluggish atmosphere, a mixture of liberalism and deism, keeping every possible excess under control. This was reflected in literature until the second half of the century.

Multatuli ("I have suffered greatly") was the pen name of Eduard Douwes Dekker. Born in Amsterdam in 1821 as a son of a ship's captain who intended him for trade, he went as eighteen-year old to Java, the main island of the Dutch East Indies, now Indonesia. After being moved from one post to another as a young colonial civil servant, he was appointed "assistant resident" in Lebak (Java) in 1857. He started to openly criticize the abuses of the colonial system and was forced to resign from office. In a state of fierce indignation he returned to the Netherlands, where he sought to disclose the state of his affairs. Nobody listened. It was from that moment on that he

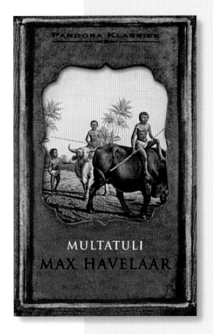

reluctantly decided to become a writer, and within thirty days he wrote *Max Havelaar of de koffyveilingen der Nederlandse Handelmaatschappij* (Max Havelaar: Or the Coffee Auctions of the Dutch Trading Company) in a hotel room in Brussels.

The novel has an imaginative composition. Effectively disguised as an innocent humoristic story, it turns out to be a combination of bright satire and bitter social complaint, ending in an appeal to the Dutch King William III to do something about it. Immediately upon publication the novel was the talk of the day. It also became the subject of fierce debates in parliament, but to the great disappointment of the author it was primarily praised for its literary qualities. D.H. Lawrence judged: "As far as composition goes, [*Max Havelaar*] is the greatest mess possible." But he also stated: "The book isn't really a tract, it is a satire. Multatuli isn't really a preacher, he's a satirical humorist. Straight on in the line of Jean Paul Richter the same bitter almost mad-dog aversion of humanity."

Was Multatuli a troublemaker, using the upheaval he caused as material for his literary genius? Or was he a naive social idealist, far ahead of his fellow citizens? Or was he, a true romantic, the intrinsic blend of those two? Critics, writers, and colonial specialists have argued about it from the start and continue to do so. From the date of publication onwards, and more particularly so after his death in 1886, many literary authors, freemasons, anarchists, socialists and freethinkers found something to their liking in his overwhelming oeuvre and in his unconventional behavior in public life. The twentieth-century novelist Willem Frederik Hermans admired the temperament and the freshness of Multatuli's writing, but still entitled his biography of Multatuli "The enigmatic Multatuli."

Artist and Community

In modern times, the relation between artist and bourgeois has changed radically from – in the terminology of the French sociologist of art Nathalie Heinich – a *régime de communauté* to a *régime de singularité*.[3] That is a transition from a situation in which the artist is embedded in the community to one in which he sees himself opposing the community.

In the Netherlands, this development has taken a rather special course. The *régime de communauté* coincided with the heydays of the liberal-bourgeois culture in the nineteenth century.[4] At the time that the *régime de singularité* started to take shape in the Netherlands, the liberal-bourgeois culture was being rapidly displaced by a "pillarized" bourgeois culture, split up along denominational lines. This pillarized culture represents the specific Dutch context to the modernist antagonism between bourgeoisie and artist, characteristic of the *régime de singularité*.[5] Hermans and Reve saw themselves confronted with this pillarized culture too. We will briefly discuss this curious history here.

In the middle of the nineteenth century, the liberal bourgeois culture was presented as universal and virtuous, and therefore worth pursuing for all. This explains the initiatives of the bourgeois elite to spread knowledge and the arts among all (read: lower) groups of the population, in order to disseminate the same enlightened, modern ideas they themselves cherished. The construction of a universal high culture happened to be a sheer necessity in an increasingly specializing, differentiating and industrializing society, which created a need for a bond to keep the growing complexity together. Literature, too, aimed at contributing to this consensus. The writer was given the role of moderator, shepherd, and educator. It was in this climate that ministers of the protestant church presented themselves as poets, performing their edifying poems at reading societies. This is the *régime de communauté* in its purest form. The entire constellation was inspired by a utopian ideal: as critical and virtuous citizens, all people are equal. Yet, this fine ideal was thwarted in no less than three ways: by mass culture, by social movements, and by the avant-garde.

Mass culture, emerging at the beginning of the twentieth century, presented a formidable competitor for bourgeois culture. It operated in the same public domain and solicited the favors of the same public. In its own way, mass culture cherished a pretense of universality too. Its cultural products were, just like those of the "official" bourgeois culture, essentially intended for everyone, regardless of his or her social, religious or regional origin.

The hegemonic pretenses of the bourgeoisie were crippled in yet another way. Despite its zeal to civilize fellowmen through education and reading societies, such attempts were only marginally successful in filtering down enlightened ideas from the upper to the lower classes in society. Moreover, their efforts were further frustrated by the churches' drive to impose more discipline on their followers. As a reaction to the rather secular body of ideas generated by the French Revolution, the churches felt compelled to increase their influence. A variety of revival and restoration movements emerged. The threat of apostasy was the whiplash, which prompted more close-knit organization of religious life. Thus the foundation of the so-called "pillars" was laid, which would leave their mark on Dutch culture well into the twentieth century. Attempts within the pillars to offer an alternative for enlightened bourgeois culture had little success, largely because the pillars were essentially unattractive for the intellectuals. The pillars were more successful in the domain of mass culture. The public broadcasting system was established in the 1920s with separate broadcasting associations. It even gloriously managed to survive the great dismantlement of the pillars in the 1960s. Only with the emergence of commercial networks, the denominational grip on the mass media seems to have finally weakened.

At the end of the nineteenth century another mutiny occurred, in the very heart of bourgeois liberal culture itself. Until the middle of that century artists and the civilized bourgeois public more or less shared the same tastes and values (*régime de communauté*). But at the end of the nineteenth century even here fissures started to show. The famous German sociologist Max Weber saw a progressive disenchantment of the world as the inevitable effect of the critical spirit of the Enlightenment and of the industrialization and rationalization of modern society. This disenchantment challenged artists to search for means of transcendence other than religion. In the Netherlands, it was not until the 1880s that art as counterculture, a compensation for the modernization process, developed in the first avant-garde movement in the Netherlands, the so-called *Tachtigers*. With its subtle character and high vocation, art loosened itself from a general audience and became something from the few for the few. While the bourgeoisie stuck to a morally more optimistic mainstream culture, the artistic elite – in a restless succession of naturalistic, symbolist, decadent, *Jugendstil*, modernist and avant-garde art – focused on a very select avant-garde audience. Thus the *régime de singularité* arrived in the Netherlands.

The idea of *l'art pour l'art* (art for arts sake), introduced by the *Tachtigers*, was much more than just an immanently artistic position. The very claim to have a right to realize idiosyncrasies in total freedom represents a radical attempt to give meaning within the new context of modern culture. Ever since, poets have endlessly squabbled about the question of literary autonomy, to the extent that a bystander might think a religious war is being waged, a war in which minor dogmatic differences are completely blown out of proportion. The trials and tribulations of this poetic fight might appear to be rather unsympathetic follies, unless one realizes that, in a way, they are a religious war indeed. In a secularizing culture, art increasingly acquired the existential value that religion had had in the past.

If we review these developments, the following picture arises. On the one side, artists increasingly claim the role of spiritual leaders, thus alienating the liberal bourgeoisie. On the other side, the bulk of the population (laborers, petty bourgeois, Catholics) escaped the enlightened tutelage of the same bourgeoisie. At the very moment the clarion blast of the *Tachtigers* resounded and the artistic elite presented themselves – with a rather pre-modern, aristocratic air – as prophets of the modern sense of life, the confessionals succeeded in organizing massive support for an ideology which in essence was anti-modern. While the ties between writers and their "natural" audience loosened, the ties between the political elite (confessional or socialist) and their ranks strengthened. At the same time, more or less independent of all this, modern mass culture began its triumphal march.

It was not until after the Second World War that this constellation gradually started to change. Several indications showed that postwar artists and writers were eager to break away from their "modernist" isolation. For Menno ter Braak – the most discussed essayist of the period between the wars – the idea of an unbridgeable gap between bourgeois and poet was still all-decisive and positively valued. Comparing the ideas of Menno ter Braak with those of Willem Frederik Hermans, it is evident that something had started to change. Hermans, be it cautiously, moved in the direction of "pop culture." In one of his most famous essays, he wrote: "The writer publicly expresses what his audience has always known but kept silent about, what it has dreamed but suppressed at the moment it awoke from its sleep." Hermans adopted a moderately elitist attitude. Certainly the writer has more nerve, but essentially he is not different from the audience. Hermans readily admitted that this implies a conviction that "deep down the audience is of the same constitution as the writer is." Yet, an antagonistic relation with the audience still existed, albeit that this was about to change rapidly. Only ten years later, several writers published a manifesto in which they voiced that they wanted to write "horny" stories for a "horny" audience. These writers seemed to seek a melting together with their audience, figuratively and literally. This was only the start of a new tradition, which has continued into the present boom in poetry slams and performance poetry. Surely, this kind of poetry is different from the homely minister poetry of the nineteenth century. But in an important way, the public-oriented poetics of much contemporary literature more resembles this minister poetry than the avant-garde poetry of the *Tachtigers*. Pop culture is a fact.

Modern Dutch literature in the 1960s found itself in a remarkable position. Until the 1960s, autonomous writers had to defend themselves against the dominant power of the pillars. With the dismantlement of the pillars in the 1960s this counter pressure fell away. At last, literary autonomy had a free rein. At least so it could have been, had it not been for the postmodern cultural leveling of pop culture. In pop culture, the antagonism between writer and bourgeois – the driving force of literary autonomy – loses much of its sharpness. Or, to phrase it in terms of Nathalie Heinich, the modernist *régime de singularité* becomes inextricably entwined in a new, postmodern *régime de communauté*.

The Assault: Writing the Second World War

The German occupation of the Netherlands (1940-1945) is either the theme or the setting of many works of Dutch literature. Literary authors – more than professional historians – have been inclined to present the occupation as a corrupting experience marked by moral dilemmas.

Willlem Frederik Hermans published several novels in which the division between good and evil appeared to be highly problematic. His *De donkere kamer van Damokles* (The Darkroom of Damocles, 1958) – one of the most acclaimed novels in Dutch literature – tells the story of Osewoudt, an utterly insignificant and weak man, who gets involved in the resistance movement. Yet, after the war he is accused of having worked for the Germans. Nothing appears to have been as it seemed, but, like the protagonist, the reader is left with many questions. Is Osewoudt a hero or a villain? The novel is loosely based on a large-scale counter-intelligence operation by the Germans, using captured resistance fighters as double agents against the Allies. The recent translations in English, French, and German triggered great critical acclaim for the novel, amongst others by Milan Kundera, who

HARRY MULISCH
THE ASSAULT

"A beautiful and powerful work. ..takes its place among the finest European fiction of our time."
Elizabeth Hardwick

Pantheon Modern Writers

praised the exploration of the fatal moral ambiguity of wartime presented in a thriller-like setting.

Harry Mulisch thoroughly examined the roots of evil in *De zaak 40/61* (The Case 40/61, 1962), a report of the Eichmann trial in Jerusalem in 1961. He sketched a disturbing image of Eichmann as a modern bureaucrat: "If during the same years not Adolf Hitler but Albert Schweitzer had been Chancellor, and if Eichmann had received an order to transport all sick negroes to modern hospitals, he would have done so without failing – with the same pleasure in his own fastidiousness as he had in the work that he has now left behind."

Mulisch's novel *De Aanslag* (The Assault, 1982) has appealed to many readers. It tells the story of Anton Steenwijk who, after the war, tries to reconstruct the sequence of events that led to the execution of his parents and brother by the Germans during the war. The starting point of Anton's quest is a rather poignant event: in an assault by resistance fighters a collaborator is killed. The incident occurs in the rather ordinary street where the Steenwijk family lives, in front of the house next door. The neighbors know that the Germans would retaliate by burning their house and decide – in a moment of alertness or panic – to drag the body in front of their neighbors' home, that of the Steenwijk family. Their plan succeeds: the Germans arrest Anton and his parents and burn their house. Only after the war Anton learns that his parents have been executed.

The attraction of the novel lies in the extreme moral complexity hidden in this rather straightforward opening scene. Who is morally responsible for the death of Anton's parents: the resistance fighters, the collaborator, the Germans, the neighbors? In a fascinating quest this tragic problem is unraveled. In 1986 Dutch director Fons Rademakers successfully adapted the novel for a movie, which in the following year won an Oscar and a Golden Globe.

Hermans and Reve in the Roaring Sixties

How did the two typically modernist authors fare under these circumstances? In the 1960s, fifteen years after their debut, both Hermans and Reve found themselves unwillingly in this peculiar pop-cultural mix. The number of readers of their work increased quickly and considerably, as a result of increased prosperity, broader education, and a growing cultural mobility. Inherently, the critical attention for their work also increased substantially. Both authors grew into media personalities, becoming public figures in a society adrift. Yet they reacted very differently to these changed conditions.

It was not until 1958 that Hermans succeeded in reaching a larger audience, with the novel *De donkere kamer van Damocles* (The Darkroom of Damocles). He gained strong literary prestige with his ruthless polemical writings (*Mandarijnen op zwavelzuur*, Mandarins on Vitriol, 1964), his brilliant poetical essays (*Het sadistische universum*, The Sadistic Universe, 1964), and, once more, a highly successful novel (*Nooit meer slapen*, Beyond Sleep, 1966). Two decades later, the Dutch literary professional community had picked up Hermans' literary ideas. His passionate hammering away at fictional writing as a craft and his ideas about the "classical novel" were planted in the minds of a whole generation of literary critics and young writers. In short, he established a literary standard. However, his nihilistic, conservative worldview did not gain that much prestige. Hermans remained the kind of contrary intellectual artist from the heyday of modernism and avant-garde. He did not see any dignity or happiness for mankind on the horizon, and excluded the possibility that life makes any sense at all. Many could not bear his gloomy skepticism. Hermans' firmament lacks any opening to metaphysical meaningfulness; it only knows the beauty of indifferent physical matter.

Reve too was a melancholic pessimist, but he looked for a kind of redemption, and in his highly ironic play with religion he found some release. He adjusted himself to the altered circumstances more smoothly. He turned out to be an artist who was perfectly able to play to a television audience. He made a few highly debated programs, which culminated in The Great Gerard Reve Show (1974).[6] This hilarious television program, containing for example a dialogue in heaven between Reve and God, illustrates the change mentioned above: some branches of literature developed into a kind of performance art, that is to say a kind of literature that is primarily an opportunity for successful television broadcasting. As a result, people could be captivated by an author, even if they had never read a word of his work nor would ever do so.

In his many novels – for instance *De Avonden* (The Evenings, 1947) and *Bezorgde ouders* (Parents Worry, 1988) – and in his extensive confessional correspondence – for instance *Op weg naar het einde* (Set Off to the End, 1963) and *Nader tot U* (Closer to Thee, 1966) – Reve played a literary game with the discourses that had been common in the pillars of yesteryears. Raised in the communist pillar, he made a jump to the Catholic pillar. It was an imaginary changeover however, because the Catholic pillar had in the meantime broken down. Reve produced "camp," using the abundant tradition of the Catholic religious imagination as material. Fighting for his own interpretation of religion in the "Donkey Case," yet very ironically subjecting himself to the Catholic rituals, Reve created extravagant cross-bonds in the Dutch culture. In doing so he translated the great themes of modernism and decadence in terms of the petty bourgeois small-mindedness that the Dutch just had overcome, but still vividly remembered.

An important factor in Reve's success was his position in the debate on the social position of writers, a major issue in the 1960s. As a symptom of the complete change of style in this era, writers demanded better payment and established a trade union. They did not even attempt to deny that, in doing so, they turned into petty bourgeois. Reve's position was ambiguous. Of course, he embraced the idea of the writer turning bourgeois, but he did this very ironically. He labeled himself not as a worker or employee, but as a grocer ("I have a shop"), and adopted the attitude of a small businessman who, by working hard, wanted to become big. While the Dutch were just trying hard to break away from their petty bourgeois image, Reve presented a picture of the author as a precautious grocer, a Catholic to boot. This telltale posture was not only part of Reve's "camp," it also was fully exploited as a commercially successful attitude, that is to say: Reve did very well with it.

Back to the Courtroom

In retrospect, the legal proceedings against Hermans and Reve turn out to be rearguard actions in the cultural system of pillarization. But they also illustrate that the religious frame of reference was still present. In defending his case, Hermans withdrew to the nucleus of the modernist poetics: the autonomous and fictional character of literature. He hung on to the "*régime de singularité*." Reve handled it differently. He chose to take full responsibility for his text, independent of all literary aspects. Obviously, he sought public recognition for his singular worldview. But the clowning and irony with which he mixed it, smuggled in an elusive kind of fiction: the fiction of authenticity. This attitude of Reve was perfectly compatible with the playful, sometimes even carnivalesque atmosphere of the roaring 1960s. With an attitude that was always controversial and consequently ambiguous, Reve may be called a true exponent of that era. Not surprisingly, the bond of friendship between Hermans and Reve was broken off in the 1960s.

Further Reading

Beekman, E.M. *Troubled Pleasures: Dutch Colonial Literature from the East Indies, 1600 1950*. Oxford: Clarendon Press, 1996.

Galen Last, Dick van, and Rolf Wolfswinkel. *Anne Frank and After: Dutch Holocaust Literature in Historical Perspective*. Amsterdam: Amsterdam University Press, 1996.

Goedegebuure, Jaap, and Anne Marie Musschoot. *A Companion to Dutch Literature*. Second revised edition. Rekkem: Stichting Ons Erfdeel, 1995.

See also the internet site of the Foundation for the Production and Translation of Dutch Literature, www.nlpvf.nl/essays

Some translations of writers mentioned:

Couperus, Louis. *The Hidden Force*. Amherst: The University of Massachusetts Press, 1985.

Hermans, Willem Frederik. *The Darkroom of Damocles*. New York: Overlook Press, 2008.

Hermans, Willem Frederik. *Beyond Sleep*. New York: Overlook Press, 2007.

Mulisch, Harry. *The Assault*. Harmondsworth etc.: Penguin, 1987.

Multatuli. *Max Havelaar or The Coffee Auction of a Dutch Trading Company*. Harmondsworth etc.: Penguin, 1987.

Nooteboom, Cees. *Rituals*. Harmondsworth etc.: Penguin, 1985.

Reve, Gerard. *Parents Worry*. London: Minerva, 1991.

Chapter 14

Three Feminist Waves

Rosemarie Buikema & Iris van der Tuin

During the past century, Dutch culture and society were shaped in important ways by the three feminist waves which thoroughly transformed the position of women in the West. This chapter cannot offer a comprehensive overview of these changes nor does it address the sheer facts and figures. Discussions about the effects of the feminist waves invariably involve key indicators and focus on questions such as: what is the proportion of women in full-time employment by now; what are their career opportunities for leading positions; what is the glass ceiling in Dutch society; what childcare facilities are available; what is the male participation rate in care and domestic work; what are the pay differences between men and women, and so on. A presentation of facts and figures can at least partly answer such questions. However, in order to understand the differences in gender relations expressed by those figures, it is essential to be informed about the history of feminist thought in the Netherlands and to be aware of the gender-specific structures of Dutch society in a transnational context.

Our purpose, therefore, is to highlight the ways in which feminism evolved in the Netherlands as an intellectual, cultural, and political movement. What have been the specific themes of first, second and third wave feminism in the Netherlands, and how can those themes be understood from a contemporary feminist perspective? In other words, what kind of continuities can we discern in feminist thought in the Netherlands during the past century, and what are its historical and geopolitical features? In this approach to feminist thought in the Netherlands – which is characteristic of the third-wave feminist method – feminism is perceived as a form of cultural legacy, while historical knowledge is reconsidered from a contemporary perspective.

This chapter will discuss three Dutch feminist cultural artifacts – two novels and one documentary – which exemplify the story of Dutch feminism in academia, art and activism. Analyzing these three waves in a chronological order will show how third-wave feminism envelops the discourses of the second and the first. The chapter will conclude with a discussion of the way in which that insight can enrich our scholarly understanding of first and second wave's artifacts.

Hilda van Suylenburg: First-Wave Feminism

Hilda van Suylenburg is a work of political fiction written by aristocratic feminist writer Cecile Goekoop-de Jong van Beek en Donk (1866-1944), which appeared in 1897 and is still considered to be the impassioned manifesto of first-wave feminism in the Netherlands. Nevertheless, there has not been much feminist academic analysis of the novel. A large number of characters cross the path of Hilda van Suylenburg, the novel's socially engaged heroine, and this ploy serves to address nearly all the crucial issues of first-wave feminism. Her encounters with men and women from all layers of nineteenth-century society are staged against the backdrop of the basic feminist question of how women can be liberated from their second-rate position. That position still is, at the time of the novel's publication, explicitly lodged in various laws intent on depriving women from a range of civil rights that today have become universally acknowledged, such as having authority over one's own body, one's children, and one's possessions; and the right to education, employment, and the vote. Even so, the novel also testifies already, in 1897, to the insight that – although legal equality is the indispensible condition for gender equality and emancipation – the feminist practice of fighting for equal rights represents in fact only a first and very rudimentary step in the right direction. It becomes clear that, apart from access to higher education, legislation on employment for women and equal pay, women have other barriers to breach, notably that of identifying with the image of womanhood that is enforced on them. Attaining first-class citizenship therefore is not just obstructed by legislation, and much work remains to be done in the domain of internalized images of womanhood and the female body. In nineteenth-century Netherlands, those images are mainly class specific.

Hilda van Suylenburg moves in the middle classes, where the obstacle to be cleared concerns the image of woman as ornament. In these circles, a young woman chiefly spends her time entertaining herself and others with the business of laying the table decorously and getting dressed in fetching gowns – functioning above all as a prop, a spectacle. Her time-consuming efforts bring her the shallow praise of her environment, but her freedom to act is marshaled by strict codes and laws. By identifying with such a position, as Hilda van Suylenburg argues in the novel, women are kept from greater and more challenging efforts. Both in the domain of the arts and in that of serving society, the identification with an existence as ornament hampers the possibility of taking seriously women's professional capacities and freedom to act. Women therefore tend to take their tendency to care and being subservient as natural givens, instead of qualities that might earn them a salary; they consider their artistic aptitude in the light of women's existence as ornament, rather than fully develop their talents. In order to break free from the internalized repression that condemns women to social invisibility and mediocrity, women need to come to a shared and self-developed analysis of their own situation. Interestingly, this strategy is usually seen as specific for second-wave feminism, but as the novel *Hilda van Suylenburg* shows, it could also be found in the first wave. Bergman, too, deploys the strategy of sisterhood in her documentary *Over the Hill,* as will be pointed out later.

Hilda van Suylenburg sets about this task by going over the many facets of the woman question with a range of right-minded and socially engaged women. Her most enthusiastic ally is Corona van Oven, a female doctor. In the nineteenth-century fin the siècle, female doctors were seen as the picture of emancipation. They typified the new and just society that was to come because they embodied the two dimensions of the first-wave ideal: subservience in freedom. This particular female doctor is having an affair with an unhappily married artist who now has discovered his true love. Many have suggested that this liaison in the novel symbolizes the reforming powers of art and science combined. Still, the protagonist Hilda van Suylenburg is a well-read and a socially aware woman who meets men and women from a range of social layers. She also propagates the perception that there is no such thing as *the* woman and that each and every woman's life is embedded in a network of social and geopolitical structures.

In fact, the novel *Hilda van Suylenburg* shows that first-wave feminism contains the germ of all ensuing feminist debates: the tension between equality and difference, the ties – as well as internal pressures – between the law and ethics, the force of structures and their effects on the individual. All these tensions can be recognized in the story of Hilda van Suylenburg. *Hilda van Suylenburg* is an example of political fiction, a genre that is usually seen to have little literary merit, because the driving force of the narrative consists predominantly of the political program, rather than literary values. Yet this novel's form is neither standard nor dull. On the contrary, it offers an understanding of the inescapable pressures of the established structures on the fight for change. Goekoop, the author who in such explicit terms addresses the stifling aspects of these structures, is also affected by these pressures. At a manifest level, *Hilda van Suylenburg* emanates the message that the hall-mark of beauty is simplicity and that all outward apparel is no more than a cloak masking vacuity. Nonetheless, extensive descriptions of external features and characteristics are offered for each new character Hilda van Suylenburg meets, with the interesting detail – entirely in line with the nineteenth-century discourse of natural history – that "good" characters are assigned noble features and that the others have to do with descriptions such as "his dark little eyes, thick, lank black hair and, right above his eyes, the highly protruding forehead of fanatics, gave him a somewhat repellant aspect."[1] As will be discussed at the end of this chapter, the body-political dimension in Goekoop's novel, a canonical manifesto of Dutch first-wave equality feminism, is best understood from the perspective of third-wave feminism, with its affirmative views on both second-wave body politics and the bodily dimension of the law and social ethics.

Joke Smit: Mobilizing Female Discontent

Anyone interested in the Dutch feminist revival during the 1970s is automatically led to the seminal article "Women and their Discon-tents" (*Het Onbehagen bij de Vrouw*) in the November 1967 issue of the leading literary magazine *De Gids*. This article by Joke Smit (1933-1981) is generally taken to signal the start of the second wave in the Netherlands. Joke Smit, a journalist and associate professor of trans-lation studies at the University of Amsterdam, still called herself Joke Kool-Smit, having not yet broken with the matrimonial convention by which women adorned themselves with their husband's names, even

as she was investigating the kind of changes she believed were necessary in order to dismantle the social inequality between the sexes. Just as the American author Betty Friedan had done previously in *The Feminine Mystique*, Smit related a number of academic studies to her own personal experiences.

"Women and their Discontents" raises almost all issues of the feminist cause in the 1970s. From legalizing abortion and free contraception to creating part-time employment and child care centers, challenging role-patterns, and improving education opportunities for women and girls. Above all, its driving force is the spitting anger that leaps off the pages.

Especially high-educated women sent Smit their adherence after reading the essay, asking her who they could join in order to "do something." Smit, too, thought she could not just leave it at that. Considering that socialism was a potential ally of feminism, she joined the Dutch social democratic labor party PvdA. Together with party-member Hedy d'Ancona she formed Man-Woman-Society (*Man-Vrouw-Maatschappij*, MVM), the first Dutch feminist action group of the second feminist wave.

In the mind of the more radical "Dolle Mina" action group and other, often younger feminists, MVM was a very moderate affair. Joke Smit and her allies did not call for sabotaging men, marriage, the family, and capitalism, but instead argued for a long march through the institutions. MVM attempted to influence political parties, trade unions, and governmental bodies. About fifteen percent of its members were male, and most members were also affiliated to either the PvdA or to the new liberal democratic party, D'66. They occasionally joined a protest march, but the core business of MVM members consisted of drafting policy papers based on the informed analyses of the employment situation, education, child care, matrimonial laws, and income tax legislation. Apart from exerting influence on the existent institutions, MVM also effectuated a few feminist institutions. In 1973, their pleas led to the formation of the Emancipation Committee that advised the government on a new phenomenon: emancipation policy. Some years later, Joke Smit and her allies were involved in creating a new ministerial position: the State Secretary for Emancipation.

MVM was dissolved in 1988, seven years after the death of Joke Smit. By then, the feminist movement consisted of a number of mostly one-issue groups and associations. MVM had been a decisive factor in the second feminist wave, but had to make way for new forms of feminism and activism.[1]

The Shame is Over: Second-Wave Feminism

Anja Meulenbelt's feminist confessional novel *The Shame is Over: A Political Life Story* (*De Schaamte Voorbij*, 1976) has a trans-Atlantic connection. The title of this confessional novel is in direct reference to an article by the American second-wave feminist Kate Millett, author of the confessional *Flying* (1974), who in her article "The Shame is Over," which appeared in an issue of the feminist *Ms* magazine, discussed the criticism her confessional novel had received. Meulenbelt's reference to one of her American sisters shows that, as of the second wave, Dutch feminists were transcending the national level; they consumed American (and British) feminist texts. *The Shame is Over* is *the* Dutch second-wave feminist manifesto. It has raised the feminist consciousness of thousands of women, and is nowadays considered to be a feminist classic, that is, a must-read. Meulenbelt herself became the feminist model for thousands of Dutch women at the end of the 1970s.

The novel *The Shame is Over* addresses both the problem of becoming an independent woman in the Netherlands after the Second World War and the problem of finding the words for expressing and narrating women's particular embodied experiences. The novel portrays a woman who strives for independence within a context that is short of role models for independent womanhood, but also explicitly addresses the issue of language. Language politics is traditionally connected to the deconstructive strand of academic feminism. Nonetheless, *The Shame is Over* makes clear how body and language politics are intrinsically connected. Meulenbelt's independence struggle could not be narrated by using the words available to her, because the cultural imaginary hardly contained any points of reference and identification. In writing, she had to invent her own terms. Several chapters in the novel are dedicated to the material and physical process of writing it – with Meulenbelt describing how, when and where she is writing and how hard it is for her to go through her diaries, letters, or scribbles on seemingly irrelevant bits of paper. The distinctive experiences of women are not merely exemplified; the construction and deconstruction of these experiences are also on the menu. It has been argued that writing *The Shame is Over* taught Meulenbelt to live as well as to write in an independent way other women could identify with. "Feminism," Maaike Meijer writes, "is the art of discovering-oneself, in life as well as writing. A language for the new take on reality has not yet come to exist."[2] She argues that the famous opening passage of the book addresses precisely this point:

> Language, my problem is language, this is not my language. I could write in colours or in wordless sounds. The scraps I find among shopping lists and notes are remote from me, or so close that I am embarrassed. Emotions that appear too sentimental or too dramatic if they are spelled out on paper. Love. Pain. Words that become shallow, or businesslike, or hard. Cunt. Vagina. Orgasm. Not my language, but as yet I have no other.[3]

Irene Costera Meijer claims that the book could only be effective in the second feminist wave of feminism because it offered words to its readers.[4] These words allowed Meulenbelt and her female readership to turn vague emotions and feelings into concrete life events, which provided them with what women had been lacking for centuries: subjectivity. Maaike Meijer argues that in deploying the language game, Meulenbelt wrote the exemplary life story of a woman in the 1970s: "She embodies the possibility of change. She represents on her own a wide range of consecutive choices modern women can make."[5]

Although both scholars touch upon the issue of language, Meijer's analysis is slightly problematic from a third-wave feminist point of view because the issue of representation is addressed as a straightforward notion. Both feminist scholars argue that Meulenbelt's novel succeeded in bridging the "I" (Meulenbelt herself; the particular life of a particular woman) and the "we" (Meulenbelt and her readers; the life women in general could identify with).[6] This connection, however, is not a clear-cut identification. Meulenbelt turns the creative use of language (deconstructive feminism) into a necessity (for difference feminism). By showing how hard it is for her to fit all those contradictory experiences into a coherent life story, Meulenbelt not only deconstructs the idea of a single model for a feminist way of life, but also shows to what extent feminism is *invested* in the idea of producing a coherent account of the life of a woman. There is a tension within *The Shame is Over* between difference (the personal of the exemplary life of a woman is political) and deconstruction (the exemplary life of a woman is a linguistic construct), while it simultaneously makes clear that the methodologies of difference and deconstruction are reciprocal in feminism.

Dolle Mina:
Second-Wave Feminism and the Media

Dolle Mina had its coming out at the end of January 1970 and became the most well-known *and* well-liked feminist action group of the Dutch second feminist wave. Inspired both by American women's liberation groups and the Dutch lighthearted countercultural movement Provo, Dolle Mina was especially popular for its playful pranks. Its feminist actions were funny and managed to shift the image of feminists as frustrated bluestockings, which had become stuck in the Dutch imaginary ever since the first feminist wave.

Dolle Mina was named after Wilhelmina Drucker (1847-1925), a famous feminist and suffragette from the first wave. One of Dolle Mina's early actions consisted of burning bras in front of the statue of Drucker in Amsterdam, paying homage to the burning of corsets by first-generation feminists. Dolle Mina would burst into silly critical songs at weddings, pinch men's bottoms in public, close down Amsterdam public toilets for men only – claiming the right to pee – and occupied newsrooms and educational institutions.

Because of this playfulness and the crafty manipulation of her image – for instance by employing good-looking young students – Dolle Mina was embraced by the Dutch media. Dolle Mina was great public relations for feminism and many women decided to join the group. But as revolutions go, the development of Dolle Mina can

hardly be characterized as well-structured, especially when satellite groups were set up in all parts of the country. Initially Dolle Mina allowed men to be part of the group. The moment that Dolle Mina decided to bar men from joining, however, marked a prominent difference with the other well-known Dutch second-wave feminist group Man-Woman-Society (*Man-Vrouw-Maatschappij*, MVM).

MVM not only continued to allow men to be part of the group, but also used a more formal, less confrontational strategy. MVM focused on talking reasonably and trying to establish agreements, often with the same officials who were made fools of by Dolle Mina. Another difference between the two organizations was that Dolle Mina focused on axes of social inequality other than gender. Its attention to class illustrates to what extent Dutch second-wave "difference feminism" allowed the differences between women to be part of its philosophy. Apart from its core business of smashing patriarchy, Dolle Mina also invested a great deal in the sexual liberation of women. The women who took part in Dolle Mina were generally somewhat younger than MVM members and less likely to have permanent jobs with the civil service or universities. Note, however, the radical element in the latter observation: it was not that typical, during the early 1970s, for married women (with children) in the Netherlands to be employed at all.

Dolle Mina silently faded away in 1977 when its initiatives and membership were absorbed by the many other groups that sprung up, representing the entire spectrum of feminist philosophies in the Dutch 1970s, such as the feminist publishing house *De Bonte Was* (representing radical feminism), *Paarse September* (lesbian feminism) and *Sister Outsider* (black lesbian feminism).

Over the Hill: Third-Wave Feminism

The work of third-wave feminists such as the Dutch documentary filmmaker Sunny Bergman allows us to show once more how contemporary feminism has a different take on the foundational debates of feminism. Both in the Netherlands and abroad, Bergman caused quite a stir with her 2007 documentary *Over the Hill* (*Beperkt Houdbaar*). Bergman is the daughter of a second-wave feminist mother whose ideas she initially opposed by becoming a model and soap star, spending a lot of time on her looks. In *Over the Hill* she analyzes the influence of the beauty industry on individual women experiencing their body. The globally disseminated images of photoshopped women's bodies make it almost impossible for women to be content with their looks. The documentary zooms in on the well-known facts of twenty-first century body politics: Brazilian women having their breasts enlarged; American women having their labia reduced; Asian women having their eyes straightened – surgeries performed mostly by male plastic surgeons, to outrageous profits, not to mention the fortunes spent by women on anti-aging creams and botox treatments. By focusing on the central conflict between interests of capital and free will Bergman addresses a central concern of the transnational post-second-wave feminist debate. The critique on sexism voiced by the first and second wave is joined by the third-wave analysis of global capitalism. Although the same beauty ideal is being propagated all over the world, the perennial question about the relationship between political structures and the individual remains: did ideas on the notion of a "makeable society" (a term that originates in 1970s Dutch socialism) and in particular the sexual revolution of the 1960s and 1970s lead to a new type of repression (the pressure to meet the ideal of the makeable body), or is the subjection to ideal types of the female body merely an individual decision?

The most spectacular scene in the documentary depicts Bergman visiting the California plastic surgeon David Matlock, who first submits her body to a thorough inspection and then tells her "you need the full works, my dear:" upper arms, belly, labia, double chin. It is a devastating diagnosis that crushes even Bergman a little, despite her strong opposition to such practices. Towards the end of *Over the Hill*, Bergman announces her wish to prepare a lawsuit against the cosmetic industry for damages caused to the female psyche, launching a website to support this case.[7] The ensuing discussions are an illustration of the continuous legacy of first and second-wave feminism in present-day feminist discussions.

Feminist criticism argues that although radical political action against the beauty industry undoubtedly has its uses, it is more effective to understand why Bergman feels crushed, despite herself, by Matlock's judgment and by the fact that road workers have stopped whistling at her since she has turned thirty. Such self-scrutiny checks the legacy of the second wave (stop stereotypical images of women, embrace difference) against practical experience. It also explores the limitations of free will (you are free to ignore the prevalent beauty ideal, to accept the wrinkles and refrain from shaving your legs). Who has the strength to resist established norms, and to what social costs? Feminist research shows, for example, that Chinese women say they have their eyes straightened not because it raises their chances of finding a marriage partner, but because it gives them a better position on the labor market, which in turn means that they can afford to spend more on the consecutive education tracks of their child.

From a third-wave perspective, therefore, it is much more effective to analyze the cause and nature of identification processes and the way one is being robbed of one's own body in global capitalism, than to simply enforce a unilateral ban on the cosmetics industry. The fact of women allowing themselves to be misled by the beauty industry can best be countered by proposing new images and offering an analysis of the interests of patriarchy and capital in promoting an inter-female competition on the most attractive body – a strategy that will be much more effective than simple prohibition.

The single most devastating achievement of patriarchy is perhaps the incapacity of women to properly support and sustain each other against patriarchal structures of interest and desire. In trying to analyze this paradoxical position for women, third-wave feminists are better equipped than their predecessors to affirm the multifarious forms of feminism and acknowledge women's difference in a geopolitical context, in the knowledge that suitable words and images for all those different situations and identifications are still wanting. As Bergman's documentary makes clear, third-wave feminists still have quite a way to go. Uniting the three main strands of feminism, she deploys "thinking equality" in protesting against sexist and maiming images of women, and "thinking difference" in advocating the rejection of prevalent images and the development of new ones. She also attempts to deconstruct the force of transnational phenomena such as capitalism and ethnocentrism, as well as of personal and subconscious identification processes.

The first-wave equality politics of Cecile Goekoop possess a "body political" dimension that was expressed by the range of female and male characters with a distribution of different attributes. Anja Meulenbelt raises a large number of feminist issues of the second wave in a complex narrative about a single, allegedly exemplary character. Sunny Bergman, finally, represents the third wave by underlining that change can only be accomplished if women try to achieve equality, difference, *and* deconstruction simultaneously. By doing so, they can develop a new language of images for women and a new solidarity with women's experiences all over the world.

Positioning Dutch Third-Wave Feminism

At the beginning of the twenty-first century the Netherlands appear to be of particular significance for feminism in both its geographical and historical position. The Netherlands is unique in its "glocal" position as a kind of "borderland" which enabled the Dutch feminist tradition to become increasingly transnational. Moreover, the development of third-wave feminism arguably also has a special prominence in this country.[8] Both in academia, art and activism, the Netherlands is located at the crossroads of Anglo-American, dominant feminist discourses and European, minor feminist traditions. From its ability to bridge these different discourses, the Netherlands takes the lead when it comes to developing innovative ones. The Netherlands, that is, does not fall into the stifling trap of the so-called Trans-Atlantic Dis-Connection, according to which Anglo-American and French/European feminisms are incommensurable, but addresses the importance and eventual *dis*advantage of the Dis-Connection for the feminist cause, allowing it to develop in the direction of transnationalism.[9]

In addition, the Netherlands has a special relation to the historical development of feminist thought. The products of contemporary Dutch feminism are characterized by a focus on cultural memory, which argues that the perspective on the history of Dutch feminism and on the manner of telling it determine the strategies of the third feminist wave.[10] That is to say that third-wave feminism in the Netherlands does not present an argument *against* the first or second feminist wave, but rather promotes a careful reading and re-reading of the feminist artifacts of the past, be it novels or pamphlets or scholarly productions. This affirmative generational approach explores a feminist future in which sexual difference is no longer strictly hierarchical, that is, privileging men at the expense of women.

The three Dutch feminist cultural artifacts that were discussed in this chapter, then, illustrate the spatiotemporal position of third-wave feminism in the Netherlands. Third-wave feminism is affirmative about feminisms of the past, especially in its orientation to the present and towards the future. The third does not offer an entirely new agenda, but relates strongly to the action plans of the first and second feminist waves. *What* contemporary Dutch feminists address has stayed the same, whereas *the way in which* they voice their claims has changed under changing political, socio-cultural, and academic processes.

When the women's movement in the West went academic in the 1980s, it was argued that feminism entails a negotiation of thinking equality, thinking difference, and deconstruction. Equality feminism was ascribed to the first wave, difference feminism to the second, and deconstructive feminism to academic feminists. Third-wave feminism shows us that the contents of the feminist discussion cannot be classified as clearly. First-wave feminists did indeed work for equal rights for women, but they also addressed the ways in which women differ from men. Alternatively, the 1970s women's movement focused on what was distinctive about women, whereas their debates testify to differences between women: a supposedly inherent femininity was simultaneously deconstructed and positioned.

Third-wave feminism is distinctive in that it envelops equality, difference, *and* deconstruction. In other words, the starting point of third-wave feminism is that every feminist standpoint is always present in the content of each feminist claim. Precisely this assumption allows for an affirmative generational politics: it is no longer necessary to *abandon* a previous feminism for the construction of a new feminist wave; third-wave feminism interrogates the analyses of its predecessors and shifts the canonical perceptions of feminism. This shifting also applies to the spatial dimensions of equality, difference, and diversity. A transnational approach to feminism also demonstrates that the three main theoretical strands are intertwined, which renders the discussion about spatial distribution irrelevant. It is no longer interesting to try to prove to what extent, say, European difference feminism is commensurable with an Anglo-American perspective on equality or diversity. The Netherlands has been able to bridge these geographical and historical differences.

Further Reading

Buikema, Rosemarie, and Anneke Smelik, eds. *Women's Studies and Culture: A Feminist Introduction*. London: Zed books, 1995.

Buikema, Rosemarie, and Iris van der Tuin. *Doing Gender in Media, Art and Culture*. Routledge: London, 2009.

Hermsen, Joke J., and Alkeline van Lenning, eds. *Sharing the Difference: Feminist Debates in Holland*. London: Routledge, 1991.

Chapter 15

Excellence and Egalitarianism in Higher Education

Jeroen Torenbeek & Jan Veldhuis

As a relatively wealthy nation with intensive international trade connections and an enthusiasm for innovation and exploration, the Netherlands has developed into a gateway of ideas and an ambitious hub of education and research. The nation's international reputation is reflected by such indicators as the number of Nobel Prize winners, the proportionally very high research output in academic journals and the global rankings of its institutions of higher education. With nearly all of its rated universities belonging to the world top two hundred according to the Chinese Shanghai, the German CHE and the Dutch CWTS (Leiden) rankings,[1] the Netherlands, as one leading British newspaper conceded, is emerging "as continental Europe's principal power in higher education."[2]

Although the Netherlands is firmly embedded in the European structure for higher education, its academic structure is also a reflection of traditions and culture that are the products of a specific national history. One of those particular constants is the desire to reconcile the appeal of egalitarianism with the drive for excellence.

Fundamental Characteristics

The Netherlands was an eager participant in the recent Bologna Process which aimed to homogenize the European higher education area. Although the Netherlands embraced the uniform organization and structure of "Bologna," it is not difficult to discover the special characteristics of Dutch education under this seemingly homogeneous surface.

A first striking trait is that higher education – as all other education – is primarily a public responsibility. This is the case in most continental European countries. In the Netherlands it means that the national government by law is responsible for the regulation of the main characteristics, such as governance, structure and quality control, and for funding – currently about eighty percent.

This directly leads to a second characteristic, which is more specific for the Netherlands: the essential equality between all institutions of higher education. In line with traditional egalitarian Dutch ideas, public funding follows the principle of equal distribution. All academic institutions receive similar funding for staff, housing and equipment.

Consequently, the third characteristic is that the quality of all institutions of higher education is largely comparable, and relatively high. The insignificant differences that remain may be attributed to geographically determined social stratification. The social elite still prefers the traditional, established universities in the urban agglomeration in the north-west and the center of the country over the oftentimes younger universities in the other regions. Qualitative differences mainly exist in the field of research, mostly resulting from the selective funding by national science foundations (quality criteria) and by private companies and semi-public organizations (contract research).

A fourth characteristic is the fact that admission into an institution of higher education is based on exit rather than entrance exams. Only a limited number of study programs – mainly in the fields of arts and life sciences – adopt additional entrance procedures, largely as a consequence of a government-imposed *numerus fixus*, a limited number of places made available to first-year students. The main reason for this absence of entrance exams is the strongly selective and profiled structure of secondary education. Three different school types in secondary education are designed to prepare for a specific form of further education. Preparatory vocational secondary education (VMBO), with a curriculum of four years, leads to senior secondary vocational education and training (MBO) – for at least another year, to fulfill the legal requirement of education until the age of seventeen. VMBO covers slightly over fifty percent of the age cohort. Senior general secondary education of five years (HAVO), which covers approximately twenty-eight percent of the age cohort, prepares for higher professional education (HBO). The six-year curriculum of pre-university education (VWO) prepares students for education at one of the research universities (WO). About eighteen percent of the age cohort enroll in these schools, which are comparable to the older gymnasia. Moreover, students choose from four different "profiles:" sciences, life sciences, economy & society, or arts & society. Each of these profiles may contain subjects required for the admission to matching study programs.

This highly selective structure in secondary education, and especially the differences in duration, content and quality between the HAVO- and the VWO-certificate, is the main reason for a fifth characteristic: the persistence of the binary system in higher education. There is a clear distinction between research-oriented universities on the one hand and institutions of higher professional education on the other. In 2008, about 200,000 students were enrolled in the thirteen research-oriented universities and eight academic medical centers that constitute the sector of tertiary education that is known as WO (*Wetenschappelijk Onderwijs*, or academic education). Only these research-based universities offer PhD programs. Another 350,000 students were enrolled in the about fifty technical or vocational institutions that constitute the sector of higher professional education known under the acronym HBO (*Hoger Beroeps Onderwijs*). Although these institutions of higher professional education have been renamed as "universities of professional education" and are given limited opportunities to develop and carry out applied research projects, the binary system is still firmly in place.[3]

A sixth feature of Dutch higher education, especially of the research universities, is its strong international orientation, both in the curricula and in the international exchange programs. Staff and student exchanges are not only stimulated by the universities themselves and by the Dutch government, but also very strongly by European programs and by European and global networks in which Dutch universities often play a prominent role, for example in the Coimbra, UNICA and Utrecht networks. Languages traditionally have had a strong position in Dutch education, with English, French and German compulsory in secondary education. In the last decades the position of French and German has weakened, mainly because English, as elsewhere, has become dominant. In 2005 English was also introduced in the curriculum in the last two years of primary school. In higher education, an increasing number of courses are offered in English, especially in the master's programs. Some programs are completely offered in English, as are the curricula of the University Colleges of Utrecht, Maastricht and Middelburg. The influx of foreign students in regular study programs and in summer schools also demonstrates the attractiveness of Dutch education abroad.

Notwithstanding the international orientation of Dutch higher education, only relatively few Dutch students spend part of their studies at a foreign university. The high quality of Dutch higher education itself and – until recently – the favorable job market for graduates may help to explain this rather homebound attitude of the students. But this is also stimulated by the attractive character of Dutch student life. The majority of Dutch students, and particularly university students, leave the parental home and rent rooms in privately owned student-houses or university housing. In university cities the student organizations traditionally dominated a large part of the students' social life, with clubs, student houses, debating societies, gala parties, formal dinners and yearbooks. Although membership of these traditional student organizations has declined from eighty to about fifteen percent in the past four decades, a great variety of other student organizations have taken their place, including many of the customs and practices of the traditional student organizations.

A seventh characteristic of Dutch higher education may have contributed to this widely developed student life, namely the government-funded system of grants and loans (*studiefinanciering*) that are available to all students for the duration of their curriculum. This grant system is based on the idea that higher education should be available and affordable to all, regardless of background or financial means. All Dutch students under thirty years of age are eligible for a grant that consists of a rather modest basic grant and free public transport. Such a grant is "performance-related," which means it has to be paid back if a student fails to earn a diploma. Depending on their parents' income, some students are also eligible for a supplementary grant. In addition to the performance-related grant, students can borrow money to help cover the tuition and additional costs. The maximum monthly support package amounts to slightly more than € 900. Many students opt to take on jobs to supplement this amount for a pleasant student life or to avoid accumulating large loans.

A final factor that continues to shape Dutch higher education is the solid governance and fairly efficient organization of the universities which is largely a legacy of the "external" democratization of higher education that took place after the Second World War. A significant increase in participation of large segments of the population was facilitated by a reorganization of secondary education that was implemented by law in the 1960s. This state-supported democratization led to a spectacular enrolment of middle and even lower income groups in universities. The student revolt, which had started already in the early 1960s, gained new support among the growing student population and young faculty in their call for democratization of university governance. The vehement student protests of 1968/1969 in many Western countries ultimately resulted in the Netherlands in "internal" democratization of universities which introduced institutionalized involvement of both faculty and students. Already in 1969 the government responded to the student protests by proposing a new law (*Wet Universitaire Bestuurshervorming*, WUB) which was accepted in 1971. It formalized co-management (*medezeggenschap*) of students, faculty and staff in all levels of university governance.

At the end of the 1980s the demand for participation, which had led to continuing unrest and instability, subsided. University governance finally has been stabilized by a new law on Modernization of University Governance (*Wet Modernisering Universitaire Bestuursorganisatie*, MUB) in 1997 which provided employees and students with an advisory voice in governance, management, and curriculum, and at the same time allowed for more efficient decision making. Dutch higher education institutions are now governed by an Executive Board (*College van Bestuur*) – consisting mostly of President, Rector and a third member. The Supervisory Board (*Raad van Toezicht*) – which appoints and oversees the Executive Board – consists of five persons with professional, corporate, governmental or academic expertise. The OECD, the Organization for Economic Cooperation and Development, the international organization of thirty affluent countries, sees so many advantages in this distinctive Dutch system of governance, which allows for both participation of stakeholders and vigorous decision making, that it suggests that this should be considered by other nations.

Education, Urbanization and Emancipation

These specific traditions and organizational arrangements of higher education are a reflection of the historical developments and national culture of the Netherlands. Intellectual cosmopolitanism and academic inquiry were greatly stimulated by the high level of urbanization which characterized the seven northern provinces of the Low Countries – Groningen, Friesland, Gelderland, Sticht (Utrecht), Oversticht (Overijssel), Holland and Zeeland – as early as the sixteenth and seventeenth centuries. These provinces formed the highly decentralized "Republic of the Seven United Netherlands." Social care and education, as provided by for example the guilds and the churches, led to relatively high levels of literacy in these urban centers. The high quality of education, in turn, greatly stimulated economic prosperity. In this period the first universities or academic schools were founded in a prosperous city of nearly each province, such as Leiden (1575), Franeker (1585), Groningen (1614), Utrecht (1636) and Harderwijk (1648). The most prosperous city, Amsterdam, founded its own *"Atheneum Illustre."* Famous seventeenth-century scientists like Regius, Willem Stratenus, Herman Boerhave and Willem Jacob's Gravesande attracted students and illustrious visitors from all over the world.

Aletta Jacobs:
Emancipation through Education

Aletta Jacobs challenged male-dominated academic education by becoming the first female medical doctor. As a leading suffragette, reformer and proponent of birth control, she went on to become an enduring inspiration for the feminist movement.

Born in 1854 into a large Jewish doctor's family in a poor peat-winning district in the north-east, Aletta Henriëtta Jacobs set her mind on becoming a medical doctor at an early age. After completing her education as pharmacist's assistant at age 16, she became the first woman to enter secondary education (HBS), if only as a listener. She subsequently received permission to attend medical classes at Groningen University and, after personal authorization from Prime Minister Thorbecke, was allowed to take her doctor's exam and to defend her dissertation in 1879, becoming the first woman in the Netherlands to do so.

Influenced by the liberal reform movement in England and unionism in the Netherlands, doctor Jacobs opened a medical practice in the working class neighborhoods of Amsterdam. As a progressive reformer she offered practical advice in child care and hygiene, denounced the living conditions of the urban poor, advocated better working conditions for salesgirls, and started promoting birth control to alleviate the plight of working class women. In spite of wide-spread resistance she became an active member of the Dutch Neo-Malthusian Society and introduced the diaphragm as contraceptive in the Netherlands.

Convinced that full constitutional equality of men and women was essential for further reform, Jacobs started a tenacious struggle for women's right to vote. Litigation to be put on the ballot failed when the highest court argued that she was ineligible for election, simply because women never had that right. After continuing to promote women's suffrage in a series of lectures and articles, she became president of the Dutch Women's Suffrage movement and editor of its journal in 1903. She held this position until 1919, successfully raising money to organize conferences and staging protest marches in The Hague. Jacobs also actively promoted international solidarity by traveling the world and seeking cooperation with like-minded activists such as Carry Chapman Catt, the powerful president of the National American Woman Suffrage Association (NAWSA). After the outbreak of the First World War her international network became a vehicle for pacifist and humanitarian initiatives, in 1915 leading to the founding of the Women's International League for Peace and Freedom in The Hague, the oldest women's peace organization in the world.

In 1917 the Dutch government, fearing widespread revolt, conceded to the growing pressure by allowing women on the ballot and at the same time introducing universal suffrage for men. Two years later a bill was passed which replaced the word "men" in the constitution by "persons," as Jacobs had argued for years. The "Jacobs Bill" eliminated constitutional gender differentiation and introduced women's suffrage in the Netherlands with the general elections of 1922.

Aletta Jacobs died in 1929. In 1935 her personal archive became the core of the International Information Center and Archives of the Women's Movement (IIAV) in Amsterdam, now a worldwide collection on the heritage of the women's movement.

In the nineteenth century, after the French occupation and the Congress of Vienna, the seven provinces were united into one nation state. Therefore the national government became a major influence in the further growth of academic education. The only three remaining universities of Leiden, Utrecht and Groningen became national universities, while the city of Amsterdam upheld its *Atheneum Illustre*, which became a national university in 1876. The new Constitution of 1848 gave great impetus to the further development of the whole educational system. During the following three decades, new laws dealing with primary, secondary and higher education were passed, creating educational opportunities for segments of society previous excluded from higher education. For the middle classes, in 1863 a new type of secondary education was introduced: the Higher Civil School (HBS), with a curriculum of three or five years, offering a preparation for positions in trade, merchant shipping, banking, industry and agriculture – but not for the "learned professions" that required a university education: church ministers, lawyers, medical doctors, gymnasium and HBS teachers, and university professors.

The Constitution of 1848 also paved the way for the emancipation of Roman Catholics and orthodox Protestants, groups that had been held back in society and education. Both religious denominations demanded access to free and government-funded education. This fundamental struggle over the schools – one of the main factors of the "pillarization" of society – was finally resolved in 1917. In a groundbreaking agreement, the national government agreed to provide equal funding for both non-denominational (public) and denominational ("private") schools. Many new Catholic and Protestant schools were founded, first at primary level, and in the second half of the century at secondary level. In higher education this process of religious emancipation led to the founding of the Protestant Free University of Amsterdam (VU) in 1879, and half a century later to the founding of the Roman Catholic University at Nijmegen (KUN) in 1923 and the Roman Catholic Higher Trade School at Tilburg in 1927. Initially, the money for the foundation of these institutions was raised by the religious communities themselves, but after a gradual increase of governmental support they were granted complete public financial funding in 1968.

It should be noted here that "private" schools and institutions in the Netherlands therefore refer to privately governed schools and institutions, which are financed with public funds. In 1991 humanists made use of the same laws to fund their own Humanistic University, and more recently Muslims started to make a strong case for an Islamic university.

Another stimulus for extension of higher education came from the developments in the field of the natural sciences and their applications in agriculture, trade, industry, and health care. The polytechnic school at Delft was upgraded to a *hogeschool*, a "College of Higher Technical Education," and three new institutions for higher education were founded: the Colleges of Higher Trade Education at Rotterdam (1913), of Higher Agricultural Education at Wageningen (1917) and of Higher Veterinary Education at Utrecht (1917). These colleges admitted students who had finished HBS, rather than gymnasium. This in turn stimulated the admission of HBS graduates to the other, older colleges of higher education, and especially those in the field of medicine and the sciences. Increasingly, the term "hogeschool" was used for practice-oriented institutions of higher professional education.

The third external factor to greatly impact the organization of Dutch higher education was the rebuilding and modernization of society after the Second World War, combined with the further socio-economic development of the northeastern, eastern and southern part of the country. This led to the foundation of Technical Colleges of Higher Education at Eindhoven (1956) in the southern province of Brabant, and in Enschede in Twente (1961) in the east, and the foundation of the University of Maastricht (1976) in the far south of Limburg. An increasing need for medical staff led to the foundation of the Rotterdam Faculty of Medicine (1966), which in 1973 merged with the College of Higher Trade into the Erasmus University Rotterdam. In 1986 the three Technical Colleges, the Agricultural in Wageningen and the Trade College in Tilburg were renamed "universities." The Veterinary School in Utrecht has already in 1925 been incorporated into Utrecht University.

Harmonization in Europe

The European Union (EU) has steadily affected Dutch higher education. The attempts to reinforce the knowledge infrastructure of the budding European organizations in the 1950s evolved into a whole range of European "framework programs" for the funding of research and development. In the 1980s and 1990s, higher education was used as a tool to help promote the participation of citizens in the European community. Hundreds of thousands of students have participated each year in exchange programs that are funded by the Erasmus and Socrates programs since 1987. This seems to indicate that the future intellectual elite of Europe has become considerably more mobile – and more Europe-minded – than earlier generations.

However, only after the signing of the Maastricht treaty in 1992 did Europe really get involved in higher education. At first, the European Commission claimed it would never strive for the harmonization of higher education, whose diversity was praised extensively. Ironically, the universities themselves had different ideas. In 1998, during the festivities for the 750th anniversary of the Sorbonne in Paris, the first plans were made to harmonize higher education in Europe. In 1999, the oldest university in the world, that of Bologna, Italy, gave its name to a major structural change in higher education when twenty-nine ministers of education signed an agreement to make academic degrees and quality assurance between their nations more compatible by bringing greater uniformity in the maze of European curricula and diplomas. Dutch universities were among the first to adopt the proposed Anglo-American system of three separate cycles for bachelor, master and doctorate (PhD) students.

It has become clear that the European Union explicitly aims at designing a new landscape for higher education, and thus provides the framework in which Dutch higher education will develop further, but likely with much diversity. We will illustrate this with two examples: the binary system, and the equality between institutions.

Most European countries have a binary system in higher education, distinguishing between universities and for example the *Fachhochschule* (in Germany), *högskolan* (in Sweden), or *hogescholen* (in the Netherlands). The division seems crystal clear: universities prepare students for academic professions or for a life in science and academia, whereas the *hogescholen* prepare students for professional practice. In other words, an academic way of thinking versus practical competencies: history of art and musicology versus art school and conservatorium, economics versus business school, philology versus journalism and computer science versus computer programming. The new landscape in Europe, however, is supposed to reduce the gap between the two categories of higher education institutions, especially by more differentiation of the tracks within each of the two categories. In an international context, this sounds logical and plausible, but it remains to be seen to what extent such a new structure imposed by Brussels will become more than a thin layer of veneer under which the binary system remains in existence. After all, in many European countries – and in the Netherlands very distinctly – secondary education has been organized in preparation for either university education or for higher vocational training.

Another important characteristic of higher education in continental Europe is its fundamental egalitarian nature, and the equal treatment its institutions receive. The policymakers in Brussels intend to end this situation before long. Differentiation will be the keyword, and the main goal is to create new qualitative heights: continental Europe should also have its Cambridge and Oxford, or its Harvard, Yale, Princeton and Berkeley. It is beyond the scope of this chapter to analyze whether this is a desirable goal and whether it can be enforced in such a manner. We may wonder, though, whether the ambition to create one or two top scientific institutions in the Netherlands, with its public structure and high quality of all universities and most institutions for higher professional education (*hogescholen*), is realistic. For one thing, this would require some fundamental choices. Should the Universities of Utrecht and Amsterdam be upgraded, leaving the other research-universities second rank? Or would it be better to opt for time-honored institutions at Leiden and Groningen? Perhaps the universities of Rotterdam and Maastricht, the youngest two, are suitable candidates? If the Technical

University Delft were made the top institute, what will be the future for the institutions in Eindhoven and Twente? And what about the world famous University of Wageningen? Since it would imply a great loss of human and physical capital, this idea is not realistic.

Nevertheless, it goes without saying that higher education should always aim for excellence. But in a densely populated country as the Netherlands with rather short distances, greater excellence can better be achieved by promoting specific top schools and top institutes *within* each of the universities and by closer cooperation between and specialization of such groups, in other words, by aiming at the creation of *Universitas Neerlandica*.

University College: Challenging Academic Traditions

In August 1998 Utrecht University opened its University College for the first 180 students, arriving from twenty-eight nations from all over of the world for a university education which was to challenge Dutch academic traditions in numerous ways. As founding father professor Hans Adriaansens phrased it, UCU intended its students "to cross the widest possible river."

The three-year English-spoken undergraduate curriculum covered a broad range of courses in Humanities, Sciences and Social Sciences. Whereas the Dutch universities traditionally require a choice for a particular field of study or academic discipline right from the start, University College mirrored English and American examples in encouraging students to first explore and develop their talents and ambitions.

University College was set up as the "International Masterclass" of Utrecht University. Students were carefully selected in an extensive process including motivation letters and interviews, emphasizing the importance of ambition and motivation. Such competition for admission may be rather common around the world, but was relatively new to the Dutch situation. By law all Dutch students who successfully complete preparatory academic education (VWO) have access to university programs. Since this makes selection "at the gate" impossible, University College invited students "behind the gate," once they were registered at Utrecht University. This was a typical Dutch way of experimenting first before adjusting rules and regulations to changed realities.

The highly selective admission to University College challenged students to live up to the expectations. Small classes stimulated active participation and allowed for individual attention to students, in contrast to the sometimes rather massive and traditional lectures – the unavoidable consequence of the democratization process in the 1970s in Dutch higher education – which provide a less challenging

and student-focused teaching format. Thus, University College stimulated an attitude more competitive than is customary among Dutch students, who may strive to do their best but not necessarily measure their accomplishments in relation to those of other students. Such competitiveness was further enhanced by the rather confined community "on campus" – another novelty in Dutch higher education. The campus, located at the former Kromhout military barracks, provided not only classrooms and ample study places, but living accommodations and three daily meals in the "Dining Hall" as well. These arrangements aimed at facilitating students in completing a calculated workload of fifty-six hours per week, as the regular annual workload for students was condensed into two relatively brief semesters of sixteen weeks, instead of the customary Dutch academic year of forty-two weeks.

Since UCU opened, the first generation of students has spread their wings to pursue further education at renowned institutions around the world, establishing the College's name in the international academic world. Every year some 200 new students are enrolled. Meanwhile, two more, similar colleges have opened their doors – University College of Maastricht University and Roosevelt Academy in Middelburg of Utrecht University – and honors tracks and talent-classes have developed in regular universities as well. The University of Amsterdam and the Free University in Amsterdam have opened the University College Amsterdam in 2009. Leiden planned the start in 2010 of a mainly on social sciences based University College. University College Utrecht was a pioneer on the road to new traditions.

Combining Quality with Equality

The OECD (Organization for Economic Cooperation and Development) provides a much valued annual analysis of the higher education system of its member countries. Its country note on the Netherlands in 2007 gave much reason to be satisfied.[4] The OECD praised the country's strong institutions for higher education maintained by public funding, with their effective governance structure, good system for quality care and also the use of English in teaching and research, producing high quality results. Scientific research is exceedingly productive: the Dutch represent only a quarter of a percent of the world population, but they account for two percent of the global scientific output.

Furthermore, the OECD report mentions the reasonable tuition fees as a strong point of Dutch higher education, as it results in affordable education. This public character has created equal opportunities for students from underprivileged social backgrounds. Yet, notwithstanding this positive characteristic of Dutch higher education, the OECD report indicates that participation of young people from lower income backgrounds, including people from ethnic minorities, does not exceed twenty percent of the age cohort (versus forty-five percent on average). Although the ethnic minority groups recently made remarkable progress, overall the problem remains serious.

There are more challenges the Dutch higher education still has to over-come, according to the OECD report of 2007. A second, unmistakable weak-ness that it points out in Dutch higher education are the relatively high drop-out rates, at thirty percent on average (except for medical sciences). It has been suggested that the issue of these drop-out rates could be remedied by "selecting at the gate," through entrance exams or weighing of final high school exam results. After all, such a selection could filter out the students lacking either talent or motivation, causing them to drop out eventually. Yet, pilot testing at Leiden University has thus far not proven a direct correlation between selection at the gate and academic success.[5] This may be due to a restriction in range, that is to say that the variation among prospective students is too small – each of them having a rather comparable upper level secondary school degree in the very selective layer structure of secondary education – and the absence of actual experience of both student and institution in the university curriculum. An instrument which has been developed is a form of "selection after the gate:" the so-called Binding Study Advice (BSA), forcing students to leave if they did not complete a minimum part of the first year curriculum. This instrument is used by an increasing number of institutions, to prevent a likely drop-out later on in the curriculum.

The Dutch educational landscape is changing, so much is clear. The open, low-threshold, concept of higher education for all seems to have outlived itself. The taboo around differentiation and selectivity has been broken, not only by Europe, but also from within. In 2004, the State Secretary for Education and Science entitled her bill "Fast track for talent." It is very likely that the future will see further differentiation in higher education. The cherished equality between universities needs to be balanced against increasing demands for more challenges and quality in the form of top institutes and centers of excellence. The consequence for the students will be more differentiation, more challenges and honors programs. Increasing numbers of ranking lists – based on student evaluations, citation indices, statistics of numbers of graduates and doctorates, opinions of colleagues and specialists – already provide proof of this growing focus on quality and quality assessments. Yet, thus far, these rankings do not seem to seriously influence students' choices. They still choose a field of study, an institution with a seemingly pleasant atmosphere, a city not too far away from home, and an appealing student life.[6]

The Dutch educational landscape is gradually changing as higher education is becoming more internationalized, globalized and harmonized. Nevertheless, just under the surface one can find the national traditions and individual characteristics that are the foundations of academic excellence and intellectual wealth.

Further Reading

Jacobs, Aletta. *Memories: My Life as an International Leader in Health, Suffrage, and Peace*, edited by Harriet Feinberg; translated by Annie Wright. New York: The Feminist Press, 1996.

Kaiser, Frans et al. *Issues in Higher Education Policy 2006: An Update on Higher Education Policy Issues in 2006 in 10 Western countries*. Den Haag, Ministerie van Onderwijs, Cultuur en Wetenschap, 2007.

Litjens, Judith. "The Europeanisation of Higher Education in the Netherlands." *European Educational Research Journal* 4, no. 3 (2005): 208-218.

Marginson, Simon, Thomas Weko, Nicola Channon, Terttu Luukkonen and Jon Ober. *Thematic Review of Tertiary Education: The Netherlands; Country Note*. Paris: Organization for Economic Co-operation and Development, 2007.

Weert, Egbert de, and Petra Boezerooy. *Higher education in the Netherlands: Country Report*. Enschede: Centre for Higher Education Policy Studies, 2008.

Witte, J., M.C. van der Wende and J. Huisman. "Blurring Boundaries: Bologna and the Relationship Between Types of Higher Education Institutions in Germany, the Netherlands and France." *Studies in Higher Education* 33, no. 3 (June 2008): 217–231.

See website of the Netherlands Organization for International Cooperation in Higher Education, www.nuffic.nl.

Contemporary
Issues

Chapter 16

Religious Diversification or Secularization?

David Bos

Amsterdam's Nieuwe Kerk is probably the country's most frequently visited church. Each year it welcomes hundreds of thousands of visitors. They do not come to this fifteenth-century "new church" for worship, however. Neither do they come to admire the building, which oddly lacks a tower. Since the 1980s, it mainly serves for exhibitions, mostly of treasures from far away and long ago.

Christianity in the Netherlands seems doomed to share the lot of past civilizations. Since the 1960s, a thousand church buildings have been closed down, and demolished or converted into museums, concert halls, apartments, restaurants, clubs, shops, or mosques. Many citizens have given up church membership. In surveys, forty to sixty percent – depending on how the question is phrased – say they do not belong to any denomination. Evangelical and Pentecostal churches, which emphasize conversion and establishing a personal relationship with Jesus Christ, do grow, but mostly by recruiting members from more conventional Protestant denominations.

This decline of religious affiliation is paralleled only by some formerly communist countries, where institutionalized religion was deliberately thwarted. In the Netherlands, by contrast, Christian political parties such as CDA participated in each and every government coalition since 1918 – except for a brief interlude between 1994 and 2002 – and exerted their influence on society, for example by prohibiting shops to open on Sundays or after 6 p.m.

It is not easy to say then whether Dutch society is secular or thoroughly religious. Many citizens themselves do not know what to make of it. Is it a hotbed of Calvinism or of secular humanism? Of Enlightenment or fundamentalism? Of merchants or ministers?

In the Beginning

As in other European cultures, the Dutch calendar testifies to a pre-Christian past. The first day of the week is not named after the Lord (*domingo, domenica, dimanche*), but after the Sun (*zondag*). Moreover, *woensdag, donderdag* and *vrijdag* refer to Germanic gods: Wodan, Donar (also known as Thor) and Freya. Little is known about their cults, because they left no texts, statues, or buildings. Public rituals took place in the open air, outside settlements. These tribes, wrote the Roman historian Tacitus, "do not consider it consistent with the grandeur of celestial beings to confine the gods within walls, or to liken them to the form of any human countenance."

Yet, in the southwest of the country now known as the Netherlands, where three European rivers run into the sea, archeologists have found hundreds of votive stones, dedicated to Nehalennia, a Dutch deity who rose to stardom in the Roman era. She started her divine career as a local celebrity, but was picked up by sailors who passed Her sanctuaries. Before going out to sea, they implored a safe return by offering Her an effigy: a Lady, sitting on a throne, with a basket full of apples on Her lap, and a dog or wolf at Her side.

Nehalennia and Her co-stars would be outshone by a foreign deity. Instead of having a proper name, He was referred to with a noun ("God"), and while He Himself had neither parents nor siblings, and tolerated no rivals, He did have a Son, born from a Virgin. This Son of God had lived and died as a human being, but had risen, and ascended to heaven – which was the prospect for all who believed in Him.

This amazing history had taken place in a country even more distant than Rome. The first to recount it in the Low Countries were priests in the slipstream of Roman legions, like the fourth-century scholar Servatius, bishop of Mosae Traiectum (Maastricht). North of the big rivers, the new religion remained almost absent. Not until the year 630, a church was built in Traiectum (Utrecht), for soldiers of the Frankish king Dagobert I, and for mission among the "Frisians." But priests would not venture among these "heathens" (from heath) or "pagans" (from *pagani*: "villagers"). For centuries, Christianity remained an urban cult.

Official and Popular Religion

Christianization was given a new impulse by Anglo-Saxon missionary monks like Willibrord, who landed in 690 CE. With the support of the pope and the Frankish king he began to convert the natives. He rebuilt Dagobert's church, and built a second one, dedicated to St Martin.[1] This Frankish saint became popular among the "Frisians," and in some regions has remained so until the present day: on November 11, children go from door to door with Chinese lanterns, singing in honor of "Sint Maarten," and collecting candy.

Willibrord and his assistants lent force to the Word by showing themselves in fine garments, with shining chalices, jewelry, books, and relics – tokens of a superior civilization. They demonstrated that the indigenous deities were powerless by violating religious taboos, and destroying holy objects. The English monk Winfrid learned the perils of this shock-and-awe strategy. When he organized a rally near Dokkum, in 754, locals took up arms, and killed some of the intruders – among them Winfrid, also known as Boniface. With him, Western Christianity lost an able missionary, but won a saint. The story of his heroic life and death was well suited for spreading the true religion – even in the nineteenth and twentieth centuries, when Catholics again confronted Dutch "paganism."

Conversion implied renouncing Germanic deities, but "superstitions" – such as "storm making," idols made of rags or dough, "filthiness in February" and "the things they do on the rocks" – proved difficult to root out.[2] Christianity held out prospects of civilization and celestial bliss, but what good was that for simple mortals, when luck was against them?

The Church in the Middle

It was only at the end of the Middle Ages that a regular church life emerged. Parish formation shaped the countryside, as craftsmen and shopkeepers settled around the house of God and that of His servant. Before the introduction of signposts, travelers found their way in the flat Dutch countryside by keeping their eyes on church towers. Village priests lived like other peasants, usually with a wife and children. What set them apart was their proficiency in rituals, and their equally esoteric ability to read and write. Their command of Latin was limited, however. One priest baptized *in nomine patria et filia et spiritus sancti*: in the name of the Fatherland, the Daughter, and the Holy Ghost.

In many city churches, the Eucharist was celebrated several times per day – on the occasion of a wedding, a funeral or in memory of someone who had died before long. Wealthy families, guilds, and other associations had "memorial Masses" read for their deceased members. Were they so worried about salvation, so anxious about the purgatory? Or did they use the church – *the* platform of Medieval society – to show how important they were?[3]

Around 1500, Amsterdam's Oude Kerk employed not only a rector and a few curates, but twenty-two other priests and sixty "altarists" or "memorists" who read Mass at more than thirty side-altars. Beside churches, every late-Medieval city of some importance also boasted a few monasteries. Amsterdam was so full of them that a blind alley was dubbed *Gebed zonder end*, "Interminable Prayer:" still an expression for endless work.

Amsterdam was also a pilgrimage destination, thanks to a miracle. In 1345, a man had received communion on his sickbed, but spat out the consecrated wafer. The maid threw his vomit into the fire, but the next morning she found the Host intact, hovering in the flames. It was placed in a special chapel, which put Amsterdam on the map of European tourism.

Revival, Reform and Revolt

In the late Middle Ages, parish priests were being overtaken from all sides. As retailers of ritual they had lost out to "altarists" and as pastors and preachers to new religious orders, who specialized in hearing confession and "talking like Brugman."[4] Literacy itself no longer impressed, now that many laymen were educated. Also when it came to piety, chastity, humility and charity, parish clergy were being surpassed, notably by lay orders like the Beguines – whose dwellings can be seen at Amsterdam's *Begijnhof* – and the Brethren and Sisters of the Common Life.

The latter group was part of an international movement, *Devotio Moderna*, which cultivated an internalized form of religion, popularized by Thomas à Kempis' *Imitation of Christ*. Its founder was Geert Groote, son of a wealthy merchant in Deventer.[5] He denounced clerical laxity and immorality and the haughtiness of building an enormous cathedral (*Dom*) in Utrecht, partly financed by selling indulgences.

More and more religious dissidents came forward, rejecting everything that stood between God and the (individual) believer. Neither the clergy, nor the nobility, but *burghers* are closest to salvation, wrote a dissident priest in

1523, "because they earn a living with their hands." Jan van Woerden practiced what he preached: he resigned as a curate, and took up baking bread. In 1525 Jan de Bakker, as he was now called, was strangled and burned – as the nation's first Protestant martyr – mainly for saying that priests were allowed to marry. Similar was the fate of Wendelmoet Claesdochter from Monnickendam, who blew it by bluntly saying: "That sacrament of yours is bread and flour to me."

Equally offensive was the stance of the Anabaptists ("re-baptizers") that people should not be christened until they had confessed their faith. This sounded radical, because baptism meant incorporation into human society. Renouncing infant baptism was therefore bound to lead to social disruption. This had become but all too clear in 1535, when Anabaptists in Amsterdam had tried to realize the Kingdom of God by getting rid of their earthly possessions – their clothes, to begin with. The authorities crushed the revolt of these naked arsonists, and had them executed: their hearts were ripped out of their bodies and flung into their faces.

Anabaptism survived, however. Menno Simonsz., another former priest, became the patriarch of a new, fundamentally non-violent generation of Anabaptists. Whereas these "Mennonites" contended themselves with a minority position, shunning all dealings with the state, followers of Martin Luther believed that all of society should undergo a Reformation, led by government. In many Central European and Nordic countries, the monarch chose Lutheranism, and his subjects followed suit. In the Low Countries, however, the authorities were not likely to do so. That is one of the reasons why religious dissent began to be dominated by followers of John Calvin, who allowed not only a top-down, but also a bottom-up, "revolutionary" Reformation.

In 1566, after decades of meeting in secret or abroad, Protestants manifested themselves with "hedge preaching:" open-air church services, usually outside cities. When the summer ended, they broke into churches, destroying statues and images. This "iconoclastic fury" (*beeldenstorm*) started in Flanders, and spread like wild fire. Within two weeks, it reached Amsterdam. The Nieuwe Kerk hastily closed its doors, but in the Oude Kerk, where a baby was being baptized, the mob got in. "You papist," shouted someone, "stop swearing the devil out of children! Baptize in Jesus' name, like the apostles did!" Then boys began to throw stones at the altars. Weyn Okkers, an otherwise respectable housewife, flung a slipper at the Virgin, and her maid Trijn violated St Roch. "Just wanted to check if it was properly fixed," she explained in court, but Weyn and Trijn were found guilty, and drowned in a wine barrel.

Public Church

Not until 1578 did the merchants who ruled Amsterdam join the Dutch Revolt. An inscription on the choir screen of the Oude Kerk commemorates this Alteration: "The abuses that crept into God's Church have been removed from here in the year seven-eight." One year later, seven northern provinces concluded an alliance, the Union of Utrecht, which stipulated freedom of conscience or religion – a radically new idea. In early-modern Europe, religion was deemed too important to leave it to individual believers, however. Wherever the Revolt succeeded, Calvinists were given dominance. For one thing, they gained all the church buildings, and customized them to their ideals. Altars, statues, and images were removed, the walls and ceilings were whitewashed, and the pews were often moved a quarter turn. Instead of facing the "choir," they were now arranged around the pulpit, so that congregants could hear the sermon – the core of Reformed worship. In the Nieuwe Kerk, on the very spot where the high altar had been, a sumptuous tomb would be built for Admiral Michiel Adriaensz de Ruyter. In other churches, too, "sea heroes" were given a saint-like position.

Reformed Sunday morning sermons often lasted a full hour. Before, after, and in-between, psalms were sung – on full notes and not accompanied by an organ, because rhythm and instrumental music were deemed profane. Communion ("Holy Supper") was celebrated a mere four times a year, and only accessible for those who had been confirmed – usually no more than a third of the Reformed "constituency."

Although the Reformed Church regarded itself as the only true religion, and jealously protected its monopoly on public worship – for example by baptizing and marrying each and every Christian – it lacked both the power and the ambition to drive the entire nation into its fold. Becoming a "broad church" would go at the expense of its purity, its resources – members being entitled to poor relief – and its autonomy. The Public Church would never become a State Church.

The Calvinist doctrine of predestination offered an explanation of this minority position: only God decided who would, and who would not be saved. War experiences seemed to corroborate this: in the southern and eastern regions that were re-conquered by "Spanish" troops, Protestants fled or defected. Even after the States General eventually prevailed, these regions remained predominantly Catholic, and that is still a basic feature of the Netherlands' religious geography.

A second feature is that the regions just north and west of the early-seventeenth century frontline would become the habitat of particularly strict Calvinists, commonly named for Staphorst (a village near Zwolle) or for the "black stockings" they allegedly wear. Even in this "Bible belt" many people celebrate St Nicholas on December 5. Honoring a "papist" saint is a lesser evil than desecrating Christmas. Thanks to emigrants, "Sinterklaas" – a deliberate corruption, meant to cover up the "saint" – also made it to the United States, be it deprived of a bishop's dignity, moral authority, and wits.

Discord and Dissent

Around 1600, the Reformed Church got caught in a dispute over Calvin's doctrine of predestination. Followers of the Leiden professor Jacobus Arminius "remonstrated" an interpretation that left more room for human choice. This theological dispute brought the Republic to the brink of a civil war, because it was connected with political explosives: the power balance between Holland and the other provinces, and that between State and Church. According to the Arminians – better known as Remonstrants – the former should govern the latter. The conflict was resolved by a church assembly held at Dordrecht, in 1618-1619. This "Synod of Dort" expelled the Arminians and condemned their teachings by proclaiming five doctrinal rules, known in English by the acronym TULIP. The T stands for "total depravity:" the view that every man – as the Heidelberg Catechism put it – is "prone by nature to hate God and [his] neighbor" and "wholly incapable of doing any good."

The Synod also confirmed that Church and State were equals – a view expressed in the name given to the small street between the Nieuwe Kerk and the city hall, now a Royal Palace: "Moses and Aaron Street." The States-General acquitted themselves of their Mosaic task by financing a new bible translation, *Statenvertaling*, which standardized the Dutch language. However, the public authorities were often slow to root out "false religion." In cities like Amsterdam, they allowed Mennonites, Remonstrants, and even Catholics to worship in "hidden churches" like "Our Lord in the Attic" – now a museum – next to the Oude Kerk. "House churches" is actually a better term, as these places were far from secret. The authorities tolerated them as long as they paid special taxes and refrained from advertising, loud talk, and nuisance, and seducing minors – conditions similar to the ones for present-day *coffeeshops*. As Jews and Lutherans were reckoned to be foreigners, they could build synagogues and churches that were anything but hidden. One now serves as the auditorium of the University of Amsterdam.

The Portuguese Synagogue: Monument of Asylum

The monumental Portuguese Synagogue in Amsterdam testifies to the prominence of religious minorities in Dutch history and forms an enduring legacy of Sephardic Jewish culture.

The first Jews who settled in Amsterdam were Catholic, at least in name. In Portugal, where they had their roots, Jews had been forcibly baptized since 1496. It was for its economic opportunities that these Sephardim (from *sepharad*: Hebrew for "Spain") came to Amsterdam, where they were welcomed for their know-how in international trade. Not before long, some of them came out as being Jewish, and began to return to their ancestral religion. Imported rabbis, teachers, cantors, and ritual butchers gradually convinced them that this implied a whole way of life. In 1614, the city allowed them to open a Jewish cemetery, in Ouderkerk (south of Amsterdam). Two years later, it ordered Jews to abstain from criticizing Christianity, and converting, circumcizing or courting Christians – implying that they *were* allowed to practice their religion. The States of Holland decreed in 1619 that every city could deal with Jews as it saw fit, without forcing them – as many foreign cities had done for centuries – to wear a distinguishing mark. "It is apparent that God wants them to stay somewhere," wrote Hugo Grotius, "So why not here."

Some Reformed theologians cried shame upon the permissiveness towards "these unclean people" with their "foolish and ludicrous

ceremonies" and "horrible blasphemies," but others hoped to win Jews for Jesus by showing them kindness. Besides, their knowledge of Hebrew came in handy. It was out of curiosity and intellectual rivalry rather than animosity that Reformed theologians organized disputations with Jewish scholars. The latter, who had often had a thorough Christian education, debated so well that the Sephardic *mahamad* ("church council") eventually ordered them to stop "provoking hatred against us among the gentlemen who live around us."

In the meantime, many Jews from Central and Eastern Europe had arrived in Amsterdam. These Ashkenazim were not by far as well educated or well off, most of them being dirt poor. Nevertheless, in 1671, they opened the first openly visible synagogue in Amsterdam – and Western Europe. But the Sephardim outshone them four years later with their *Snoga* or *Esnoga*. Designed by the city architect, with reminiscences of the Temple of Salomon, it was the world's largest synagogue, which soon became a must-see for foreign visitors and served as an example for synagogues all over the world.

The Portugese Synagogue became home to the seminary *Ets Haim* ("Tree of Life") which owns the largest Sephardic library in the world. After a donation by librarian David Montezinos in 1889 it holds thirty thousand printed works and five hundred manuscripts that cover all aspects of Jewish studies and cultural history. The "Livraria Montezinos" was placed in UNESCO's Memory of the World Register in 2004.

The Portuguese Synagogue was left intact by the Nazis and their helpers during the Second World War. The building was restored in the 1990s and still serves the religious purpose for which it was built.

Kingdom Come

For the Reformed Church, the nineteenth century began with a bang. In 1795, French troops and homebred revolutionaries toppled the *ancien régime* and its Public Church. They outlawed public religious display, closed down the faculties of theology, did away with supervision of schoolmasters by Reformed pastors, and announced that the latter would have to be paid by their congregants. For the "formerly dominant church" the end seemed near.

But the bang blew over. Revolutionaries made way for Napoleon, and after him, King William I restored the education and payment of Reformed clergy. On March 30, 1814, he was "sworn in and invested in state." The King was not crowned, and neither would his successors be – not for want of a crown, but for lack of a state church, with a bishop to do the job. The ceremony did take place in a church, however: the Nieuwe Kerk, of course.

Like Napoleon, William valued religion as an instrument for nation-building. He reorganized the Lutheran, the "Israelite," and the Reformed Churches. Since the "Synod of Dort," the latter had had a decentralized structure because the States General, weary of church infighting, had not allowed any more national synods. But a unitary state needed a unitary church. In 1816, government imposed a centralized form of church governance, which contained no provisions to safeguard doctrinal purity. Calvinism was deemed an obstacle for making the Church broad enough to include a nation of faithful citizens.

Dissatisfaction with this lack of ideological discipline, with the centralization of church governance, and with liturgical renewal – hymns, rhythmic singing, and organ music – broke out in the 1830s. Hendrick de Cock, a handful of fellow-pastors, and thousands of members seceded from the Reformed Church, and established a denomination of their own. They called it *gereformeerd* – the Dutch word for "Reformed" that had been common until the end of the eighteenth century, when the more indigenous sounding term *hervormd* came into vogue. The authorities broke up their church services, imprisoned them, and quartered soldiers in their houses. Frustrated by this lack of religious freedom, many emigrated to the United States, where they founded Dutch Reformed Churches.[6]

Freedom, Equality and Brotherhoods

Beside orthodox Calvinists, Catholics and liberals, too, were displeased with the autocratic regime. Their time came with Thorbecke's 1848 Constitution that again promised equal treatment. In 1853, almost three centuries after the Dutch Revolt, Roman Catholic bishops returned on the scene.[7] Protestant commentators raised a hue and cry, prophesying censorship, Inquisition, and burning heretics at the stake – doom scenarios that sound quite familiar to twenty-first-century ears.

Down-to-earth Protestant theologians were worried, too, because they foresaw that bishops would outshine them as opinion leaders. They defended their status by emphasizing a strong point: their openness to scholarship. In 1857-1858, the reverend Conrad Busken Huet published *Letters on the Bible*, explaining that Holy Scripture was "purely a human creation." This enraged orthodox Protestants, who gained power through democratization: in 1869, members of the Reformed Church were given the right to elect members of church boards and, indirectly, pastors.[8]

Amsterdam's first "democratically elected" pastor was Abraham Kuyper. In 1870, he held his inaugural sermon in the Nieuwe Kerk. Ten years later, he presided the inaugural ceremony for a neo-Calvinist "Free University" there. And another six years later, he and his supporters *sawed* their way in – the dramatic culmination of the 1886 *Doleantie*: a second, bigger secession. Kuyper and his followers soon merged with the Seceders of 1834. Besides inventing neo-Calvinism, he re-invented his community as an ethnic minority, with usages of its own. Pronouncing the final, silent e in *HEERE* ("LORD") and the "ch" in *Christus* ("Christ") as [khristus] instead of [kristus] became a shibboleth of *gereformeerden*. It placed them on an equal footing with Catholics, who had southern roots and led the way in "pillarization."[9]

Discipline and Emancipation

Since the 1795 Revolution, public schools were no longer Reformed, but they continued to offer a non-sectarian, ethical form of Christianity. Jews hardly objected, but Catholics and Orthodox Protestants did – the former because there was too much Bible talk, the latter because there was too little. They agreed to disagree, and founded private schools – for which they jointly demanded public funding.

The 1917 Pacification gave them this, and to this day, two thirds of all schools are, at least nominally, Catholic or Protestant. Aside from schools, many other "pillarized" organizations were founded to screen the faithful from siren songs of modernity. Socialism became a redoubtable competitor for the *Hervormde Kerk* in areas where class-conflicts were rife. This explains why the first regions with a high percentage of non-members were Zaan and Friesland, not the *Randstad*. All over the country, many *hervormden* quit in the 1920s, when for the first time they were asked to pay a contribution. Money was needed, now that the "silver cord" between state and church was gradually being untied.

During the Second World War, when it was confronted with Nazism, the *Hervormde Kerk* began to stand for its convictions. After the war, too, it pronounced upon many questions, often taking a progressive stance. In 1952 it stated that there was nothing wrong with sex, that it was not mainly meant for procreation, and that birth control was therefore allowed. With statements like this, it distanced itself from the Catholic Church, which – thanks to high birth rates – outnumbered it since 1930. Since 1960, there are even more Catholics than all Protestants taken together – yet still many Dutch will say that theirs is a nation of Calvinists. Whereas in 1809, fifty-five percent belonged to the *Hervormde Kerk*, in 2000 this was true of just eight percent. In 2004, *hervormden*, Lutherans, and mainline *gereformeerden* merged into a new Protestant Church in the Netherlands (PKN).[10]

Well into the 1950s, the Dutch Catholic Church remained the most conservative in Europe. In 1954 the bishops forbade the faithful not only to join the Labor Party, but also to read social-democratic newspapers or listen to "red" radio programs. Discipline worked: it kept Catholics on the straight and narrow, while urging these formerly second-rate citizens to rule the country. But Catholic intellectuals felt that pillarization had resulted in fossilization, and cautiously pleaded for change.

The tide turned in their favor in 1958, with the advent of Pope John XXIII. Within a few years, the Dutch Catholic Church became the most progressive in Europe – exemplified by the 1966 international bestseller *New Catechism*. Whereas Pius X and Pius XI had called Dutch Catholicism exemplary, the Vatican now began to worry. From 1970 onwards, it curbed progressivism by parachuting conservative bishops. Then the percentage of Catholics began to drop: from forty-one percent in 1971 to seventeen percent in 2000. When John Paul II visited the country in 1985, he encountered empty streets, and a deputy of the laity who talked to him like a Dutch uncle.

Mosques in the Polder: Corner Stones or Stumbling Blocks?

Like headscarves, mosques are visible indications of religious difference which tend to spark heated debates on things unseen.

Although the Kingdom of the Netherlands had considerably more Muslim than Christian subjects until Indonesia gained independence in 1949, the first mosque in The Hague. Its founders came from Surinam and belonged to the Ahmaddiyya movement – which is deemed heretical by most other Muslims. Since the municipal authorities did not approve the design until it had been stripped of all typically Oriental or Muslim features, the Mobarak Mosque initially looked rather like a nursing-home. The two small portal turrets it now sports were added in the 1960s, and the minaret as recently as 2005.

The Turkish and Moroccan "guest workers" who came to the Netherlands in the 1960s had even less conspicuous places of worship. As far as these young men were observant Muslims, they performed their ritual prayers in a quiet corner of the cramped boarding-houses where they lived or the factories where they worked in shifts. Religion became more important to them when they brought their wives and children over, which made them directly responsible for their children's education. Moreover, after many had lost their jobs in the 1970s they derived a sense of dignity (or even superiority) from their religion.

Numerous factory-buildings, cinemas, schools, and churches were converted into mosques, often including classrooms, offices, a tea-house or two, and shops. At present, there are some 450 official mosques, which come under various denominations. Some of them are controlled by foreign governments, others reject "State Islam" – but not always "Petrol Islam" – and promote views that are either considerably stricter or more liberal.

A growing number of mosques are newly built. In public discussions on such projects, the architectural design is usually interpreted as a direct indication of the religious community's integration into Dutch society. Large buildings with tall minarets and other "ethnic" features are deemed triumphant, backward intrusions upon mainstream Dutch society – much like neo-gothic Catholic churches were in the late nineteenth century.

After its completion, Rotterdam's Essalam Mosque – commissioned by a Dubai sponsor – will be the second largest in Europe. But will it get a full house? Even though many Turkish-Dutch and Moroccan-Dutch youth strongly identify as Muslims, and eagerly observe Ramadan, very few of them go to the mosque. The imams who lead prayer and preach there on Fridays often only speak Turkish or Arabic, and are hardly familiar with Dutch society.

Many young Muslims find spiritual guidance on the Internet, where "cyber muftis" – often based in the Middle East – offer interpretations of Islam which pretend to be pure and universal, devoid of "cultural accretions" and "superstitions." To counter such foreign influences, and offer an alternative to imported imams, a Dutch university training for Muslim clergy was established in 2005. Soon, the first students will graduate. Much is expected from these home-grown imams, but will mosques want to employ them?

Born-Again Citizens

Have the Dutch had it with religion? Since 1983, the Constitution no longer mentions churches. But in those same years, a Christian peace movement (IKV) organized the largest political demonstration in Dutch history, and thousands discovered post-Christian spirituality: Bhagwan, New Age, or psychic-healer Jomanda. Broadcasted charity collections, funerals of celebrities, and silent marches – invented by nineteenth-century Catholics to evade the ban on processions – mobilize and move masses of people. Religion, the provision of meaning and belonging, has grown more diverse. But citizens no longer agree to disagree. Since 1989, when Muslims rallied against Salman Rushdie, strong religious convictions are in bad odor – the smell of burning books, buildings, and bodies. Newcomers are taught to separate church and state, but in order to "integrate" them, that sacred principle is often violated, for example by government attempts to educate "enlightened" imams.

Saying "God bless the Netherlands" is not done, even at the end of the annual Speech from the Throne. But the two euro-coin still bears the motto "God be with us." Civil religion – connecting the nation, its monarchy and some Supreme Being – comes to light most clearly on May 4, when the queen approaches the National Monument on Dam Square, after listening to a speech from the country's highest pulpit, in the Nieuwe Kerk. And then, all observe two minutes of silence.

Further Reading

Bodian, Miriam. *Hebrews of the Portuguese Nation: Conversos and Community in Early Modern Amsterdam.* Bloomington: Indiana University Press, 1997.

Coleman, John A. *The Evolution of Dutch Catholicism, 1958-1974.* Berkeley: University of California, 1978.

Knippenberg, Hans. "The Netherlands: Selling Churches and Building Mosques." In *The Changing Religious Landscape of Europe*, edited by Hans Knippenberg, 88-106. Amsterdam: Het Spinhuis, 2005.

McLeod, Hugh. *Religion and the People of Western Europe, 1789-1989.* Oxford: Oxford University Press, 1997.

Rooden, Peter van. "Long-term Religious Developments in the Netherlands, ca 1750-2000." In *The Decline of Christendom in Western Europe, 1750 2000, edited by Hugh McLeod and W. Ustorf, 113-129.* Cambridge: Cambridge University Press, 2002.

Sengers, Erik, ed. *The Dutch and Their Gods: Secularization and Transformation of Religion in the Netherlands since 1950.* Hilversum: Verloren, 2005.

Chapter 17

Immigration and Multiculturalism

Han Entzinger

The prevailing self-image of the Dutch has always been one of a strong international orientation and an open mind towards influences from abroad: an open society with open borders. The Dutch prided themselves on their tolerance for other cultures and religions, and they were believed to welcome immigrants and refugees from all over the world. In the late twentieth century the Netherlands had become one of the countries in Europe with the largest share of foreign-born residents. Its generous and respectful policies of multiculturalism served as a shining example for other immigration societies. Since the turn of the millennium, however, the Dutch mind appears to have been closing at an unprecedented speed. Immigration is now seen as a major problem, as a threat to social stability and to Dutch culture. The murders of politician Pim Fortuyn (2002) and film director Theo van Gogh (2004), both of them outspoken antagonists of immigration, in particular from Muslim countries, shocked the nation. In the 2009 European elections Geert Wilders's anti-immigration and anti-Islam Freedom Party (PVV) became the second largest party of the country, only three percentage points behind the Christian Democrats (CDA).

Why this sudden change? Is immigration really undermining the country's stability and culture, as certain antagonists claim? Is it really challenging the country's identity, or would that identity have changed anyway, even without migration? What are the main arguments used in the current debate on immigration and how valid are they? These are some of the questions to be dealt with in this chapter. Before analyzing the current debate, however, an overview of the highlights of Dutch immigration history, with an emphasis on the past half a century will be presented.

A Brief History of Immigration

Already in the seventeenth and eighteenth centuries, the Republic was a safe haven for Protestants and Jews persecuted elsewhere in Europe.[1] Particularly welcome were those who brought along entrepreneurial skills and money. Without immigration, the Dutch "Golden Age" would have been much less prosperous. Over many years, tens of thousands of migrant workers from neighboring countries came to work in agriculture, industry or shipping. Many of them settled for good. Numerous family names that now seem utterly Dutch, in fact have French or German roots. In the year 1700, for example, forty percent of the population of Amsterdam were foreign-born. The role of the Dutch in international trade and in colonizing other parts of the world could never have been a success without an ability to adapt to highly different conditions and cultures. Even the tulip, the ultimate national symbol, was, in fact, imported from Turkey in the fifteenth century.

Much of the late nineteenth and early twentieth centuries were characterized by an emigration surplus. Many Dutch left the country for one of the colonies – above all for the Dutch East Indies – or they emigrated to the "New World." After the Second World War this pattern reversed once more. Since then, immigrants have been arriving from former colonies, from labor recruitment countries around the Mediterranean Sea, from other countries in Europe, and, increasingly, from all over the world. The recent history of immigration to the Netherlands and the immigrant presence in the country are not drastically different from those in nearby West European countries. Currently, about eleven percent of the Dutch population of 16.5 million people are foreign-born and for that reason can be qualified as immigrants. If one includes the so-called second generation (that is to say their Dutch-born children), the percentage goes up to twenty.

Thus, one in five persons living in the Netherlands is either an immigrant or a child of an immigrant. These figures include people with a background in other EU-countries, in Western countries outside the European Union as well as in pre-independent Indonesia. The number of residents with "non-Western origins," as official Dutch statistics call them, stands at around 1.8 million, just over one-tenth of the population. Among these "visible minorities" three communities stand out in size: Turks, Surinamese and Moroccans, each numbering between 300.000 and 400.000.

The Turkish and the Moroccan communities are legacies of the so-called "guest worker" policies in the late 1960s and early 1970s, which were followed by a rather generous program of settlement and family reunion. Most migrants from Surinam arrived in the 1970s, when this former Dutch colony acquired political independence. Since the late 1980s the origins of immigration have become much more diverse. The end of the Cold War led to a significant growth of East European migrants and of asylum seekers, some of whom later acquired refugee status. Besides, growing numbers of Dutch and foreign residents find their spouses in other countries. In recent years, the number of highly skilled migrant workers has also increased, although many of them do not settle permanently. Meanwhile, follow-up migration among the three largest "non-Western" communities, the Turks, the Surinamese and the Moroccans, is continuing, albeit at a much slower pace than before.

Foreign citizens constitute only a minority of all people of immigrant descent. In fact, only 4.5 percent of the population of the Netherlands do not hold a Dutch passport, less than in most nearby countries. This is largely an effect of a generous naturalization policy in the past and the fact that nearly all (post-)colonial migrants hold Dutch passports anyway. Yet, unlike many other immigration countries in Europe, citizenship is not generally considered as the primary distinguishing factor between migrants and the native population. Rather, ethnic origin tends to be more relevant in the public perception as a means of differentiating between *them* and *us*. The Dutch have even coined a term for this: the Greek-based word *allochtoon* (non-indigenous) refers to someone whose ethnic roots lie outside the Netherlands and who, for that reason, can be differentiated from *autochtoon* (indigenous), the native Dutch. An interesting, but unresolved question, of course, is whether an *allochtoon* can ever become *autochtoon* and, if so, at what stage in the integration process or even after how many generations.

Settlement patterns of people with an immigrant background, irrespective of where one places the defining boundary between *allochtoon* and *autochtoon*, are quite unbalanced. As in most other countries in Europe, migrants tend to be overrepresented in the larger cities and underrepresented in the countryside. Initially, most migrants came to the cities, where employment and educational opportunities were best. Once migrant communities had settled there, follow-up migrants tended to join them, taking advantage of the increasing social and geographic mobility of the original population, who had left the least attractive housing to the new arrivals. The largest four cities in the country (Amsterdam, Rotterdam, The Hague, and Utrecht) house only thirteen percent of the total population of the Netherlands, but they accommodate over thirty percent of all immigrants. In Amsterdam and Rotterdam almost half the population has an immigrant background (first and second generation), as do two-thirds of the school-aged children and youth in these cities. In certain neighborhoods only a small *autochtone* population of students and pensioners has stayed behind.

Indonesian *Rijsttafel*: Sharing the Table

Classical integration theory argues that immigrants preserve their food habits long after they have become assimilated into their new surroundings. Many tend to abandon their language, culture and music more readily than their food. It may take up to several generations before the immigrant offspring have taken on the same diet as their native peers. This is certainly true for many newcomers in the Netherlands. Admittedly, the relatively unsophisticated traditional Dutch cuisine may not have been too appetizing to them anyway.

What is often overlooked, however, is that newcomers may also influence local cuisine. This is how Americans – and the world – got their *pizzas*, how *chicken tikka masala* became a standard dish in the United Kingdom, and why the French have taken on *couscous*. The Dutch have their own version of this culinary creolization: Indonesian *rijsttafel* (or "rice table"). *Rijsttafel*, now a favorite in numerous Indonesian restaurants around the country, was unknown until after the Second World War. In fact, it is an invention of the Dutch colonial elite in the Netherlands East Indies, who were the only ones able to afford serving up to some fifteen or even twenty local dishes all at the same time in one meal – each of them in a little bowl, along with some rice. The Indonesians themselves were far more modest, limiting themselves to just one or two of these dishes, or even just a bowl of fried rice.

After Indonesia's independence, over three hundred thousand "repatriates" – made up of the Dutch colonial elite as well as Indonesian Dutch of mixed origin (*Indische Nederlanders*) – came to the Netherlands. They brought *rijsttafel* with them, and introduced it into Dutch cuisine. Surprisingly, given the fact that most dishes are very spicy, *rijsttafel* quickly became rooted in its new surroundings. Some Dutch restaurants abroad even feature Indonesian *rijsttafel* as their most typical Dutch dish. Since people have begun to travel the world more, cooking in the Netherlands has become more international, as in many other countries. However, good old *rijsttafel* remains an interesting example of how migration may affect eating habits in two directions.

Over half a century has passed since the large scale immigration from Indonesia. A third generation has come of age and, sadly, the typical colonial *Indische* culture in the Netherlands has almost disappeared. "Indisch" has become a remnant of the past – or *tempo doeloe*, Malay for "the old times." The fact that about three out of four people with a background in Indonesia have married a native Dutch person may have contributed to this. However, every Dutchman knows what *nasi goreng, babi panggang, gado gado, sambal goreng boontjes* and *saté* means and many do like it a lot. Who would have predicted that three hundred and fifty years of colonial heritage once would pass through the stomach?

First Steps Towards Integration

In the aftermath of the Second World War, the beginning of large-scale immigration and the emergence of the welfare state more or less coincided in time.[2] No wonder that, in the 1950s, it was mainly through a number of well-chosen social policy measures that some 300,000 so-called "repatriates" from Indonesia were encouraged to assimilate into Dutch society, with which most already had a certain familiarity. Later, in the 1960s and 1970s, social policy again played a crucial role in the reception and guidance of newly arriving immigrants, low skilled "guest workers" from Southern Europe, Turkey, and Morocco, as well as people from Surinam. A major difference, however, was that these migrants' residence was seen as temporary, both by the Dutch authorities and by most migrants themselves. As a consequence, no efforts were made this time to promote integration. On the contrary, migrants were encouraged to retain their cultural identity. The official justification was that this would help them reintegrate upon their return to their countries of origin. One of the most outspoken expressions of this approach was the introduction of mother tongue teaching for migrant children in Dutch primary schools as early as 1974. The authorities also facilitated migrants in setting up their own associations and consultative bodies.

This approach of creating separate facilities based on community identities was not new to the Dutch. Under the segregated system known as pillarization (*verzuiling*) various religious and ideological communities had long had their own institutional arrangements, such as schools, hospitals, social assistance agencies, newspapers, trade unions, political parties, and even broadcasting corporations. Within the limits of the law, each community was free to create its own arrangements. This enabled them to preserve their specific identity and to "emancipate" their members in their own way.[3] Since the late 1960s, however, pillarization has lost ground. Yet, it was generally believed that what did not work anymore for the population as a whole might be good for the migrants who, after all, were perceived as fundamentally different from the Dutch and as people in need of emancipation. Until about 1980 the promotion of institutional separation could easily be justified with an appeal to the migrants' presumed temporary residence. However, this institutional separation persisted even after the Dutch government finally acknowledged that most migrants would stay and should be encouraged to integrate.

The path that was envisaged for integration was remarkably similar to the one that had worked in the past for the religious and ideological "pillars." It was a combination of combating social deprivation through selected support measures provided by the then still generous welfare state, promoting equal treatment, and encouraging "emancipation," while aiming at the preservation of the communities' cultural identity. To this end the migrants were labeled *ethnic minorities*, and the policy on their behalf became known as *Minorities' Policy*. Interestingly, a country with remarkable ethnic homogeneity now introduced the notion of ethnicity as a basis for differential policymaking. The authorities and a vast majority of the population were convinced that this was the best way to promote the "emancipation" of migrants. It was this policy of deliberate separation that drew worldwide attention from protagonists of multiculturalism.

However, doubts were voiced about the effectiveness of this minority policy.[4] Some critics claimed that stressing ethnic differences would risk perpetuating them and would therefore become an obstacle to the migrants' fuller social participation, a phenomenon known as *ethnicization* or *minorization*. This was all the more worrying, since the economic downturn in the early 1980s had left large numbers of low skilled workers – often of immigrant origin – without a job. By 1990, more than one third of all Turkish and Moroccan men in the Netherlands were unemployed; unemployment rates for women were even higher. Most of the Dutch considered it inappropriate to encourage these immigrants to return, since the Dutch economy owed so much to them. Consequently, however, immigration became a growing burden for welfare and social policy regimes. Yet it was widely considered to be politically incorrect, if not racist, to discuss this in public.

Nevertheless, dissatisfaction grew under the surface. In 1991, the leader of the conservative Liberal Party (VVD), Frits Bolkestein, triggered a first public debate about immigration, which focused on the presumed incompatibility of Islam and "Western values." His remarks were influenced by the Rushdie affair in the United Kingdom and by recurrent disputes in France about the wearing of headscarves in public schools. Concerns grew in the Netherlands that the strong cultural relativism which had inspired the Minorities' Policy tended to perpetuate the immigrants' marginal situation rather than foster integration.

After the 1994 parliamentary elections the Christian Democrats (CDA) remained outside the government for the first time in almost a century. Traditionally, they had been the heralds of pillarization. This explains why the new coalition of three non-religious parties, headed by Labor Party (PvdA) leader Wim Kok, was now able to shift the policy focus from respecting cultural diversity to promoting the immigrants' social and economic participation. Significantly, the Minorities' Policy was renamed *Integration Policy*. From that moment on, culture was largely seen as a private affair; providing jobs to immigrants had become the main policy objective. Mother tongue teaching was removed from the core curriculum and later disappeared from the schools altogether. Besides, it was recognized that the migrants' lack of integration was also due to their insufficient familiarity with the Dutch language and society. A program of mandatory Dutch language and *inburgering* ("civic integration") courses was launched, which every newly arriving migrant from outside the European Union would be obliged to attend.

The ambition to improve the migrants' position in employment, education, housing, and other significant spheres of society proved to be quite successful. Registered unemployment among *allochtonen* dropped dramatically, though it still remained substantially above the national average. It was generally assumed, however, that it was the prospering economy rather than targeted government policies that had led to this improvement. Also in education the position of *allochtonen*, particularly of the second generation, improved significantly during the later 1990s. Although they were still overrepresented in lower forms of secondary education, their participation in higher education went up rapidly and their school dropout rate declined. The housing situation of immigrants no longer differed significantly from that of the native population of similar income levels. In other words, immigrant integration, measured by the traditional standards, advanced. The Dutch believed they were on the right track.

Problematizing the Issue

Nevertheless, certain problems related to immigration proved to be more persistent. The still rather amateurish integration courses failed to meet the rising expectations about the Dutch language proficiency of immigrants. Growing segregation led to a decrease in inter-ethnic contacts both at schools and in immigrant concentration districts. The still pillarized school system reinforced existing patterns of segregation and facilitated Muslims in establishing Islamic primary schools, some of which failed to meet Dutch standard quality norms. Even more worrying were the high delinquency rates among certain immigrant communities, which, at first, were mainly seen as a result of the lack of opportunities and of discriminatory practices. Later, the inability of immigrant parents to raise their children in a Western environment and, increasingly, their unfamiliarity, if not disagreement with Western values such as equality and tolerance were blamed for faltering integration and high crime rates. Finally, concerns were growing, though seldom expressed, about the relatively strong reliance on various social policy provisions among ethnic minorities.

At the start of the new millennium, two contradictory narratives began to emerge in the Dutch public debate on integration. The "official" one expressed that considerable progress had been achieved in all major indicators, such as participation in employment, in education and housing. Overall, the second generation was doing significantly better than their parents, particularly among the Surinamese. The continuing identification among Turks and Moroccans with their countries of origin and with Islam was taken as a sign of a successful multiculturalism: institutional integration could indeed go hand in hand with preservation of the original cultural identity. The sharp rise in naturalizations during the 1990s was yet another sign that growing numbers of immigrants saw a future for themselves in the Netherlands.

The competing view was much less optimistic. Paul Scheffer, a publicist and a prominent member of the Labor Party, was among the first to voice this view openly. In a much-debated article called *The Multicultural Tragedy* he stated that Dutch multiculturalism had failed.[5] Instead, he argued, a new ethnic underclass was emerging of immigrants who did not identify sufficiently with Dutch culture and society, and who were unwilling and unable to integrate. Scheffer voiced the concern that many Dutch people felt – but did not express – about continuing immigration, stagnant integration, increased segregation and a rapidly growing Muslim population. Scheffer argued that this would eventually undermine social cohesion and the functioning of the liberal democratic state, particularly because of the supposedly illiberal ideas of the Muslims. He accused the Dutch elite of having remained largely indifferent to these developments. Their cultural relativism had allegedly prevented them from demanding the newcomers to adapt. Respect for cultural difference had prevailed over understanding the needs of the less privileged members of the native population.

In this climate of increased sensitivity regarding immigration in general and Islam in particular, the terrorist attacks of September 11, 2001, in the United

States reinforced the impression that a "clash of civilizations" was imminent.[6] Around that same time the star of Pim Fortuyn suddenly began to rise on the Dutch political stage. Fortuyn was not really against immigrants as such, but his primary concern was the assault on democratic liberties that might result from the presence of so many people unfamiliar with Western values, particularly Muslims. Further immigration, he argued, would only exacerbate these problems. Fortuyn was killed by an animal rights activist nine days before the parliamentary elections of May 2002. His newly established party, however, came in second in these elections and became a partner in the new government coalition. This coalition proved to be very unstable, and was soon replaced by a more stable coalition that embarked on a tough anti-immigration agenda, which included the curtailing of family migration and the promotion of returns. Soon thereafter, immigration to the Netherlands dropped significantly. Between 2004 and 2007 the country's migration balance was negative, for the first time in four decades. In that period, Poland and Lithuania were the only two other EU-countries where emigrants outnumbered immigrants.

Integration policy also took a more assimilative direction. The dominant view became that migrants were to blame for their slow integration and should take the initiative to step up this process. Some lip service was paid to the idea that integration should be two-sided and that the established population should also leave some space to the newcomers, but only a few concrete policy measures pointed in that direction. Acquiring Dutch citizenship, for example, was made much more difficult and expensive, which provoked a plunge in naturalizations. At the request of the city of Rotterdam, the stronghold of Pim Fortuyn, a new law was passed which enabled local authorities to prevent people with low incomes (that is to say immigrants) from settling in certain neighborhoods. Enrollment in mandatory integration courses was enforced, even for *allochtonen* who had already been living in the country for decades. Passing the integration exam became compulsory, and failing to do so now led to a fine and to denial of permanent settlement rights. Most of the new measures left little or no room for a public recognition of the migrants' cultural identity. This led to the paradox that the same migrants who had been encouraged to preserve their own identity in the days of multiculturalism, were now blamed for their lack of identification with Dutch culture.

The emphasis in the integration debate has shifted quite clearly from promoting a fuller social participation for immigrants towards requesting newcomers to assimilate to Dutch culture and to assume a "Dutch identity."[7] Understandably, this has provoked fierce discussions on the nature and contents of that identity. The most outspoken feature of this "culturalization" of the immigration debate has been the growing emphasis on Islam as a major cause of many integration problems. Although less than half of all non-Western *allochtonen* in the Netherlands are Muslims, many *autochtonen* now consider Islam and its perceived expansiveness and oppressiveness as the root of all evil. They see the growing presence of Islam as a threat to the Dutch liberal and permissive attitudes on issues such as sexuality, equal rights, freedom of religion, and freedom of expression. In fact, Theo van Gogh was murdered in 2004 by a Dutch-born Muslim fundamentalist of Moroccan background who felt the film director had insulted Islam. This murder provoked strong reactions among large segments of the native population, who tended to be blind to the fact that the vast majority of Muslims in the Netherlands also strongly disagreed with the killing.

Since then, immigration and integration have risen to the top of the political agenda. Attitudes towards these issues have become much tougher, not only in politics, but also in society at large. Undoubtedly, the frequent linking of Islam, immigration, and security has had a negative impact on public opinion among both *autochtonen* and *allochtonen*. Surveys indicate a decline in acceptance of cultural diversity, once considered a trademark of the Netherlands.[8] Several members of parliament and celebrities, some of immigrant origin themselves, have been threatened and are now under constant security protection. One of them is Geert Wilders, the leader of the newly established Freedom Party (PVV), which has a strong anti-Islam and anti-immigrant agenda and which, according to opinion polls in 2009, is favored by about one-fifth of the electorate.

Ahmed Aboutaleb: Multicultural Mayor

Just days before the United States elected Barack Obama as its first non-white president in November 2008, a similar milestone was reached in the Netherlands. For the first time in history, a Dutch Moroccan became mayor – not just of a small village, but of the second largest city in the country: Rotterdam, with 600,000 inhabitants.

That new mayor was Ahmed Aboutaleb, born in 1961 in Morocco. At the age of 15, he migrated to the Netherlands, where his father had arrived as a "guest worker" some years before. He received his training as an engineer and held several positions in journalism and in Dutch public administration before becoming the founding director of Forum, a publicly financed information and advocacy agency for multiculturalism. After he acquired a feel for politics in that position, Aboutaleb was elected an alderman to the Amsterdam local government in 2004. Only months later, film director Theo van Gogh was murdered by a radical Muslim of Dutch-Moroccan descent. In the grim aftermath Ahmed Aboutaleb, together with Amsterdam's mayor Job Cohen, was able to defuse tensions, both on the Moroccan and on the Dutch side. He proved to be a real bridge-builder, not by talking softly about the need for mutual understanding, but by demanding that the Moroccans step up their integration efforts and consider the Netherlands unequivocally as their first home.

After it had supported multiculturalism for many years, the Dutch Labor Party (PvdA), of which Aboutaleb meanwhile had become a prominent member, was eager to hear this message from someone who had been an immigrant. When Labor joined the national government after the November 2006 elections, Aboutaleb became the Deputy Minister for Social Affairs and Employment. His nomination did not pass without political turmoil, as several parties on the right saw his dual citizenship as a sign of disloyalty to the Netherlands. Aboutaleb survived a vote of no confidence in parliament and he was confirmed in office. In fact, the Moroccan law would have made it impossible for him to relinquish his Moroccan citizenship, even if he had wished to do so.

Two years later he became mayor of Rotterdam, by appointment of the national government upon nomination of the city council, as is customary in the Netherlands. Local politics in Rotterdam had been sharply divided since Pim Fortuyn's party *Leefbaar Rotterdam* ("Liveable Rotterdam") won the local elections of 2002, ending ahead of Labor, which had governed the city since times immemorial. In 2006, Labor had taken the lead again, mainly as a result of a huge turnout among the Rotterdam immigrant communities. Understandably, "the Liveables" were seeking revenge. At first, they strongly objected to Aboutaleb's nomination, again because of his two passports, but they soon realized that the new mayor's rather hard line on integration came close to theirs. Nevertheless, Aboutaleb does not face an easy task. Although a Dutch mayor is supposed to stand above all parties, he often has to maneuver very skillfully. In a socially, ethnically and politically polarized city like Rotterdam this certainly is a challenge, even for an immigrant as successful as Ahmed Aboutaleb.

Open Borders, Closing Minds?

Why has this dramatic turnaround occurred? Anti-immigration sentiments have also been growing elsewhere in Europe, but nowhere has the swing been as huge as in the country once reputed for its tolerance. Of course, the economic crisis and the rise of Islam as a political force may serve as explanations. These, however, are worldwide phenomena and there are no reasons to believe that these have hit the Netherlands harder than other European countries. It is more likely, therefore, that the explanation should be found domestically. In mainstream politics – not just the Freedom Party – the belief is widespread now that earlier policies of multiculturalism must be held accountable for the immigrants' lack of integration. Recognizing and facilitating their cultural identity has kept immigrants in the margins of Dutch society. In hindsight, what had worked in the days of "pillarization" for the emancipation of native religious and ideological minorities should not have been copied for immigrant ethnic minorities with strong attachments to other countries and to Islam, a world religion not rooted in the European traditions.

In this view, multiculturalism has perpetuated the immigrants' marginality and explains their perceived lack of loyalty as well as the emergence of social tensions and delinquency.

To what extent do such views reflect reality? There is ample research evidence that most people of immigrant background living in the Netherlands are faring quite well.[9] An all-party parliamentary committee concluded in 2004 that "in most cases immigrants have integrated remarkably well and that this has occurred in spite of public policies rather than as an effect of these."[10] Research among Rotterdam youngsters of Turkish and Moroccan descent also indicates that their integration, as measured by all traditional standards, has progressed substantially over the past ten years.[11] Their social situation has become more similar to that of their *autochtone* peers, and so have their ideas, views and expectations on almost everything, except religion and issues related to it. At the same time, however, both *allochtonen* and *autochtonen* mutually perceive a widening of the cultural distance between them and an increased discrimination. Turkish and Moroccan youngsters, especially the more highly educated, are less optimistic about their own future than Dutch youngsters and also less optimistic than they were ten years ago.

Such findings, confirmed by numerous other research outcomes, may lead to the conclusion that, in fact, immigrant integration has been quite successful in most cases, but that the dominant definition of "successful integration" has changed meanwhile. Undoubtedly, Dutch society has changed profoundly in the last few decades. Immigration has contributed significantly to these changes. Large segments of the native Dutch population perceive this as a threat, and see immigration and Islam as a major scapegoat for changes that may have gone too fast. Some recent dramatic events have reinforced thinking in terms of *us* and *them* or, for that matter, in terms of *autochtonen* versus *allochtonen*. One should wonder, however, whether the initial multiculturalist approach must not also be seen in this perspective. Was it really as genuine and hospitable as most people believed in the earlier days of large-scale immigration? After all, facilitating immigrants to retain their own cultural identity may also have served as a ready excuse for not letting them become part of mainstream society. To the first generation such a marginal situation may still have been acceptable, but the second generation that has since come of age tend to claim a fair piece of the pie. It seems time for the Dutch mind to open up, even more so since closing the borders to new immigration has proved to be impossible.

Further Reading

Ederveen, Sjef, et al. *Destination Europe: Immigration and Integration in the European Union.* The Hague: CPB/SCP/CBS, 2004.

Gijsberts, Mérove. *Ethnic Minorities and Integration: Outlook for the Future.* The Hague: Social and Cultural Planning Office (SCP), 2005.

Lucassen, Leo, and Rinus Penninx. *Newcomers: Immigrants and Their Descendants in the Netherlands, 1550-1995.* Amsterdam: Aksant, 2002.

Sniderman, Paul M., and Louk Hagendoorn. *When Ways of Life Collide: Multiculturalism and its Discontents in the Netherlands.* Princeton: Princeton University Press, 2007.

Chapter 18

Law in Action

Freek Bruinsma

The postal code of the Red Light District in Amsterdam is 1012. Coalition Project 1012 is a joint effort of public authorities, private citizens and local businesses to counter the degradation of the district. It assumed its full-fledged form with a budget of forty-five million euros at the end of 2007. The Project aims to abolish the criminal infrastructure of women trafficking, drug dealing and money laundering. Repression of prostitution is not its goal. Prostitution was allowed in Amsterdam as far back as 1413 when the city decreed: "Because whores are necessary in big cities and especially in cities of commerce such as ours – indeed it is far better to have these women than not to have them – and also because the Holy Church tolerates whores on good grounds, for these reasons the court and sheriff of Amsterdam shall not entirely forbid the keeping of brothels." Prostitution has been made legal in 2001, although a brothel keeper needs a license and new licenses for window prostitution are only issued for two locations. The municipal authorities retain some control because they can refuse contracts, subsidies or permits if they have serious doubts about the integrity of the applicant.

Beleid: Combining Bottom-Up and Top-Down Strategies

Because of its non-legalistic leanings, law in action in the Netherlands can be characterized as pragmatic. A basic tenet is that rules should only be applied if they serve a goal, and not for their own sake. The dominant train of thought is that rules cannot cover everything, and compliance needs agreement. There is even a word for it. *Beleid* is a concept which is difficult to translate, as it is an integral part of Dutch culture and society. The English equivalent "policy" covers only half of its meaning. Characteristically, an authoritative dictionary of the Dutch language offers contradictory definitions of *beleid*. On the one hand, it lists that *beleid* means to manage and administer (*besturen*) on the basis of facts and expertise, which seems to imply top-down planning. On the other hand, however, it defines the term as a considerate approach (*bedachtzaamheid*), preferably by hearing all those concerned and giving them a say. These definitions may seem contradictory: one can either take decisions against the wishes of at least some of those concerned or one can come to an agreement with mutual consent, which implies non-decisions in the case of a veto or resistance. In theory and practice *beleid* is a mixture of both. *Beleid* is the art of rule-making and rule-implementation in context. It uses bottom-up and top-down strategies at the same time.

The egalitarian facade of *beleid* hides a solid tradition of authority. Up to the 1960s this could be characterized by the concept of "pillarization" (*verzuiling*). Each pillar – the Reformed, the Catholic, the liberal and the socialist pillar – had its own elites that maintained moral and social control within. Although the pillars imploded in the 1960s, all attempts to increase democratization by introducing a referendum, an elected mayor or lay representation in the professional judiciary have failed. These initiatives were doomed because direct democracy and participation interfere with *beleid*, which the elites prefer to develop in negotiations rather than by public vote. *Beleid*, then, is also a mix of elitist rule and popular influence.

Pragmatism is conditioned culturally as well as structurally. According to the sociologists Geert Hofstede and Gert-Jan Hofstede the Netherlands share an extremely feminine culture with the Scandinavian countries, stressing values such as equality, solidarity, sympathy for the weak, and resolution of conflicts by negotiation and compromise.[1] A need to negotiate and to compromise is structurally embedded in politics as there is never one party gaining an absolute majority. As a consequence, Dutch politicians are used to wheeling and dealing. This is particularly true for the Christian Democrats who have participated in all coalition governments since 1917 but for an interval from 1994 until 2002. On the one hand, moral crusades thus never found an unmitigated outlet in moral legislation, and, on the other hand, the Christian Democrats could always veto attempts to legalize practices that they considered immoral. Only during the brief interlude when the Christian Democrats were out of office, the coalition of socialists and liberals managed to lift the ban on brothels (2000), euthanasia (2001) and same sex marriages (2001). Since Christian Democrats, together with social-democrats and a small orthodox Christian party, formed a coalition government in 2006, a new tendency to restore conservative values has become apparent, as illustrated by "Coalition Project 1012" or the ban on tobacco smoking in cafes and restaurants, introduced in 2008.

Two policy areas may help illustrate Dutch law in action: the approach to crimes without victims and the practice of institutionalized consultation with interest groups that is called the "poldermodel."

Pragmatism Towards Crimes Without Victims

Although abortion and euthanasia, alcoholism and drug addiction, prostitution, gambling, pornography, and homosexuality might be criminal according to the statutes, these various kinds of behavior have been labeled "crimes without victims."[2] Philosophers might argue that there are victims, yet such crimes refer to strongly demanded goods or services, creating a black market and a subculture when legally proscribed. The lack of a complainant makes criminal law difficult to enforce.

This is pragmatism at its best. Since there are no sound practical reasons to outlaw crimes without victims, the law in action calls for a policy (*beleid*) of non-enforcement. For decades the law in the books symbolically reflected moral condemnation, while the practice was permissive. Pragmatism uses the tool of a sliding scale: at the one extreme a blind eye is turned to vices with minor ramifications such as drug abuse in private, and at the other extreme strict law enforcement is called for when the stakes are high, as in the case of the production and trade in hard drugs. In the absence of a yardstick the cases in-between are of course the difficult ones: what is the approach to hard-drug addicts, and to the suppliers of soft drugs? In theory, pragmatism tackles these questions one by one and by trial and error, trying to strike a balance between a counter-productive zero tolerance and an unproductive wait-and-see attitude. In practice, however, the facts are quite often decisive, resulting in an unfounded and half-hearted "yes." Pragmatism prefers inconsistent outcomes over blind rule enforcement.

In the 1970s a committee of experts, chaired by a neurologist, laid the basis for the Dutch policy of tolerance with regard to soft drugs. The committee refuted the stepping-stone hypothesis which held that a cannabis user runs a high risk of becoming a heroin user, and recommended different approaches to soft drugs and to hard drugs. Since the criminal law allows, but does not compel the prosecution services to bring a crime to court, non-prosecution can be a matter of policy (beleid). The guidelines that set explicit standards for prosecution and non-prosecution with regard to drugs were adopted in 1976 by the most left-wing government in Dutch history, the Den Uyl coalition government (1973-1977).[3] These prosecution guidelines elaborate on the distinction in the Opium Act between "soft" and "hard" drugs, and add a second distinction between consumption and production. Possession of soft drugs was considered negligible up to thirty grams, small amounts of hard drugs could be ignored except where there are prior convictions; occasional dealing within a pattern of addiction would be penalized with fines, yet systematic and quasi-professional dealing, especially importing and exporting, was penalized with stiff prison sentences.

This was only half of the story, however, namely the story of law in books. The other half, law in action, was that the police anticipate beleid of the prosecutors and took it as a starting point for setting their own priorities at grassroots level. They tried to get professional dealers in hard drugs convicted, but they would not take any action if they came across small-scale dealing in hard drugs. It was difficult to say when and where, and as a consequence also why and why not, the law would be enforced.

Obviously the borderlines between permitting the small-scale use of soft drugs and prosecuting large-scale dealing in hard drugs are continuously challenged. What should be done with hard-drug addicts whose welfare benefits are not sufficient to cover the daily costs of their addiction and who therefore turn to crime? A fine makes less sense than a free and state-controlled distribution of the heroin substitute methadone.[4] How does one defend the quality checks on ecstasy pills at rave parties? The authorities are of the opinion that if one cannot eradicate illegality it is better to monitor illegal situations in the interests of other concerns, such as public health. Should the police show an interest in the supply of soft drugs to coffeeshops? Police closed some of the fully equipped and computerized greenhouses, only to give the competitors new opportunities.

The year 1996 marked the end of the heydays of the drugsbeleid. New guidelines for (non-)prosecution were published. While the basic distinction between soft and hard drugs was preserved, the allowable amount of soft drugs for personal use was significantly reduced from thirty to five grams.

Several municipalities at the national borders have decided to a further reduction to three grams, for sale only to registered members of a particular *coffeeshop*. The Dutch drug policy remains a bone of contention in European politics.[5] In the absence of state-controlled growing, the illegal cultivation and trading of Dutch cannabis (*nederwiet*) has become big business. Only twenty percent of production is for domestic consumption by an estimated number of 400,000 cannabis consumers, leaving half a billion kilo *nederwiet*, representing a market value of two billion euros, for export – tax free, of course, since it is illegal.

Coffeeshops: From Permissiveness to Control

In the Dutch language the word *coffeeshop* is used for a bar that serves soft drugs rather than coffee. This very Dutch institution resulted from the prosecution guidelines of 1996 that tried to regulate drug use and separate soft drugs from hard drugs. A *coffeeshop* had to meet specified requirements to be tolerated: no sale of hard drugs and alcoholic drinks, no selling to minors, a maximum of five grams for each transaction, no more than five kilos of soft drugs in stock, no advertising and no nuisance to the neighbors.

Only 105 of the 443 municipalities have one or more *coffeeshops*. Most of them are in the larger cities, mainly in Amsterdam. Fully aware of the weak public support for the *coffeeshops*, local authorities

have reduced their number by stricter implementation of the rules from 1,004 in 1995 to 702 in 2007. Amsterdam in particular witnessed a dramatic decline: from 450 in 1995 to 228 in 2007. After the Christian Democrats returned into the national government in 2006 the number was further reduced by stipulating that a *coffeeshop* would not be tolerated within five hundred meters of a school. The mayor of Amsterdam openly regretted that this government policy led to the closure of another forty-three *coffeeshops*, because he feared that illegal and irresponsible drug runners would fill the gap.

The *coffeeshop* has lost much of its innocence as a symbol of the underground youth culture, however. About eighty percent of the license holders in Amsterdam and Venlo (a provincial town in the south of the Netherlands near the border with Germany) was discovered to have an average criminal record of six offenses. Also, drug tourism could not be avoided in a Europe without borders. Almost all customers of the *coffeeshops* near the borders came from Belgium, France, and Germany. The biggest *coffeeshop* with a license for a bar and a restaurant, Checkpoint in Terneuzen (photo), near the border with Belgium, attracted more than 900,000 tourists a year who spent an estimated seven million euros, until it was forced to close in 2008. Moreover, with so much local experience in vegetable gardening, it did not take long to produce *nederwiet* of potent quality, thus blurring the distinction between soft and hard drugs. After the ban on tobacco smoking in pubs in 2008, *coffeeshops* had to find other ways for consumption on the spot than smoking the usual blend of *nederwiet* and tobacco.

Apart from *coffeeshops* there are smart shops that sell hallucinogenic mushrooms (180 in 2007) and grow shops that sell seeds and equipment for growing marihuana (from 106 in 1999 to 375 in 2007). The suicide of a seventeen-year old French girl in Amsterdam in 2007 provided the minister of Public Health with sufficient support for putting 126 types of hallucinogenic mushrooms on the list of proscribed drugs the following year, depriving smart shops of their main source of income. Grow shops are still legal, but no one knows for how long.

The Balancing Acts of Euthanasia

At issue is the art of following a *beleid* that balances between enforcing rules in a way that is not so strict as to become formalistic and not so lenient as to lose control. While the Dutch *drugsbeleid* illustrates the latter, the legalization of euthanasia, which took a long gestation period of a *beleid* of prosecution guidelines, is much more balanced. This second example introduces a more respectable group, namely doctors who occasionally assist in terminating a patient's life. Terminal care is part of every medical practice of the general practitioners who provide the primary health care in the Netherlands. Most requests for euthanasia are dealt with in this context. Whereas drug tourism is a serious problem, any fear of euthanasia tourism to the Netherlands is unfounded: euthanasia is carried out within the context of a long-standing relationship between the doctor and the patient.

Parliament passed a Euthanasia Bill in April 2001, which went into force in 2002. The first section of Article 293 of the Criminal Code still threatens someone who takes the life of another at the explicit and earnest request of the latter with a maximum sentence of twelve years of imprisonment. But a new second section exempts a doctor from criminal liability, provided (s)he has met criteria which have been developed in the case law and informs the municipal coroner immediately after the lethal act. Whereas the non-prosecution *beleid* concerning soft drugs stands in isolation, the non-prosecution *beleid* concerning euthanasia was a process of fine-tuning consisting of leading cases submitted to the Supreme Court of the Netherlands (*Hoge Raad*), and prosecution guidelines in close concert with the professional association of doctors (Royal Dutch Medical Association, KNMG).

Beleid started to play a key role in the early 1990s when the conditions for non-prosecution were laid down. The government wanted to know more about the practice of euthanasia before embarking on new legislative attempts, and needed the cooperation of doctors.[6] The KNMG was willing to cooperate in return for clear prosecution guidelines, in order to make sure that doctors who assisted terminally ill patients to end their life did not have to fear prosecution. *Beleid* allows for a gray zone between what is lawful and what is unlawful, at the same time trusting that doctors will not decide imprudently. This is not equivalent to a right to non-prosecution, because in every report of an unnatural death the prosecution takes a decision on the merits of the case. The most important condition for non-prosecution is a procedurally controlled ascertainment of the patient's death wish, which must be verified by a second practitioner. These and other requirements have been developed in the case law of the Supreme Court.

According to the requirements of the Burial Act a doctor has to certify each case of death. The notification procedure specifies the questions that the doctor has to answer under two headings: natural or unnatural death. Before this provision of the Burial Act came into force in 1993, a survey among doctors revealed that less than twenty percent of all cases of physician-assisted death were reported. Similar surveys carried out in later years showed a much higher percentage of forty-one in 1995 and further increases to fifty-four percent in 2001, and eighty percent in 2005. At the end of 1998 five regional advisory bodies, consisting of three experts (in law, medicine and ethics) were established between the doctor who helped a patient to die and the prosecutor who can still charge the doctor. Their task is to evaluate the doctor's decision. In only three of the 2,123 voluntary reports of unnatural death in 2000 did they come to the conclusion that the euthanasia decision had been wrong, but none of these cases were pursued.[7] The purpose of the advisory bodies is to persuade doctors to report more honestly, in order to bring euthanasia out into the open.

By the same token, in spite of the notification procedure and the *beleid* of non-prosecution, many cases of euthanasia used to be reported as natural deaths, which was an easy way out if the doctor wanted to avoid trouble himself or for next of kin of the deceased. After euthanasia was legalized another more legitimate evasion has become more popular, namely palliative sedation by means of a strong tranquillizer.[8] Although the advisory bodies have strictly speaking become superfluous after legalization, they are still thought to be useful. In the new Act the advisory bodies only have to inform the Public Prosecution Service when they have found that the requirements have not been met.

The *Poldermodel*

The reconstruction after the Second World War laid the foundations for what has been coined the *poldermodel*. The term "polder" – reclaimed land – refers to the Dutch struggle against the water and the miraculous transformation of water into land. Metaphorically, however, *poldermodel* stands for decision making on the basis of mutual trust and consensus building. In the strong version it denotes corporatist self-government: the programs of the welfare state such as health and social insurance, unemployment and workers' compensation schemes were administered by tripartite bodies consisting of representatives of employers and employees – the two groups the Dutch call the "social partners" – and independent experts appointed by the government.

With an eye on the less extensive welfare programs of the other member states of the European Economic Community a consensus emerged since the 1970s that the Dutch welfare state might be out of control: the deficits in the public budget increased and loopholes undermined the fairness of the welfare policies. In the self-regulatory administration of the social security system, for example, nobody had a sufficient incentive *not* to grant disability pensions or early retirement plans. Employers who wanted to get rid of elderly workers, because they were often sick or simply undesirable, could remove them from the payroll by offering long sick-leave or early retirement. Both could easily agree to a benefit scheme, as the costs were to be paid by the collective insurance scheme. Doctors were inclined to help, and the insurance administration saw little chance to resist the consensual determination of the employer, employee and medical officers in exploiting the collective funds.

To avert the threat of direct government intervention, employers and unions accepted that something had to be done and concluded the Wassenaar Agreement of 1982. Measures against the self-service arrangements of the welfare state have been taken, and by cuts in spending the public budget has decreased from sixty-seven percent of the Gross Domestic Product in 1983 to less than half after 1999. At the beginning of the twenty-first century both employers and employees gave up control over the implementation of social security, and therewith the weak version of the *poldermodel* supplanted the strong version of corporatist self-government.

The weak version of the *poldermodel* can be credited for this recovery from the budgetary crisis. It consisted of a cultural mix of consensus, egalitarianism and what Francis Fukuyama called "trust."[9] In low-trust societies, such as the United States, law is a substitute for trust. In high-trust societies, such as the Netherlands, law in action is non-legalistic and consensual. Institutionalized consultation is a weaker version of the *poldermodel* than corporatist self-regulation, but more efficient because the government is the only player with the powers to end the discussion and to take decisions against the wishes of the other participants.[10] It is in this spirit that the Social and Economic Council (*Sociaal-Economische Raad*, SER) functions as an advisory body for parliament and government. It is very influential when the composite parts – employers, employees and independent experts – agree on the socio-economic *beleid* for the years to come. The *poldermodel* is at risk if one of the participants does not show the self-restraint required by the system. For this reason the income of the Prime Minister (€ 181,000 in 2009) is adopted as a cap to limit the higher incomes in the public and the semi-public sector.

Subsidies: Good Intentions, Bad Results

Subsidy is an important instrument of the welfare state and open-ended subsidizing is one of the factors that contributed to the budgetary crisis at the end of the twentieth century. Three subsidies deserve special attention because means and ends were unrelated: ends belonged to the political realm of ideals, whereas means became goals for subsidy recipients.

As a token of the appreciation of their heroism in the resistance movement during the Second World War, a unique subsidy system for sculptors and painters was introduced in 1949 (*Beeldende Kunstenaarsregeling*, BKR). In 1952 the BKR supported a mere 142 artists for the equivalent of € 136,363. In 1982, 3,295 artists together received almost sixty million euro. Budgetary reasons put an end to this grant scheme in 1987.

The manner in which these art subsidies were awarded illustrates the concept of *beleid*. Artists submitted their art works to local committees of art experts, including practicing artists. The committees advised on the quality and the price to be paid. The price, on average almost three times the market value, was converted into a welfare benefit for a specified number of weeks. New art works could be submitted only afterwards. Thanks to the BKR all government buildings in the Netherlands are decorated with works of modern art, but most subsidized art works have been stored away for many years, only to be auctioned off or returned to the artist in the 1990s.

Between 1978 and 1989 investments were subsidized by the state on the basis of a tax reduction (*Wet Investeringsrekening*, WIR). Approximately twenty-five billion euros were spent. It started as a socialist idea to influence business investment plans in politically correct directions, but it ended in a gift scheme for all kinds of business activities. The Netherlands became a tax haven and goal displacement took place: the subsidy did not function as an investment incentive, but became a source of quibbles between corporate lawyers and the Dutch tax department. At the end of February 1989 news leaked out that the scheme would end in a few days time. The last weekend of February 1989 notary offices worked round the clock to register an additional and very final € 454 million in WIR claims.

The migrant worker and his family became the object of subsidized activities in the late 1990s. From 1998 to 2002 the sum total spent to improve their position in society rose from the equivalent of € 680 million to € 1.5 billion. Three different public consultancy firms came to the same conclusion: wasted money. The subsidies were based on the incorrect assumption that foreigners would become quasi-Dutch if asked to take lessons in the Dutch language and in cycling for example, while they would receive money to maintain their own cultural identity at the same time. Integration while preserving one's own identity ("*integratie met behoud van eigen identiteit*"), as the paradoxical *beleid* slogan stated. As a result, the Netherlands has become a multicultural society where different ethnic communities live apart together.

Gedoogbeleid and Elusive Responsibilities

The contrast between the approach of command and control on the one hand and *beleid* on the other is strongest in the practice of the "administrative policy of tolerance" (*gedoogbeleid*). It means that administrators accept deviations from the letter of the law. This policy of tolerance is adopted as a fallback in cases where *beleid* does not work. Too much *gedoogbeleid* results in a shadow administration which becomes a legal order of its own. It consists of written administrative decisions that allow individuals and corporations to transgress the law, judges to uphold these decisions, and academics to study and comment on the gray administrative policy as if it constituted the official legal order.

One particular event brought two leading cases before the Supreme Court. Contrary to the rules, a local official had allowed polluted dredgings to be dumped in a nature area. The Supreme Court ruled in the ensuing lawsuits that i) civil servants are not liable to punishment if the wrongdoing fits within the pattern of the municipality's *gedogen*, and ii) municipalities are not liable to punishment if the offence has taken place in the context of a public task (the local council is supposed to exercise control).[11]

The dire consequences of this case law for third parties were brought to light by two disasters. A firework factory exploded in the middle of the city of Enschede on May 13, 2000. In total, twenty-three people died in the ensuing inferno, and part of the town was reduced to a ruin. Two nagging questions can be asked. Why was there such a factory in a city? The answer: it has been here since a long time and it has some leverage on the municipality because of its importance for the local economy and the labor market. What about the permission required? The answer: in fact, the factory had permission for only three containers, but another four were tolerated. In a second disaster fourteen youngsters lost their lives and more than three hundred were seriously burned on New Year's Eve 2001 when a fire broke out in an overcrowded bar in Volendam that lacked the proper emergency exits. It turned out that the manager did not possess the required permits, but was allowed to continue his business because of his influential position as successful businessman in a small community. The parents of the victims erected a memorial that reads: "Due to indulgence and negligence we lost our children and thus our desire to live."

In both disasters the prosecution refused to instigate proceedings because of the case law, in the absence of which other authorities were asked to investigate the disasters in a non-committal and therapeutic way.[12] In a third disaster only public authorities were involved. Awaiting their expulsion eleven refugees died in a fire in the night of October 27, 2005, while they were locked in a temporary detention center near Amsterdam Airport Schiphol. An official investigation concluded a year later that "no or fewer casualties would have been deplored if the authorities had complied with the rules." Two ministers resigned, one for each of the two coalition parties, yet one of them returned in the new cabinet at another post. Repair legislation, introducing legal responsibility for civil servants, is in preparation.

It may be difficult to translate the concept of *beleid*, but it is even harder to translate its extended and, at the same time, contradictory version of *gedoogbeleid*, and it is almost impossible to understand its rationale. Readers who are used to thinking in terms of a system of checks and balances will be surprised to hear that legitimate powers are very illusive in the Netherlands. The civil service is a complex of more or less independent agencies, each with its own *beleid* towards their own client groups, with minimal judicial review. The same readers will be pleased to hear that the leading circles in the Netherlands agree with them: Coalition Project 1012 is a good example of the new approach.

Further Reading

Boekhout van Solinge, Tim. *Dealing with Drugs in Europe: An Investigation of European Drug Control Experiences; France, the Netherlands and Sweden*. The Hague: BJu Legal Publishers, 2004.

Bruinsma, Fred J. *Dutch Law in Action*. Second edition. Nijmegen: Ars Aequi Libri, 2003.

Hondius, Ewoud, M.J. Chorus and Piet-Hein Gerver, eds. *Introduction to Dutch Law for Foreign Lawyers*. Fourth edition. Deventer: Wolters Kluwer, 2004.

Griffiths, John, Heleen Weyers and Maurice Adams. *Euthanasia and Law in Europe*. Oxford: Hart Publishing, 2008.

Hofstede, Geert, and Gert Jan Hofstede. *Cultures and Organizations: Software of the Mind*. Second edition. New York: McGraw-Hill, 2005.

Chapter 19

Living with Water

Rob van der Vaart

"How do we manage to do this? Such a small country. So much water and a climate that is changing. And yet remaining in balance. Quite difficult! But together with you we provide dry feet and clean water. Dive into that!" This is the voice-over of the television ad of the government campaign "The Netherlands Lives with Water" that was launched in spring 2008. The ad shows a green raft in the shape of the Netherlands that floats in the sea. On the raft groups that represent the Dutch population keep their balance, such as an ice skater, a young couple, and soccer fans in orange clothing. The advertisement invites citizens, consumers and NGOs to visit the campaign website and help provide solutions to the problems the Netherlands faces as a result of climate change.[1] In this way the national government hopes to create more understanding and public support for its water policy, which requires sacrifices from everyone and a long-term vision.

What an individual Dutch citizen can do to keep the country safe and dry is far from obvious. Most of them hardly have a choice, as most large cities and economic activities are concentrated in the low part of the country. Protecting the west of the country against risks of flooding is a matter of consistent and long-term government planning and of structural investment in security given the potential hazards of the current era of climate change.

This chapter will focus on the issues raised by this government television ad: water consciousness in Dutch society and the policy alternatives for a sustainable future. The stakes are high. It is expected that during the twenty-first century the sea level will rise by at least sixty centimeters. In north-western Europe, climate change will result in a higher frequency of extreme weather conditions, with strong storms and heavy rains. Intensive rainfall will result in higher peaks in the discharge of the big rivers, especially the Rhine and the Maas. This excess river water will flow into the North Sea, but less easily than today, because of the rising sea level. On top of all this, the Dutch subsoil, already partially below sea level, is slowly sinking. Ground water seepage is an increasing problem.

The combination of a low-lying country and climate change creates risk. Risk is chance – of the occurrence of flooding – multiplied by costs in terms of casualties and destroyed infrastructure. The flooding risks under changing climate conditions are particularly high in the west of the Netherlands: it is a low part of the country (chance) that is densely populated (costs). Water consciousness in all layers of Dutch society – politicians, public and private sector, civil society – and water policy are therefore very important issues. Before moving to these issues, this chapter will first address major issues in Dutch water history.

The Beemster Polder:
Masterpiece of Designed Reclamation

In 1607 a group of Amsterdam merchants and administrators decided to start a major infrastructural project, the reclamation of the Beemster, a large lake north of Amsterdam with a perimeter of almost forty kilometers. The group saw this project as a good investment opportunity. The flourishing and growing city of Amsterdam and other cities of Holland needed increasing amounts of farming products, and the reclamation of the lake would create new land for farming. It would also put an end to the regular flooding during storms of land around the big lake.

Engineer Jan Adriaenszoon Leeghwater coordinated the actual reclamation process. A high and strong dike was constructed around the lake, and a ring canal was dug outside this circular dike. With the help of forty-three windmills, the lake water was pumped into the ring canal. Leeghwater used an ingenious system of placing the windmills in rows, pumping lake water out step by step, up to the level of the ring canal. Already in 1612 the lake was dry and the actual arrangement of the polder could start.

The chessboard layout of roads, ditches, and parcels in the polder is typical of Renaissance geometrical landscaping design. The Beemster polder is internationally famous for its parcellation pattern and design principles. This is one of the reasons why the polder was

included in the UNESCO World Heritage Register. The struggle against water, the reclamation of land since the Middle Ages and developing into ever bigger water management and reclamation projects: it is all condensed in the example of the Beemster polder.

For a long time, windmills were used to keep the water in the Beemster polder at an acceptable level for farming. Obviously, the polder would have filled up with water again if it had been left to itself. Land below sea level requires constant pumping. During the nineteenth century steam-driven pumping installations were introduced, replaced later on by diesel and electric pumps. Because of these innovations, many of the windmills have disappeared. Today, the Beemster polder has a sophisticated system of water level control, with five sections of the polder each with different water levels. Arable farmers need other water tables than cattle farmers, and village residents need very high groundwater levels since the pile foundations under their houses would rot when low groundwater would expose them to oxygen.

Beemster is just one out of dozens of lakes that were reclaimed since the sixteenth century. Over time, technological innovation allowed for bigger or deeper lakes to be reclaimed. Reclamation of the Haarlemmermeer, where Amsterdam Airport Schiphol is located, only became an option in the nineteenth century thanks to steam power. The largest-scale projects were realized during the twentieth century, with the reclamation of three huge sections of the IJsselmeer, the freshwater lake that originated out of a corner of the sea after the completion of the Afsluitdijk. Together they now form the new province of Flevoland, a new space for farming, recreation, urbanization, and nature.

Water Management in the Past

"God created the world, but the Dutch created Holland," according to a popular expression. The people who over the centuries inhabited the territory now known as the Netherlands have indeed changed the physical appearance of the country dramatically. It is true, to some extent, that the country was "conquered from the water."

The Dutch coastline looked radically different two thousand years ago. The southwest of the country was mostly sea with some small islands. The dunes of the west coast were already in place, but behind the dunes was an unstable region in which the big rivers were free to change their course from time to time and where major sea floods sometimes created new lakes. The north was an indented coast with the current islands (Waddeneilanden) still more or less connected to the mainland by a stretch of salt marshes. The Zuiderzee in the center of the country was smaller and its connection to the North Sea was no more than a narrow bottleneck cutting through the indented north coast.

The Roman Empire extended as far to the north as the river Rhine. During the rise of the sea level in the third and fourth centuries CE people living in the north (particularly in what is now the province of Friesland) started to create artificial molds (*terpen*), made of clay, manure and waste materials, for protection against sea floods. Over the centuries, these molds could reach a level of about seven meters above the sea and became big enough for permanent settlement.

During medieval times, inhabitants of the north and southwest of the country gradually started to construct dikes between their settlements and the sea to protect themselves from very regular flooding. This resulted in more sedimentation that enlarged useable land. Over time the new sediments could be incorporated as new farmland by constructing new dikes facing the sea. Over the centuries, this process resulted in the formation of the northern coastline and the northern and southwestern islands as we know them today.

People living in the central river district, on the sandy and slightly higher levees alongside the rivers, also responded to flooding risks by constructing low dikes: at a right angle to the river just upstream from the settlement and parallel to the river behind their settlements, causing flooding waters to find a course behind their settlements and back into the river further downstream. These early forms of flood-protection were very local: continuous and integrated larger-scale dikes were only constructed from the late medieval times onward, when more centralized and stronger governance structures were put into place.

A major transition in settlement took place around 1000, when inhabitants of the northern and western parts of what is now the Netherlands started to move into the vast expanses of bogs and moors. These relatively inaccessible peat bogs were drained and cultivated by groups of new settlers. The long-term effects were immense: it created the rural landscape with narrow parcels, many ditches, and windmills that one now considers "typically Dutch;" it gradually lowered the land surface because of drainage (shrinking of the dehydrated peat layers), and it resulted in the habitation of the western part of the country, which became a core region during the Golden Age.

The peat bogs were not only turned into farmland. Peat stabbing was an additional source of income: peat could be dried and then sold as source of energy for cooking and heating. With the growth of the cities, the market for turf also expanded. Easily accessible peat packages, those above the groundwater level, were first exploited. The demand was such, however, that later on peat was even extracted from below the water level. Holes in the landscape were the result: new and often large lakes, created by the work of thousands of turf cutters.

The presence of all the lakes, particularly in Holland, not only limited the agricultural surface and therefore farm production, but also created a new danger for local inhabitants. When storms would sweep up the water surfaces, flooding was always a risk. People spoke of the almost permanent threat of the "water wolf." Therefore, from the sixteenth century onwards, the reclamation of these lakes started, a process that over the centuries would incorporate ever bigger former lakes into the land surface, as a result of improving technology.[2] Until the nineteenth century, flooding remained a fact of life for inhabitants of the river district and some of the coastal regions.

Between 1750 and 1800 alone 152 floods occurred in the central part of the country. The situation started to improve with the creation of a national agency for water management in 1798, now known as *Rijkswaterstaat*, the Directorate-General for Public Works and Water Management. With the gradual improvement of dike systems and water management, the frequency of floods decreased. But sometimes people were reminded of the "water wolf:" a major storm flood swept over Zeeland and parts of Flanders in 1808, resulting in a major sea dikes improvement program; another devastating storm flood hit the Zuiderzee in 1916. And in the river district the floods of 1855, 1861, and 1926 proved that the river dikes could not offer complete safety. Major infrastructural improvements took place during the twentieth century. In 1932 the Zuiderzee, in the heart of the country, became the IJssel-meer when the closing dam (Afsluitdijk) was completed. And in the southwest of the country an enormous coastal flood protection project was started after the Great Flood of 1953: the Delta Works.

The Great Flood:
Inducement for the Delta Works

What happened during the cold winter night preceding February 1, 1953, is collectively remembered by the Dutch as a national disaster. An enormous storm raised the tide and the power of waves hammering the coast. As a result many dikes in the southwest of the country gave way. 1,836 people died, 200,000 hectares of land were flooded, and 72,000 people became homeless. Surviving victims from Zeeland, the west of Brabant and the islands of South Holland were evacuated to other parts of the country. Money and clothing were collected all over the country and international emergency aid arrived. Yet, it could have been much worse. If the river dikes of South Holland had also given way, some of the deepest parts of the country would have flooded, with water levels locally rising to seven meters. More than 30,000 people would have perished.

Ironically, major plans for flooding protection in the country's southwest had already been on the table for decades. But during the crisis of the 1930s, the Second World War and the post-war reconstruction years, dike improvement was not a priority. But in 1953 Dutch politics and society had to learn by shock. Shortly after the disaster, an ambitious plan for storm surge protection in the Southwest was accepted by Dutch parliament: the so-called "Delta Plan."

The most visible result of the Delta Plan is the string of dams that connect the islands and close off the estuaries from the North Sea. The roads on top improve the accessibility of Zeeland enormously. The inner waters are now compartmentalized by additional dams more inland, which serve water management functions and add to the accessibility of the area from the southern *Randstad* region.

The storm surge barriers in the Oosterschelde are exceptional. The environmental awareness of the 1970s made it unacceptable that the highly valuable brackish and tidal ecosystem of the Oosterschelde would be destroyed by closing it off completely from the sea. The compromise was a masterpiece of engineering: a barrier with compartments that are open during normal weather conditions, but that can be closed by huge steel panels in case of storm.

The southernmost estuary, Westerschelde, was not sealed off at all by a barrier, since the Westerschelde is the access route for the harbors of Antwerp and Ghent, in Belgium. Instead, the sea dikes around it were fortified. The absence of a dam here implies that the most southwestern part of the Netherlands, Zeeland Flanders, did not benefit from improved accessibility like the other parts of Zeeland. In the 1990s it was therefore decided to create a road tunnel of 6.6 kilometers, with its deepest section sixty meters under sea level, connecting Zeeland Flanders with the rest of Zeeland.

The Delta Plan not only raised the safety level of the country's southwest, but also boosted economic development, particularly in Zeeland. The area is now more accessible for tourists, commuters to the Rotterdam urban area, and industrial and other companies.

New Water Policy

The fear of flooding gradually disappeared into the background of the Dutch collective memory after the Great Flood of 1953. In the absence of further flood disasters, water consciousness waned during the second half of the century. People in the rapidly urbanizing low-lying parts of the country generally assumed that flooding risks were now under control thanks to solid dikes and to the vigilance and expertise of the engineers of *Rijkswaterstaat*.

It came as a complete surprise to many people, therefore, that about 200.000 people had to be evacuated from the river area in 1993. The level of the river water had risen to the very top of the dikes and dike sections. Saturated with water and under enormous pressure, they might just have given way and collapsed. In the end, none of this happened, neither in 1993, nor when similar circumstances occurred in 1995, but the almost-disaster of 1993 proved that complete safety is an illusion, particularly in conditions of climate change. Periodically raising the dikes is not a sustainable solution because the volume of water that may be contained in the riverbed will rise with the height of the dikes, and increase the disastrous effects if a dike would collapse.

The 1993 and 1995 events, combined with a generally broader awareness of the potential effects of climate change for the Netherlands, resulted in a major shift in water policy. The government report on water policy for the twenty-first century, issued in the year 2000, was entitled "A Different Approach to Water."[3] The first chapter, "Rising Sea Level and Subsiding Land," sets the context of climate change and Dutch physical-geographical conditions. The key question of the report is how to increase the amount of space for water. Urban as well as rural areas should make an end to the established practice of getting rid of excess water (after heavy rains, for example) as soon as possible. This practice of "efficient" water management bestows an extra burden on the main arteries of the water system: the rivers. It should become common practice to enlarge the capacity for local water storage and groundwater infiltration. Rivers should have more space for their water, too, and not just high dikes to contain the water. This policy was further elaborated in the so-called Spatial Planning Key Decision "Room for the River" (2006).[4] It entails a smart mix of various measures, adapted to local circumstances and possibilities, creating more room for the rivers Maas, Rhine, and IJssel, such as removing obstacles in the river beds, broadening or deepening the river bed and creating bypasses. Approximately € 2.5 billion will be spent on this program until 2015.

This shift in water policy implies a fundamentally new attitude towards water: it is no longer the enemy to be contained, but rather the co-inhabitant of the country that demands its own room and space. "Living with Water" is the slogan of the national campaign for water consciousness. In the new rhetoric water may be seen as an opportunity or as a friend, be it a very expensive friend. The Delta Commission, installed for exploring needs for flood protection until 2100, concluded in 2008 that more than hundred billion euro will be needed during this century to ensure a climate-proof future for the country.[5]

Water-Conscious Citizens?

Water consciousness is one of the key words in recent Dutch water policy.[6] It is considered to be essential for popular support for an expensive water policy and for responsible action by all relevant actors – municipalities, investors, and society at large – with regard to water issues. But what exactly is "water consciousness" (waterbewustzijn)? Some Dutch scholars have suggested the following definition: water consciousness is the awareness and understanding that the consequences of any decision related to water (issues) should weigh heavily in the actual decision.[7] In this definition knowledge and understanding are linked to decisions and action. Furthermore, its neutral phrasing is remarkable: the definition does not refer to dangers or threats. Experts tend to agree that the promotion of water consciousness should not entirely focus on the negative (water as a threat), but equally on the positive (water as an opportunity). In the case of the Netherlands, potential water opportunities are manifold: the water-rich country as a location factor for companies and as an asset for attracting tourists; water management expertise as an export product; or water as an experience factor in neighborhoods or recreational areas. Yet, in the international use of the concept "water consciousness" some experts tend to focus on the problematic side of water, such as the increasing global scarcity of drinking water and the effects of climate change for coastal cities.[8]

Water consciousness is not automatically present in a country such as the Netherlands. Modernization and technological progress have resulted in a general feeling that safety from floods is self-evident. Clean water and a safe environment are perceived as "products," automatically delivered at certain costs.

Do the Dutch know and care about water issues? A 2005 survey showed that water is clearly a low interest issue.[9] In answer to the question "What do you seriously worry about?" respondents – predictably – mentioned increasing violence, erosion of norms and values, terrorism and extremism, and cuts in social security. The issue "rising water levels (sea, rivers, groundwater)" ranked twelfth: only nine percent of the respondents were worried about it. The survey also showed that the Dutch are not really interested in water management. The majority is satisfied when water management is well organized at the lowest possible costs. Any sense of involvement or urgency is missing from the survey results; a representative sample of the national population expresses a relaxed, uninvolved and consumerist attitude towards water issues.

An interesting aspect of water consciousness is the personal responsibility of citizens. Some people buy a house with a beautiful view alongside a lake or river. Millions of Dutch citizens buy or rent houses in parts of the country that may be meters below sea level. Who is to be held accountable for the damage in case of a flood? The legal context of the issue nicely demonstrates the dilemmas: in case of calamities no one can be held personally accountable, although personal legal accountability does apply in cases of negligence. But where is the line between calamity and negligence to be drawn in cases of flooding? Floods in the densely populated western part of the Netherlands may result in astronomical damage. It is understandable that the government is looking for legal openings towards "shared responsibility and accountability." Nevertheless, water insurance is a legal minefield. One interesting example concerns a major residential area to be developed in the Zuidplaspolder, adjacent to the city of Gouda, a location approximately six meters below sea level. In case of a flood, the area would be very badly hit: it is one of the lowest points in the Netherlands. Who would have to pay the costs for casualties and material damage? Are the inhabitants to some extent accountable, because they have knowingly and willingly bought houses there? Are the project developers and the municipality legally responsible because of their decision to develop the area? Or should the government have been stricter in its spatial planning regulations and never have allowed development here in the first place? Or could the water boards, responsible for dike maintenance, be accused of negligence because they had been able to foresee the risks?

Accountability in a case like this is clearly a Gordian knot. The example shows that water consciousness – seriously weighing the water factor in decisions – not only applies to citizens, but probably even more to all actors involved in urban and regional planning and development such as politicians, planning experts, civil servants, and project developers.

Water-Conscious Professionals?

Professionals in the water sector, such as the civil engineers working for the Directorate-General of Public Works and Water Management (*Rijkswaterstaat*) or for the water boards, are certainly aware of short-term risks and long-term challenges of flooding. In their professional life, they are "living with water" on a day-to-day basis. They know that it is essential to set land aside for future infrastructural needs and that a consistent national water management policy requires planning over several government terms. They also know that market pressure for urban development can jeopardize long-term water management priorities and should therefore be controlled rather strictly. But they are also aware that the success of water management since the 1950s has decreased water consciousness in Dutch society. An urban legend has it that a text posted on a wall of the Directorate-General for Public Works and Water Management reads: "Lord, give us our daily bread, and now and then a minor flood," since a near-disaster would enhance public awareness of the need for consistent water policy and water management.

But it is not for professionals in the water sector to decide on spatial development and the dynamics of land use. The practice of spatial development is a domain in which many actors have a role to play: local, regional, and national politicians and civil servants, real estate developers, land speculators, farmers, environmental pressure groups, and many more. Urban and regional planning is a complex process that by nature requires the weighing of all kinds of interests. The interests of the water sector – climate-proof solutions that diminish rather than enlarge future flood risks – is just one set of interests out of many. The key issue is to what extent all other interest groups and actors take water seriously in their approaches, actions, and decisions. What about the water consciousness of all actors involved in local and regional planning?

A hypothetical case may illustrate what is at stake here. Imagine a medium-sized city along one of the big Dutch rivers. The local administration knows exactly which areas within its borders have been reserved for implementing the "Room for the Rivers" project until 2015. These areas, for instance little stretches of land next to the river dikes, will remain untouched for other forms of development. But the local authorities are thinking ahead and are planning a new residential area and business park to be realized from 2013 onwards. One potential location – location A – is on farmland quite close to the river. The farmers are willing to sell, the site looks promising to attract new inhabitants, and environmental groups have few objections. Location A, however, is adjacent to the land reserved for the "Room for the River" water management project. Location B is farther away from the river, on the other side of town. It has an attractive landscape of dispersed villas, some farmland, a horse riding center, and some forest. The rich villa dwellers fiercely oppose the idea that their neighborhood would become more urbanized. Environmental groups are equally against it, because of the interesting flora of this mixed landscape. Local farmers are less willing to sell their land than farmers at location A; they prefer the more profitable piecemeal sales to individual newcomers who want to construct new villas in the area. Representatives of the water sector, however, advise against location A since the site might be needed in the decades after 2030 for further dike improvement works in order to avoid future floods. Local authorities, developers, farmers, and environmentalists in turn argue that 2030 is far away and that future technologies may very well solve the problem in other ways that make other places along the river more suited for extra water management projects. And in the end, against the advice of the water sector, location A is chosen and formally approved by the province.

Territorial development and national land-use dynamics are the result of thousands of decisions like this one, some local, others regional or national, sometimes in line with the water sector advice, other times against such advice. Bringing all micro-decisions in line with long-term water interests would require eco-dictatorship, which of course is equally inconceivable and undesirable. In our democratic market economy, all will depend on the level of water consciousness of all parties involved. The national government has taken two important measures for stimulating the inclusion of water issues in daily planning practice at all levels. One is the so-called Water Impact Assessment (*watertoets*). The other is the National Administrative Agreement on Water (*Nationaal Bestuursakkoord Water*, NBW).

Water Impact Assessment (WIA) became mandatory in November 2003. For every new spatial plan, such as a local plan or a regional plan, the water board of the region will give a written advice. Local planners have to explicitly present in their final plan how and to what extent they have taken this advice into account. Water issues can no longer be by-passed or neglected in territorial planning. But final decisions in planning can still go against the advice of the water sector. WIA was evaluated nationally in 2006, showing that this young planning instrument will need further fine-tuning.[10] Often WIA had only marginal effects because the location of the development was already beyond discussion, financial instruments for including water interests in local and regional planning were lacking and the parties involved spoke different "languages."

The National Administrative Agreement on Water (NAAW) involves national government, all provinces and municipalities, and all water boards. The agreement was signed in 2003 in order to tackle the big challenges of water management in the twenty-first century "jointly and in an integral way." Large-scale spatial reservations, for "Room for the Rivers" projects for example or for future coastal improvements, require integrated action and short communication lines. Quick repair of weak spots in the national flood protection system, such as relatively weak dike sections, equally requires collaboration and efficient communication. Evaluation of the NAAW in 2006 showed some shortcomings rather similar to those of the Water Impact Assessment. And again there is considerable confusion about money: which division of government has to pay for what and what exactly is the financial role of the water boards that manage regional water systems?

Towards a Sustainable Future

In the face of climate change and a subsiding underground, large parts of the Netherlands are confronted with major challenges in preventing floods in the near and more remote future. In its approach to tackling the issue, the country is going through a transition in governance style: from a technocratic and scientific style, dominated by the rather closed "state in the state" *Rijkswaterstaat*, towards an integral and participatory style, characterized by slogans such as "The Netherlands Lives with Water" and "Room for Water." Efforts are made to involve civil society, the private sector, and all sectors of government in concerted action, and to raise water consciousness among citizens, planning professionals, and other groups.[11] The transition is still in its take-off phase and the gap between national strategic vision and practical implementation at the local level is still considerable. The Netherlands seems to be going through a learning process, in which many groups of actors still have to get used to taking water issues seriously in their thinking and in their actions.

A sustainable future for the country, with its concentration of population and its main economic infrastructure exactly in low-lying areas, depends very much on improved water consciousness, to prevent irreversible planning decisions that go against the interest of water management. And it will also create a basis of public support for consistent long-term policy for preventing future floods. There are no guarantees: neither for mentality change, nor for flood prevention. The transition might become a success and result in a broadly shared sense of urgency and direction, but it is just as well possible that the state will have to take very strict control over market pressures and decisions of individuals in order to avoid unacceptable risks for the future.

Further Reading

A Different Approach to Water: Water Management Policy in the 21st Century. The Hague: Ministry of Transport, Public Works and Water Management, 2000. www.waterland.net.

Hoeksema, Robert J. *Designed for Dry Feet: Flood Protection and Land Reclamation in the Netherlands*. Reston: ASCE Press, 2006.

Spatial Planning Key Decision "Room for the River": Investing in the Safety and Vitality of the Dutch River Basin Region. The Hague: Ministry of Transport, Public Works and Water Management, 2006. www.ruimtevoorderivier.nl.

Ven, Gerard van de, ed. *Man-Made Lowlands: History of Water Management and Land Reclamation in the Netherlands*. Utrecht: Matrijs, 1993.

Water Vision: Safeguarding our Future: The Government's Vision of National Water Policy. The Hague: Ministry of Transport, Public Works and Water Management, 2007. www.verkeerenwaterstaat.nl.

Working Together with Water: A Living Land Builds for its Future; Findings of the Deltacommissie 2008. Deltacommissie, 2008. www.deltacommissie.nl.

Chapter 20

In Foreign Eyes

Jaap Verheul

The Netherlands has evoked divergent images in the eyes of foreigners. Although one of the most densely populated countries in the world, it is cheerfully associated with windmills, tulips, wooden shoes, and green polders where black-and-white cows peacefully graze. In its picturesque inner cities people joyfully ride their bicycles along the canals. People speak their minds freely, are averse to authority and dogma, and tolerate different opinions and religions. This image of free expression, independence and open-mindedness, however, is easily turned into the dystopian picture of permissiveness and moral bankruptcy. In recent years foreign media have routinely associated the Netherlands with drugs, prostitution, child pornography, abortion, euthanasia and other controversial "ethical issues." The term "Dutch disease" has been coined to criticize an over-generous welfare state doling out earnings from natural resources to voluntarily unemployed citizens and recent immigrants instead of investing them in industry. Yet the same nation was hailed to offer a "polder model" of consensus-based cooperation between employers, workers and the government to overcome economic crises. The only way to understand these paradoxes is to explore the history and function of these conflicting images of Dutchness, which often tell us more about the writers who produced them than about their topic.[1]

Envy, Fear, and Wonder

The Dutch began to appear on the mental horizon of other nations after they became a geopolitical and cultural power to be reckoned with at the beginning of the sixteenth century. True, the inhabitants of the swampy river delta near the North Sea had been noticed and described by some travelers and writers in earlier centuries. The Roman historian Tacitus in his *Germania* offered an ethnography of the Germanic tribes that formed a looming threat at the periphery of the Roman empire in the first century CE. He described the red-haired Batavians that lived in the area that later became part of the Netherlands as especially given to drinking, fighting, and gambling. In later centuries some travelers encountered these ominous territories for missionary work, trade or political negotiations. But for the most part the inhabitants of the delta remained hidden at the periphery of the shifting empires.

The dwellers of the river delta suddenly abandoned this obscurity to enter the world stage when Northern provinces rebelled against the powerful Habsburg Empire of King Philip II and declared independence in 1581. The new political entity was formally recognized in 1648 as the Dutch Republic of the United Provinces, but had already become a source of amazement during the audacious war against its former ruler. Many diplomats, soldiers, traders, scholars and other travelers who found their way to this new center of power and culture, reported back about this marvel of Calvinism, republicanism and prosperity, for the first time creating an image of the Netherlands as a unique political and cultural entity in Europe.

One of the first influential observers of the new republic was the Italian trader Lodovico Guicciardini, the nephew of the famous historian, who had settled in Antwerp as a commercial agent. The young Guicciardini published a lively history of the Low Countries in 1567, one year before the Dutch Revolt broke out. His *Descrittione di Tutti I Paesi-Bassi* meticulously described each region and city in great detail, but also provided information about folklore, languages, and the prosperous economy of the rebellious region. Guicciardini attempted to describe the Dutch national character; he praised the common sense and diligence of the merchants, the ability of the craftsmen, the reading and writing skills of the farmers and peasants, but also found the Dutch stingy, greedy, and prone to drinking. His well-timed book was reprinted over thirty times in the following century and was translated into many languages, introducing the identity and culture of the newly created nation to a European public.

The European neighbors soon found reason to envy and fear the new republic when it became a prosperous trading nation that sailed the seas in search of new markets and customers, and also proved a formidable naval power. England in particular fought a series of costly maritime wars in the seventeenth and eighteenth centuries over control of the seas and trading routes. The English developed an elaborate anti-Dutch narrative of morality and national folklore that would be disseminated into Western culture. Playwrights in Shakespeare's days, for instance, wrote farces that poked fun at Dutch sexual morals by displaying Dutch women invariably as plump and men as inebriated. Similarly, English publications attacked their Dutch opponents by arguing that they "are more famous for their Industry and Application, than for Wit and Humour."

Not surprisingly, most English invectives were directed against the maritime presence of the Netherlands. At the beginning of the first Anglo-Dutch naval war, statesman and poet Andrew Marvell effectively expressed the irritation of his countrymen in his satirical poem "Character of Holland." Although written in 1653 it would remain a staple of anti-Dutch expressions in the English language well into the nineteenth century. That Marvell ran the full gamut of maritime stereotypes is already clear from his oft-quoted first stanza:

> Holland, that scarce deserves the name of land,
> As but th' off-scouring of the British sand;
> And so much earth as was contributed
> By English pilots when they heav'd the lead;
> Or what by th' ocean's slow alluvion fell,
> Of shipwrack'd cockle and the mussel-shell;
> This indigested vomit of the sea
> Fell to the Dutch by just propriety.

Similar images of sea, rivers and mud, and, of course, the windmills, clogs and the dikes that the Dutch developed to cope with their aquatic enemy, would remain associated with the image of Dutch society for many centuries. The Netherlands, rhymed poet Samuel Butler, was not a normal country, but: "A land that rides at anchor, and is moor'd, / In which they do not live, but go a-board."[2] Literary representations of this naval competition survived well into the eighteenth century as images of evil captains and untrustworthy merchants found their way into Daniel Defoe's famous adventure novel *The Life and Adventures of Robinson Crusoë* (1719) and Jonathan Swift's *Gulliver's Travels* (1726).

But the educated English reading public also learned about the origins of the wealth and power of its perpetual maritime enemy from a number of travel journals that appeared during the seventeenth century. The most influential and enduring analysis, however, was offered by diplomat and statesman William Temple who had been ambassador to the Netherlands and befriended the Dutch ruling elite and nobility. He published his *Observations upon the United Provinces of the Netherlands* in 1673, one year after the Republic suffered a disastrous defeat against its English, French, and German enemies. Nonetheless, Temple continued to believe in their mutual interest and impressed upon his readers the many reasons why the Dutch had become "the Envy of some, the Fear of others, and the Wonder of all their Neighbours." He gave a detailed and informed overview of the history, institutions, geography, religion, trade and economy of the Netherlands and warned his readers that the power of the Netherlands was much greater than the number of its inhabitants suggested. "Holland is a Countrey," he insisted, "where the Earth is better than the Air, and Profit more in request than Honour; Where there is more Sense than Wit; More good nature than good Humour; And more Wealth than Pleasure." Temple's work was immediately translated into Dutch, French, German, and Italian, and it became a bestseller that influenced the image of the Netherlands until well into the eighteenth century. Temple later became instrumental in the marriage between stadholder William III and Mary, the daughter of the English king James II, which led to William's accession to the throne during the Glorious Revolution of 1688, an event that can be described as a true invasion of Dutch power and culture into the court and culture of England.[3]

Cradle of Freedom and Tolerance

While the English view of the Netherlands was characterized by jealousy and competition, French and German intellectuals during the Age of Reason discovered it as a beacon of freedom and tolerance in a world that remained obscured by monarchical absolutism. After all, the Dutch Republic had offered asylum to many refugees who had been persecuted for their religious or political views, and had provided an intellectual haven for those who sought scholarly innovation and publishing houses for controversial ideas. The seventeenth-century French philosopher René Descartes, for instance, studied and taught in the Netherlands for most of his life and especially treasured the freedom and safety from oppression in his host nation. "Which other country," he insisted, "where one can enjoy full freedom, where one sleeps with less concern, where there are always foot soldiers at large to protect you, where poisoning, betrayal and conspiracies are hardly known, and where so much is left of the innocence of our forefathers?"[4]

The philosophers of the French Enlightenment warmly embraced the Dutch Republic in their battle for tolerance, religious freedom and progress. Voltaire, the most influential of these *philosophes*, traveled to the Netherlands frequently, visiting his publishers, studying with the famous scholars at the University of Leiden, or pursuing love interests. In his many letters and books Voltaire sang the praises of the freedom, tolerance and egalitarianism of Holland which he found sadly missing in France, where he had been incarcerated and expelled for his political views. He jealously reported how he encountered the stadholder strolling without lackeys in the middle of the crowd as an example of Dutch modesty. In his famous historical overview of human progress, the *Essai sur les Moeurs* (1756), Voltaire has sympathetically described how the Dutch republic had rebelled against the cruel despotism and religious persecution of Philip II and had subsequently defended its liberty with labor and sobriety.

Like many foreign travelers, Voltaire was sometimes frustrated by Dutch daily life when he encountered obstacles of bureaucratic lethargy, bourgeois complacency or sly greediness. He once decried Holland as a phlegmatic hell, and after one particularly aggravating encounter with his publisher was rumored to have left the country with the angry alliteration "Adieu, canaux, canards, canaille" (Goodbye, canals, ducks, and thugs). More importantly, Voltaire repeated many popular stereotypes concerning Dutch greediness and hypocrisy in his fictional works, most notably in *Candide* (1759). Yet, in spite of their disappointment in contemporary Holland, Voltaire and other advocates of rational science and tolerance such as Denis Diderot and Montesquieu continued to underscore the importance of Dutch history in the cause of human progress and civil freedom.[5]

In contrast to the feverish optimism of the Enlightenment and the nationalist ambitions of the early nineteenth century the Netherlands sometimes suggested an image of decline to its European neighbors. They derided the complacent and pipe-smoking Dutch who traveled in slow tow barges as the "Chinese of Europe." Yet at the same time the heroic history of the Dutch Revolt and the Golden Age became a popular theme, as it conveniently served as an example for political theories about popular sovereignty and emerging ideas about national identity. It was no coincidence that Robert Watson, a historian from Scotland – a hotbed of nationalist resentment and political theory – published an influential *History of the Reign of Philips II* about the Dutch Revolt in 1777, which was reprinted six times in the following decades. This work, in turn, proved an inspiration for German writers and scholars who struggled with the problem of German national unity. Johann Wolfgang Goethe worked no less than fifteen years on his successful play *Egmont* (1788) about one of the influential supporters of William of Orange, because he saw this episode as a "turning point in the history of states" that illuminated the essential problems of his day. Also taking his cue from Watson, his close friend Schiller wrote a play about *Don Karlos* (1787), the troubled son of Philip II who sympathized with the people who revolted against his father. He subsequently published a historical overview of the first years of the Dutch revolt, which he planned as the first installment of an ambitious series about revolutions and conspiracies. He, too, saw the establishment of Dutch freedom as one of the most important achievements in world history.

This idealistic and romantic perspective also radically changed the American perception of the Netherlands. In the first years of independence the young American Republic looked with mixed feelings to its fellow republic across the Atlantic. Americans had inherited much of the popular anti-Dutch folklore from England and its founding fathers were largely disappointed in their dealings with the Dutch Republic. Instead of the expected model of republicanism, the Netherlands became a byword for all shortcomings of federalism that the American Constitution was intended to avoid. Immigrants of Dutch stock, too, were often displayed as representatives of outmoded traditions that conflicted with modern citizenship. The Dutch families that dominated upstate New York were easy targets for literary wits such as Washington Irving who poked fun at the Dutch heritage in his stories "Rip van Winkle" and "Sleepy Hollow," and the *History of New York* (1809) that was written under the pseudonym of the Dutch historian "Diedrich Knickerbocker."

But when educated Americans on the East Coast began to explore the languages and cultures of continental Europe in the early nineteenth century as an alternative to their former mother country, they, too, discovered the attractive richness of Dutch history. It was the Bostonian historian John Lothrop Motley who successfully presented the Dutch Revolt as a precursor to the American Revolution in his highly popular *The Rise of the Dutch Republic*, which was published in 1856. He not only compared Dutch founding father William of Orange to George Washington, and his Catholic enemy Philip II to King George III, but convincingly argued that the Dutch had effectively started an Atlantic revolution that, by way of England, had brought democracy and freedom to America. With this bestseller and its two sequels Motley laid the basis for an enduring pro-Dutch sentiment in American popular culture.

This new-found ideological affinity developed into a true *Holland Mania* at the turn of the century. American painters flocked to picturesque fishing villages in the Dutch bible-belt, Dutch architecture with stepped gables and verandas was imitated in the American Midwest, Dutch traditional costumes and furniture became collector's items, and intellectuals replaced the Pilgrim Fathers with Peter Stuyvesant as the true founder of their nation. This naive, utopian and decisively pastoral construction of a pre-industrial "Holland" – as the nation affectionately was called after its largest province – characterized by sailing ships, quaint cobbled alleys, and cohesive coziness was extremely appealing to an American nation undergoing a rapid and sometimes painful process of industrialization and urbanization. A romantic, historicized and somewhat stagnant Holland became a blissful counterpoint to the grim realities of modernity.[6]

As tourism developed during the nineteenth century out of a romantic quest for authenticity and exoticism, this picturesque image of the Netherlands found its way into travel guides. It is no coincidence that the first tourist guidebook ever to be printed, John Murray's famous *Red Book* of 1834,

Hans Brinker: Morality Behind the Dikes

The book that most successfully embedded the pastoral image of the Netherlands in American popular culture is the children's novel *Hans Brinker: or, The Silver Skates* by Mary Mapes Dodge. Published in 1865 in the wake of a brutal Civil War, it offered American readers a welcome image of a quaint and sturdy world unspoiled by strife and moral failure. The book was filled with stories of civil courage, perseverance, industry and Christian charity, placed in an idyllic landscape of frozen canals and small cities that showed "a bewildering jungle of houses, bridges, churches, and ships, sprouting into masts, steeples, and trees." As she explained in her book, Dodge considered Holland as "Odd-land or Contrary-land; for in nearly everything it is different from other parts of the world." *Hans Brinker* was primarily written as a morality tale about an alternative world to instruct young American readers.

Mary Mapes Dodge (1831-1905) was a well-educated, young widow from New York who started to work as a writer and editor in order to support herself and her two sons. After she had successfully published a number of children's stories she was inspired to write about the Netherlands by reading John Motley's works on the Dutch Revolt. She diligently collected information on Dutch history, literature, and art, and learned many stories from a befriended Dutch immigrant family. Dodge craftily assembled all these assorted details and anecdotes in her story about the fifteen-year-old boy Hans Brinker and his little sister Gretel who participate in a skating match to earn the coveted Silver Skates and pay for medical treatment for their ill father. Their friends meanwhile embark on a skating tour through the country, and through the eyes of these small children the reader in passing learns about the Dutch landscape, museums, architecture, and traditions.

The most famous story inside the novel relates the heroic feat of "The Hero of Haarlem," the small boy who saves the country from flooding. Returning in the evening from an altruistic errand to bring cakes to a blind man, he notices a tiny stream of water seeping through a small hole in the dike. Acutely aware of the impending danger that the dike might collapse, the boy decides to stop the leak by thrusting his chubby little finger in the hole. In spite of darkness, cold and fear the little hero perseveres until he is discovered the next morning and villagers come to the rescue.

A stunning 300,000 copies of *Hans Brinker* were sold in the first year, and the subsequent 180 American editions and translations brought the total to seven million. The story was adapted into plays, movies and musicals, and became an enduring global icon of Dutch perseverance and courage. Although a few Dutch translations appeared, and the Dutch tourist industry felt forced to provide some statues and a museum, the story never resonated in the Netherlands. *Hans Brinker* above all remains a product of the American imagination.

led its readers first to Holland, followed by Belgium and the Rhineland. "Upon the whole," the English publisher claimed, "Holland may be considered as the most wonderful country, perhaps, under the sun: it is certainly unlike every other." Murray extensively discussed the complicated system of dikes, canals, polders, sluices, and windmills that kept the country dry. But he was especially amazed by the Dutch cities: "They are so thoroughly intersected by canals, that most of the streets might more properly be termed quays, lined with houses and bordered with rows of tall trees. The canals swarm with the picturesque craft, whose gilt prows, round sterns, and painted sides are rendered so familiar beforehand to all who know the paintings of Cuyp, Vandervelde, and other Dutch artists."[7] As his example was followed by Kurt Baedeker, Eugene Fodor and the many other guidebook authors, this seductive vernacular of Dutchness entered the global language of mass tourism, country promotion, world fairs, and theme parks.

Dutch Dystopia: Permissiveness and Ethical Issues

Although this picturesque image of Holland never disappeared from international mass culture, it was supplemented by a dystopian perspective on Dutch society during the 1960s. In the culture wars that raged over morality and diversity in the United States and Western Europe, conservative commentators and intellectuals used the Netherlands as a convenient symbol for all the developments in modern society that they decried. Whether they were debating greater sexual freedom, or civil liberties, drugs and the mounting ambitions of national governments in providing social welfare through taxation, the Netherlands could be relied upon to provide anecdotal evidence. Although the Netherlands dealt not much differently with these issues than, say, Belgium, Germany or Scandinavian countries, the frankness and public character of the political discussions about ethical issues and welfare reform made it into an especially accessible case study.

International newspapers and magazines began to turn out gloomy articles about permissiveness and moral decay in the Netherlands. The magazine *Time* characteristically voiced American disapproval in a 1978 issue with the rhetorical question "Drawing The Line: Has Permissiveness Gone Too Far?" Its cover cartoon showed a Dutchman in business suit with wooden shoes who uses a big fountain pen to draw a big line across the page, separating the idyllic picture of Holland with tulips and a windmills from a huddled mass of squatters, intellectuals, unwed mothers, drug addicts, and other outcasts who were casting murky glances at the Holland that was suddenly denied to them. Readers were treated to a picture of a welfare state gone awry: street violence, vandalism, uncontrollable "squatters" who took over the inner cities, drug abuse, drug tourism, and, of course, wayward sexuality. The red light districts, free distribution of pornography, availability of abortion, and "lesbian couples who have children by artificial insemination paid for by the national health plan," were presented with hardly concealed amazement.[8]

American filmmaker Quentin Tarantino opened his neo-noir movie *Pulp Fiction* (1994) with an effective play on this dystopian perspective on Dutch society by letting two gangsters (played by Samuel L. Jackson and John Travolta) discuss a trip to Amsterdam as they drive to a hit job. When his colleague incredulously asks whether smoking hashish is really legal in Amsterdam, John Travolta's character eagerly explains the Dutch policy towards soft drugs: "Yeah, it breaks down like this: it's legal to buy it, it's legal to own it and, if you're the proprietor of a hash bar, it's legal to sell it. It's legal to carry it, which doesn't really matter 'cause – get a load of this – if the cops stop you, it's illegal for them to search you. Searching you is a right that the cops in Amsterdam don't have." They immediately decide to retire to the Netherlands after their criminal career. In Tarantino's highly ironic narrative the Dutch dystopian reputation is craftily inverted into a criminal utopia. Although Dutch policy towards soft drugs is not that different from other European nations and even many American states, the "coffeeshops" where the sale of small quantities of cannabis or "soft drugs" is condoned made drug use seem pervasive to uninformed outsiders and attracted "drug tourists" from other countries. Accordingly, the Netherlands has faced mounting pressure to change its policy from other EU partners, most notably the French who condemned it as a "narco state."

The main example of Dutch moral decay, however, was found in its attitude towards euthanasia. "Among its other singular attributes," *Time* found, "the Netherlands is the only European country considering the legalization of euthanasia – or mercy killing, as the Dutch prefer to call it." By using the term "mercy killing," which was never used in the Netherlands, the article suggested a similarity with Nazi extermination programs during the Second World War which other foreign commentators also found compelling. The Vatican for instance routinely argued that the line between Dutch and Nazi euthanasia was blurring because both were "authorizing the state to put an end to lives of people no longer economically useful to it."[9] Ironically exploiting that assertion, British novelist Ian McEwan turned the Dutch euthanasia practice into the lethal weapon of choice in the duel which ends the life of two protagonists in the novel *Amsterdam* (1998).

In the early 1980s, this moral criticism was also applied to Dutch foreign relations when conservative historian and commentator Walter Laqueur coined the term "Hollanditis" to describe the pacifist neutralism that swept over Western Europe like a contagious disease. A highly influential voice in the US foreign policy community, Laqueur published his article with the ominous title "Hollanditis: A New Stage in European Neutralism" in *Commentary*,

Frau Antje: Ambassador of Dutchness

Perhaps the most recognizable symbol of the Netherlands in neighboring Germany is "Frau Antje". The wholesome young girl in traditional costume who cheerfully advertises cheese and other dairy products represents "typical" Dutch culture, although both her role and appearance have reflected the changes in Dutch-German relations.

Frau Antje was invented by the national dairy organization in 1961 to promote Dutch cheese on German television. Evoking upright modesty and cleanliness, she brought the pastoral images of the Netherlands to life. Her folkloristic fantasy dress was based on traditional costumes worn in Volendam, the small fishing village on the IJsselmeer well known to tourists, but adapted to represent the red, white and blue of the national flag. The smiling Dutch cheese girl was preferably displayed against the background of green pastures, tulips, windmills, and, of course, the black-and-white cows that produced milk for "real cheese from Holland."

In her friendly, Dutch-accented German Frau Antje shared cheese recipes with German housewives and made countless appearances at fairs, sports events, television shows, and political campaigns. Although she remained totally unknown in her country of origin, the jovial cheese girl soon became a celebrity in her own right who was well-known to over ninety percent of the Germans. Accordingly, the export of Dutch cheese to Germany grew from twenty-eight thousand tons in 1954 to over 200,000 tons at the end of the century.

Although Frau Antje was born in the pre-modern world of folklore and idyllic tradition, even she fell victim to the forces of modernity. Just when Dutch export managers began to worry that the stereotype of the cheese girl was so old-fashioned that it would hinder the promotion of high-tech products, in 1984 one of the models who often played Frau Antje posed for the German edition of *Playboy* – without her traditional costume. Ten years later conservative German magazine *Der Spiegel* canonized the dystopian image of Holland in an article aptly titled "Frau Antje's Change of Life." Its argument that the Dutch period of tolerance was coming to an end was effectively illustrated by a Sebastian Rügen cartoon that displayed a defiant looking Frau Antje who smoked a hash cigarette, showed marks of drug needles, and carried a crumpled Heineken beer can with discarded wooden shoes and tulips. The backdrop of smoke-erupting green houses played on the negative German stereotype of Dutch agricultural industry which produced tomatoes that were so tasteless that they were nicknamed "water bombs."

Rügen's iconic cartoon, which evoked a wave of anger and shock in the Netherlands, but was followed by many similar images in European magazines, symbolized the soured image of the Netherlands in foreign eyes. Yet, after relations between Germany and the Netherlands improved at the end of the century, Frau Antje sprang back to life as a modern, efficient and environmentally friendly ambassador of Dutch culture and, of course, cheese.[12]

---

the leading opinion magazine of the neoconservative movement in the United States. He warned his readers that the cultural revolution of the 1960s now threatened to turn the Netherlands into "one of the weakest links in the Western alliance."

American neoconservatives added a new chapter to this dystopian narrative in the wake of the terrorist attacks of September 11, 2001 when they cited the Netherlands as an example of failed multiculturalism and European elitism. Conservative journalists described the political murders of populist party leader Pim Fortuyn in 2002, and filmmaker Theo van Gogh two years later, as a "Dutch 9/11." They argued that the resulting political turmoil showed that even the Dutch had accepted the limits of tolerance and recognized the threat posed by its Muslim immigrants. Conservative media warmly embraced Somalian-born member of parliament Ayaan Hirsi Ali, who had become one of the most vocal critics of Islam in the Netherlands. She was listed as one of the hundred most influential people in the world by *Time* magazine in 2005 and joined the neoconservative think tank the American Enterprise Institute after she decided to give up her parliamentary seat when her citizenship was called into question. In many books in which American conservative journalists attacked the European tolerance towards Islamic extremism, the Netherlands is described as a particularly disappointing example.[10]

Usable Dutchness

Dutch culture and society are evidently many things to many people. Although some of these utopian and dystopian images may be based on travel experiences, international exchanges, journalistic inquiries or even scholarly research, they derive their appeal and significance from forces and needs originating beyond Dutch borders. Essentially, foreigners embrace or reject aspects of Dutch society to define or reinforce their own national identity. Opposition to other cultures and societies is an indispensable ingredient in each national identity. Consequently, the Dutch "other" has been used to legitimize geopolitical ambitions or facilitate domestic debates about the relationship between government and citizen, the moral and ethical fabric of society, and integration and diversity. In that sense "Dutchism" may be added to infamous essentialist concepts such as Orientalism and Occidentalism.

Yet constructions of Dutch identity have also fostered international dialogue and friendly rebuke. When citizens of Western European countries are asked to define the national character of their Dutch neighbors they describe them as exceptionally ambitious and emotional, but also kindly think of them as helpful, rational, efficient, independent and far more honest than the Dutch consider themselves. The Dutch, with their trading nation with many international connections, have always been fascinated by their foreign reputation and immediately translated descriptions of observers such as Lodovico Guicciardini and William Temple into their own language. They were also keen to learn about their own past from historians such as John Lothrop Motley, Simon Schama, Ernest Zahn, Jonathan Israel and Russell Shorto. Dutch readers even took foreign criticism in stride and turned judgemental essays by expats and immigrants into a popular literary genre. They were eagerly informed by Portuguese writer José Rentes de Carvalho that they are complacent, narrow-minded and utterly joyless, they proved willing to be told by American sociologist Derek Phillips that their academic and moral standards were weak, they were chastised in essays by Algerian-French journalist Sylvain Ephimenco for being too lenient towards immigrant minorities, and they even digested the sardonic ethnography of *The UnDutchables* by American writers Colin White and Laurie Boucke in translation. Foreign perceptions of the Netherlands, then, have served as a convenient mirror to the spectator and as a carnival mirror for the Dutch.[11]

Further Reading

Buruma, Ian. *Murder in Amsterdam: The Death of Theo van Gogh and the Limits of Tolerance.* New York: Penguin, 2006.

Galema, Annemieke, Barbara Henkes and Henk te Velde, eds. *Images of the Nation: Different Meanings of Dutchness, 1870-1940.* Atlanta, GA: Rodopi, 1993.

Goodfriend, Joyce D., Benjamin Schmidt and Annette Stott. *Going Dutch: The Dutch Presence in America, 1609-2009.* Leiden: Brill, 2008.

Krabbendam, Hans, Cornelis A. van Minnen and Giles Scott-Smith. *Four Centuries of Dutch-American Relations, 1609-2009.* Albany: State University of New York, 2009.

Stott, Annette. *Holland Mania: The Unknown Dutch Period in American Art and Culture.* Woodstock: Overlook Press, 1998.

Notes

Chapter 1

1 Coos Huijsen, *De Oranjemythe: Een postmodern fenomeen* (Zaltbommel: Europese Bibliotheek, 2001).

2 Incidentally, largely on personal merit, Prince Claus became one of the most beloved members of the royal family, and his death in 2002 was mourned by many.

3 The Netherlands Antilles is scheduled to be dissolved as a political entity in 2010, when the five islands – Curaçao, Bonaire, Sint Eustatius, Saba and Sint Maarten – will acquire a new constitutional status within the Kingdom. See: www.minbuza.nl/en

4 The Dutch constitution refers to the head of state as "king," regardless of whether a man or a woman fulfils the position.

5 B.P. Vermeulen, A.P. Krijnen and D.A. Roos, *De Koning in het Nederlandse staatsrecht* (Nijmegen: Ars Aequi Libri, 2005), 25.

6 Walter Bagehot, *The English Constitution* (1867).

7 J.J. Vis, "De staatsrechtelijk ruimte van koningin Beatrix," in *De stijl van Beatrix: De vrouw en het ambt*, ed. C.A.Tamse (Amersfoort: Balans, 2005), 27-53.

8 Jan W. Van Deth and Jan C.P.M. Vis, *Regeren in Nederland: Het politieke en bestuurlijke bestel in vergelijkend perspectief* (Assen: Van Gorcum, 2006), 94-95.

9 Rudi B. Andeweg and Galen A. Irwin, *Governance and Politics of the Netherlands*. Third revised edition (London: Palgrave Macmillan, 2009), 82.

10 Joop J.M. van Holsteyn and Galen A. Irwin, "Never a Dull Moment: Pim Fortuyn and the Dutch Parliamentary Election of 2002" in *West European Politics* 26, no. 2 (April 2003), 47-50.

11 Rudi B. Andeweg and Galen A. Irwin, *Governance and Politics of the Netherlands* (London: Palgrave Macmillan, 2009), 62.

12 Monique Doppert and Mariette Hermans, eds., *Beatrix: Koningin van alle Nederlanders* (Amsterdam: Van Gennep, 2005).

Chapter 3

1 Russell Shorto, "Going Dutch" *The New York Times*, 3 May 2009, New York edition, p. MM42, www.nytimes.com. Actually, not all Shorto's income was taxed at fifty-two percent. This figure only applies to his income over € 54,776 (2008).

2 Gøsta Esping-Andersen, *The Three Worlds of Welfare Capitalism* (Cambridge: Polity Press, 1995).

3 Robert E. Goodin, Bruce Headey, Ruud Muffels and Henk-Jan Dirven, *The Real Worlds of Welfare Capitalism* (Cambridge: Cambridge University Press, 1999).

Chapter 4

1 Statistical data about the *Randstad* tend to vary across sources. The reason is that the outer limits of the *Randstad* area are not fixed. There is not one clearly defined and unambiguously demarcated *Randstad* region.

2 Paul M. Hohenberg and Lynn H. Lees, *The Making of Urban Europe, 1000-1950* (Cambridge: Harvard University Press, 1985), 227.

3 Henk Engel, "Randstad Holland in Kaart/Mapping Randstad Holland," *OverHolland* 2 (2005): 3-10, 23-44.

4 The province of Flevoland should in fact be included in these data, which is not the case here. This province was created in 1986 and consists of the so-called IJsselmeer polders (in translation: North East Polder, East Flevoland, South Flevoland, subsequently reclaimed since the 1940s). The new town of Almere, in South Flevoland, is part of the Amsterdam urban agglomeration and therefore also part of the *Randstad*.

5 VINEX stands for "Vierde Nota Ruimtelijke Ordening Extra," a 1995 planning memorandum from the Ministry of Housing, Spatial Planning and the Environment.

6 The data used here are from the Central Bureau of Statistics (www.statline.nl). The number of so-called "Western" immigrants has also risen sharply: to approximately 1.5 million people (nine per cent of the population). They are mainly concentrated in border regions (marriage partners) and in the big cities (expats working for international companies and institutions).

7 See for example Sako Musterd, "Segregation and Integration: A Contested Relationship," *Journal of Ethnic and Migration Studies* 29, no.4 (2003): 624-641.

8 Patricia van Ulzen, "Beelden van Steden," *City Journal* 9 (October 2007): 9-13; Patricia van Ulzen, *Imagine a Metropolis: Rotterdam's Creative Class,* 1970-2000 (Rotterdam: 010 Publisers, 2007).

Chapter 7

1 Jan Luiten van Zanden, "Economic Growth in the Golden Age: The Development of the Economy of Holland, 1500-1650," in *The Dutch Economy in the Golden Age: Nine Essays* edited by Karel Davids and Leo Noordegraaf, Economic and Social History in the Netherlands vol. 4 (Amsterdam: NEHA: 1993), 20 (table 4).

2 Jaap Jacobs, *New Netherland: A Dutch Colony in Seventeenth-Century America.* The Atlantic world vol. 3 (Leiden: Brill, 2005).

3 Anne Goldgar, *Tulipmania: Money, Honor, and Knowledge in the Dutch Golden Age* (Chicago: University of Chicago Press, 2007).

4 Jan de Vries, *European Urbanization, 1500-1800* (London: Methuen, 1984), 39 (table 3.7).

5 Herbert H. Rowen, *The Princes of Orange: The Stadholders of the Dutch Republic* (Cambridge: Cambridge University Press, 1988).

6 Wantje Fritschy, "A '*Financial Revolution*' Reconsidered: Public Finance in Holland During the Dutch Revolt, 1568-1648," *Economic History Review* 56 (2003), 57-89; Marjolein 't Hart, "The merits of a financial revolution: public finance, 1550-1700," *A Financial History of the Netherlands*, edited by Marjolein 't Hart, Joost Jonker and Jan Luiten van Zanden, (Cambridge: Cambridge University Press, 1997), 11-36.

7 Jan Luiten van Zanden and Maarten Prak, "Towards an Economic Interpretation of Citizenship: The Dutch Republic Between Medieval Communes and Modern Nation-States," *European Review of Economic History* 10 (2006), 111-45.

8 R. Po-chia Hsia, H.F.K. van Nierop, eds., *Calvinism and Religious Toleration in the Dutch Golden Age* (Cambridge: Cambridge University Press, 2002).

9 Benjamin J. Kaplan, *Divided by Faith: Religious Conflict and the Practice of Toleration in Early Modern Europe* (Cambridge: Harvard University Press, 2007).

10 Klaas van Berkel, Albert van Helden, Lodewijk Palm, eds., *A History of Science in the Netherlands: Survey, Themes, and Reference* (Leiden: Brill, 1999), chapters 1 and 2; C.D. Andriesse, *Titan: A Biography of Christiaan Huygens* (Utrecht: Universiteit Utrecht, 2003), 19; Steven Nadler, *Spinoza: A Life* (Cambridge: Cambridge University Press, 1999), chapters 1-2.

Chapter 8

1 James R. Kennedy, *Nieuw Babylon in aanbouw: Nederland in de jaren zestig* (Amsterdam: Boom, 1995); James R. Kennedy, *Een weloverwogen dood: euthanasie in Nederland* (Amsterdam: Bert Bakker, 2002).

2 Benjamin J. Kaplan, *Divided by Faith: Religious Conflict and the Practice of Toleration in Early Modern Europe* (Cambridge: Harvard University Press, 2007); John Marshall, *John Locke, Toleration and Early Enlightenment Culture* (Cambridge: Cambridge University Press, 2006).

3 Ad van der Woude and Jan de Vries, *The First Modern Economy* (Cambridge: Cambridge University Press, 1997).

4 Karel Davids and Jan Lucassen, eds., *A Miracle Mirrored: The Dutch Republic in European Perspective* (Cambridge: Cambridge University Press, 1995).

5 Herman Obdeijn and Marlou Schrover, *Komen en gaan: Immigratie en emigratie in Nederland vanaf 1550* (Amsterdam: Bert Bakker, 2008).

6 Jonathan Israel, *The Radical Enlightenment: Philosophy and the Making of Modernity, 1650-1750* (Oxford: Oxford University Press, 2001).

7 Steven Nadler, *Spinoza: A Life* (Cambridge: Cambridge University Press, 1999).

8 Wijnand W. Mijnhardt, "The Construction of Silence: Religious and Political Radicalism in Dutch History" in *The Early Enlightenment in the Dutch Republic*, ed. Wiep van Bunge, 231-262 (Leiden: Brill, 2002).

9 Joost Kloek and Wijnand Mijnhardt, *1800: Blueprints for a Society* (London: Palgrave/ MacMillan, 2004).

10 Peter van Rooden, *Religieuze regimes: Over godsdienst en maatschappij in Nederland 1570-1970* (Amsterdam: Bert Bakker, 1995).

11 Jerrold Seigel, *The Idea of the Self: Thought and Experience in Western Europe since the Seventeenth Century* (Cambridge: Cambridge University Press, 2005); C.G. Brown, *The Death of Christian Britain: Understanding Secularization, 1880-2000* (London: Routledge, 2001); Peter van Rooden, "Oral history en het vreemde sterven van het Nederlandse Christendom," *Bijdragen en Mededelingen betreffende de geschiedenis der Nederlanden* 119 (2004): 524-551.

Chapter 9

1 Arend Lijphart, *The Politics of Accommodation, Pluralism and Democracy in the Netherlands* (Berkeley: University of California Press, 1968).

2 Hans Daalder, "On the Origins of the Consociational Democracy Model" in *Consociationalism, Pillarization and Conflict-Management in the Low Countries*, ed. M.P.C.M. van Schendelen, special issue, *Acta Politica* 19, no. 1 (1984): 97-116.

3 See for a more general discussion of the "frozen" nature of the Dutch political system in a comparative perspective: Stefano Bartolini and Peter Mair, *Identity, Competition, and Electoral Availability: The Stabilisation of European Electorates, 1885-1985* (Cambridge: Cambridge University Press, 1990).

4 See Kees Schuyt and Ed Taverne, *1950: Prosperity and Welfare. Dutch Culture in a European Perspective*, vol. 4 (Basingstoke: Palgrave Macmillan, 2004).

5 See for instance R. Inglehart and W. Baker, "Modernization, Cultural Change and the Persistence of Traditional Values," *American Sociological Review* 65 (2000): 19-51; C.S. van Praag and W. Uitterhoeve, *25 Years of Social Change in the Netherlands: Key Data from the Social and Cultural Report* (The Hague: SCP, 1999).

6 Jan Lucassen and Rinus Penninx, *Newcomers: Immigrants and Their Descendants in the Netherlands, 1550-1995* (Amsterdam: Het Spinhuis, 1997).

7   See for a discussion of the developments leading to the events of 2002, H. Pellikaan,
    T. van der Meer and S.L. de Lange, "The Road from a Depoliticized Democracy to a
    Centrifugal Democracy," *Acta Politica* 38 (2003): 23-49.

8   James Kennedy, *Nieuw Babylon in aanbouw: Nederland in de jaren zestig* (Amsterdam:
    Boom, 1995).

Chapter 10

1   Peter Romijn, *Burgemeesters in Oorlogstijd: Besturen tijdens de Duitse Bezetting* (Amsterdam:
    Balans, 2006).

2   J.C.H. Blom, "De vervolging van de joden in internationaal vergelijkend perspectief," in
    Crisis bezetting en herstel: Tien studies over Nederland, 1930-1950 (The Hague: Nijgh &
    Van Ditmar, 1989). Historian Nanda van der Zee in her book *Om erger te voorkomen:
    De voorbereiding en uitvoering van de vernietiging van het Nederlandse jodendom* (Amsterdam:
    Balans, 1997) for instance, questioned to what extent Wilhelmina actually spoke out against
    the persecution of the Jewish citizens. For an overview of recent research on the Holocaust
    in the Netherlands see Ido de Haan, "Breuklijnen in de geschiedschrijving van de joden-
    vervolging: Een overzicht van het recente Nederlandse debat," *Bijdragen en mededelingen
    betreffende de geschiedenis der Nederlanden* 123, no. 1 (2008): 31-70.

3   Gerard Trienekens in his *Voedsel en honger in oorlogstijd, 1940-1945. Misleiding, mythe en
    werkelijkheid* (Utrecht, Antwerpen 1995) argued that the myth of the hunger winter was
    largely exaggerated since the majority of the Dutch population was not undernourished.
    And Herman Klemann concluded in *Nederland, 1938-1948: Economie en samenleving in
    jaren van oorlog en bezetting* (Amsterdam: Boom, 2002) that the Dutch economy was not
    systematically destroyed during the war, but on the contrary was doing quite well and had
    actually been growing until 1944, since Dutch companies tended to cooperate rather that
    commit sabotage.

4   L.J. de Jong, *The Netherlands and Nazi Germany* (Cambridge: Harvard University Press,
    1990). The other two authoritative historians of the first generation were Abel Herzberg,
    who published *Kroniek van de jodenvervolging, 1940-45* in 1950, and Jacques Presser, whose
    impressive 1965 study *Ondergang* was translated as *Ashes in the Wind: The Destruction of
    Dutch Jewry* (London: Souvenir, 1968).

5   In his controversial study *Grijs verleden: Nederland en de Tweede Wereldoorlog* (Amster-
    dam: Contact, 2001) Chris van der Heijden questioned whether the general population
    was as "black and white" as they had been portrayed in earlier studies. He suggests most
    people were simply trying to survive, not making any conscious choices to do either
    "good" or "bad," and therefore we should be very careful in judging behavior in retrospect.
    Ad van Liempt showed how easily some Dutch citizens had been willing to betray Jews for
    money (7.50 guilders per person) in his book *Kopgeld: Nederlandse premiejagers op zoek
    naar joden, 1943* (Amsterdam: Balans, 2002). Gerard Aalders analyzed in *Nazi Looting:
    The Plunder of Dutch Jewry During the Second World War* (Oxford: Berg, 2004) why the
    percentage of Jews deported from the Netherlands was considerable higher than from
    other European nations.

Chapter 11

1   Museums all over the world have Dutch seventeenth-century art included in their collections.
    In the Netherlands the collections of every museum – be it a national, provincial or municipal
    museum – includes seventeenth-century art. Of course the primary museum is the national
    museum: the Rijksmuseum in Amsterdam. Smaller but absolutely marvelous is the Maurits-
    huis Museum in The Hague.

2   Evert van Uitert, Louis van Tilborgh and Sjraar van Heugten, *Vincent van Gogh: Schilderijen*, Catalogue (Rijksmuseum Vincent van Gogh/Rijksmuseum Kröller Müller, 1990).

3   Vincent van Gogh, letter to Emile Bernard, Arles, c. July 25, 1888.

4   The Van Gogh Museum in Amsterdam has the largest collection of works by Van Gogh in the world. The second largest collection is in the Kröller-Müller Museum in Otterlo, a wonderful museum in a beautiful location. All these museums have very good websites, in Dutch as well as in English.

Chapter 12

1   Ben van Berkel, quoted in the leaflet on the occasion of the publication of Ben van Berkel, Caroline Bos, *Move*. 3 vols. (Amsterdam: UN-studio/Goose Press, 1999).

2   The paradox is that most of these churches were built in areas where the Catholics formed a minority, because in the other areas the Protestants were allowed to keep the old churches they occupied since the reformation.

3   Hetty Berens, ed., *P.J.H. Cuijpers (1827-1921): The Complete Works* (Rotterdam: NAi, 2007).

4   Sergio Polano, ed., *Hendrik Petrus Berlage: The Complete Works* (1987; Milano: Electa, 2002). For translations of the most influential theory: Ian Boyd White and Wim de Wit, eds., *Hendrik Petrus Berlage: Thoughts on Style, 1886-1909* (Santa Monica: Getty Center for the History of Art and the Humanities, 1996). Still the best sourcebook for direct inspirations: Pieter Singelenberg, *Berlage: Idea and Style; The Quest for Modern Architecture* (Utrecht: Haentjes, Dekker en Gumbert, 1972).

5   Wim de Wit, ed., *The Amsterdam School: Dutch Expressionist Architecture, 1915-1930* (Cambridge: MIT, 1983); Maristella Casciato, *The Amsterdam School* (Rotterdam: 010, 1996). Also much context in: Manfred Bock, Sigrid Johannisse and Vladimir Stissi, *Michel de Klerk: Architect and Artist of the Amsterdam School, 1884-1923.* (Rotterdam: NAi, 1997).

6   Shortest introduction in: Noud de Vreeze, *Woningbouw, Inspiratie & Ambities: Kwalitatieve Grondslagen van de Sociale Woningbouw in Nederland* (Almere: Nationale Woningraad, 1993). The book contains a lot of photographs and plans from the period 1901-1989. In favor of modern architecture but still very readable: Donald I. Grinberg, *Housing in the Netherlands* (Delft: Delft University Press, 1977).

7   Ed Taverne, Cor Wagenaar and Martien de Vletter, eds., *J.J.P. Oud, 1890-1963: Poetical Functionalist; The Complete Works* (Rotterdam: NAi, 2001).

8   Herman van Bergeijk, "Willem Marinus Dudok: An Architect and a Municipal Official" *Rassegna*, 75 (1998): 52-69. For a different opinion: Donald Langmead, *Willem Marinus Dudok: A Dutch Modernist* (Westport: Greenwood, 1996).

9   Joris Molenaar and Anne Mieke Backer, et al., eds., *Van Nelle: Monument in Progress* (Rotterdam: De Hef, 2005), not only tells the history of the firm and the building but also shows the restoration and alternation from offices and production lines into a "Design Factory."

10 Aaron Betsky, et al., *Living in the Lowlands: The Dutch Domestic Scene, 1850-2004* (Rotterdam: NAi, 2004), catalogue for the semi-permanent exhibition in the NAi. Among the contributions are: Marinke Steenhuis, "Middelburg 1940: A New Historic City Centre" which focuses on the plan by P. Verhagen; Jean-Paul Baeten, "Model for a New Society" discusses the changing concepts and forms in Pendrecht and Alexanderpolder Rotterdam 1947-1965; Ellen Smit, "Nagele: A Modern Village for Farm Workers" talks about the exceptional village of Nagele, compared to the more traditional villages in the new polders (1947-1956).

Chapter 13

1   See their correspondence: Willem Frederik Hermans and Gerard Reve, *Verscheur deze brief! Ik vertel veel te veel; Een briefwisseling* (Amsterdam: De Bezige Bij, 2008).

2   See about these cases: Jan Fekkes, *De God van je tante: Ofwel het ezel-proces van Gerard Kornelis van het Reve* (Amsterdam: Arbeiderspers, 1968); Klaus Beekman and Ralf Grüttemeier, *De wet van de letter: Literatuur en rechtspraak* (Amsterdam: Polak & Van Gennep, 2005) and Frans A. Jansen's chapter on Hermans and Frans de Rover's on Reve in M.A. Schenkeveld-Van der Dussen, ed., *Nederlandse literatuur: Een geschiedenis* (Groningen: Martinus Nijhoff, 1993). Citations are from these publications; our translation.

3   Nathalie Heinich, *Être artiste: Les transformations du statut des peintres et des sculpteurs* (Paris: Klincksieck, 2005).

4   Joost Kloek and Wijnand Mijnhardt, *1800: Blueprints for a Society* (London: Palgrave, 2004).

5   See also Frans Ruiter and Wilbert Smulders, *Literatuur en moderniteit in Nederland, 1840-1990* (Amsterdam: Arbeiderspers, 1996).

6   See website "Geschiedenis TV-kanaal," http://geschiedenis.vpro.nl.

Chapter 14

1   Cecile Goekoop-de Jong van Beek en Donk, *Hilda van Suylenburg* (Amsterdam: Scheltema & Holkema, 1897) [our translation].

2   Maaike Meijer, "15 oktober 1976: Anja Meulenbelt Publiceert 'De Schaamte Voorbij': De Tweede Feministische Golf en de Literatuur," in: *Nederlandse Literatuur: Een Geschiedenis,* ed. M.A. Schenkeveld-van der Dussen (Groningen: Martinus Nijhoff, 1993), 820 [our translation].

3   Anja Meulenbelt, *The Shame is Over: A Political Life Story*. Translation Ann Oosthuizen (1976; London: The Women's Press, 1980), 3.

4   Irene Costera Meijer, *Het Persoonlijke Wordt Politiek: Feministische Bewustwording in Nederland 1965-1980* (Amsterdam: Het Spinhuis, 1996), 224, 228.

5   Maaike Meijer, "De Schaamte Voorbij," 822 [our translation].

6   Idem., 819-25; Costera Meijer, *Het Persoonlijke Wordt Politiek*, 215, 234 ff.

7   www.beperkthoudbaar.info.

8   Étienne Balibar, "Europe as Borderland" (The Alexander von Humboldt Lectures in Human Geography, Radboud University Nijmegen, 2004).

9   Domna C. Stanton, "Language and Revolution: The Franco-American Dis-Connection," in *The Future of Difference*, ed. Hester Eisenstein and Alice Jardine (Boston: G.K. Hall, 1980), 75-87.

10   Rosemarie Buikema, "Literature and the Production of Ambiguous Memory," *European Journal of English Studies* 10, no. 2 (2006): 187-99.

11   See also Marja Vuijsje, *Joke Smit: Biografie van een feministe* (Amsterdam: Atlas, 2008).

Chapter 15

1   See for these rankings: *Academic Ranking of World Universities*, Institute of Higher Education, Shanghai Jiao Tong University, www.arwu.org; Centre for Higher Education Development (CHE) in Germany, www.che-concept.de; Centre for Science and Technology Studies (CWTS), Leiden University, the Netherlands, www.cwts.nl. In each of these three rankings Utrecht University is positioned first within the Netherlands, Amsterdam University or Leiden University mostly second and third.

2   Martin Mince, "US and UK fill top 10 places," *The Times Higher Education Supplement,* 9 November 2007.

3 Simon Marginson, Thomas Weko, Nicola Channon, Terttu Luukkonen and Jon Oberg, *Thematic Review of Tertiary Education: The Netherlands; Country Note* (OECD, 2007).

4 Denny Borsboom, "Selectie aan universiteiten is lege huls" *NRC Handelsblad*, 6 September 2006, www.nrc.nl/opinie.

5 "Studenten negeren ranglijsten massaal", *NRC Handelsblad*, 8 December 2005, www.nrc.nl/dossiers/hoger_onderwijs.

Chapter 16

1 Martinus (316-397) was a Roman soldier, named after Mars, who converted to Christianity and became bishop of Tours (France). The coat of arms of the city of Utrecht refers to the legend that once, when he met a naked beggar, he tore his cloak in two and gave away one half.

2 These and other ritual practices are mentioned in an eight-century "Short index of super-stitions and paganisms." See Joris van Eijnatten and Fred van Lieburg, *Nederlandse religie-geschiedenis* (Hilversum: Verloren, 2005), 57.

3 Llewellyn Bogaers, *Aards, betrokken en zelfbewust: De verwevenheid van cultuur en religie in katholiek Utrecht, 1300-1600* (Amsterdam: Vrije Universiteit, 2008).

4 "Praten als Brugman" is a Dutch expression, commemorating the rhetorical skills of a fifteenth-century Franciscan itinerant preacher. Even before the Reformation, sermons in the Low Countries often took a full hour.

5 Deventer, a city on the river IJssel, was part of the Hanseatic League: an international trade network. See W.P. Blockmans, "The Formation of a Political Union, 1300-1600" in *History of the Low Countries*, eds. J.C.H. Blom and E. Lamberts (New York: Berghahn, 1999), 76-78. Deventer had a famous school, where Erasmus of Rotterdam received a large part of his education. As a boy, Desiderius Erasmus attended the then famous school at Deventer. See Johan Huizinga, *Erasmus and the Age of Reformation* (1924; London: Phoenix, 2002).

6 See James C. Bratt, *Dutch Calvinism in Modern America: A History of a Conservative Subculture* (Grand Rapids: Eerdmans, 1984).

7 The Old Catholic Church, which resulted from the 1723 "Utrecht Schism" was already allowed to have its own bishops. See Gian Ackermans, *Herders en huurlingen: Bisschoppen en priesters in de Republiek, 1663-1705* (Amsterdam: Bert Bakker, 2003).

8 See my *Servants of the Kingdom: Professionalization among Ministers of the Nineteenth-Century Netherlands Reformed Church*. Translated by David McKay (Boston: Brill, forthcoming).

9 See Peter van Rooden, "Long-term Religious Developments in the Netherlands, ca 1750-2000" in *The Decline of Christendom in Western Europe, 1750-2000*, eds. Hugh McLeod and W. Ustorf (Cambridge: Cambridge University Press, 2002), 113-129. This, and many other relevant English articles are available on the author's web page: www.xs4all.nl/~pvrooden/Peter/english.htm.

10 *Gereformeerden*, too, had suffered from secularization and secessions. In the mid-1920s, for example, discord broke out over the question if in Paradise, the snake had audibly spoken. A much bigger schism took place in 1944, after the *Gereformeerde* Synod had imposed Kuyper's doctrine of baptism.

Chapter 17

1 The most comprehensive overview of Dutch immigration history is to be found in: Leo Lucassen and Rinus Penninx, *Newcomers: Immigrants and Their Descendants in the Netherlands, 1550-1995* (Amsterdam: Aksant, 2002).

2 I have analyzed Dutch immigration and integration in the past fifty years in more detail in: Han Entzinger, "Changing the Rules While the Game Is On: From Multiculturalism to

Assimilation in the Netherlands," in *Migration, Citizenship, Ethnos*, eds. Y. Michal Bodemann and Gökçe Yurdakul (New York: Palgrave MacMillan, 2006), 121-144.

3   The most authoritative analysis of Dutch *pillarization* has been offered by Arend Lijphart, *The Politics of Accommodation: Pluralism and Democracy in the Netherlands* (Berkeley: University of California Press, 1975).

4   A major eye opener for many was the report *Allochtonenbeleid*, written in 1989 by the Scientific Council for Government Policy (WRR), a think tank close to the prime minister's office. A political breakthrough only came several years later. An English summary of the report, entitled *Immigrant Policy*, was published by the Council in 1990.

5   Paul Scheffer, "Het Multiculturele Drama" ["The Multicultural Tragedy"] *NRC Handelsblad*, 27 January 2000. An English translation of this article has been published as Paul Scheffer, "The Land of Arrival," in *The Challenge of Diversity: European Social Democracy Facing Migration, Integration and Multiculturalism*, ed. René Cuperus, Karl A. Duffek and Johannes Kandel (Innsbruck: Studien Verlag, 2003), 23-30.

6   As first predicted by Samuel Huntington in 1993. See also: Samuel P. Huntington, *The Clash of Civilizations and the Remaking of World Order* (London: Touchstone, 1998).

7   In 2007, the Scientific Council for Government Policy (see note 4) published a report on Dutch identity: Wetenschappelijke Raad voor het Regeringsbeleid, *Identificatie met Nederland* (Amsterdam: Amsterdam University Press, 2007). At the presentation ceremony of the report Princess Máxima remarked that "*The* Dutch identity does not exist." This comment, which was meant to be self-evident, provoked fierce political debates in the weeks thereafter and thus illustrated how sensitive these matters have become. See also chapter 1.

8   See for example: Mérove Gijsberts, *Ethnic minorities and Integration: Outlook for the Future* (The Hague: Social and Cultural Planning Office, 2005); Paul M. Sniderman and Louk Hagendoorn, *When Ways of Life Collide: Multiculturalism and its Discontents in the Netherlands* (Princeton: Princeton University Press, 2007).

9   This is reflected – among others – by regular publications of the Netherlands Institute for Social Research (formerly Social and Cultural Planning Office, SCP) and by Statistics Netherlands (CBS) on the development of integration, such as Jaco Dagevos and Mérove Gijsberts, eds., *Jaarrapport Integratie 2007* (The Hague: SCP, 2007); *Jaarrapport Integratie 2008* (The Hague: CBS, 2008).

10 This was what Stef Blok, MP and chair of the Commission, stated upon presentation of its final report: Tijdelijke Commissie Onderzoek Integratiebeleid (Commissie Blok), *Bruggen bouwen. Deel 1: Eindrapport*. Tweede Kamer, vergaderjaar 2003-2004, 28 689, no. 9 (2004). Interestingly, the leaders of most major parties in parliament had already distanced themselves from this conclusion before the report had even been released. Apparently, certain messages are more welcome than others.

11 Han Entzinger and Edith Dourleijn, *De lat steeds hoger: De leefwereld van jongeren in een multi-etnische stad* (Assen: Van Gorcum, 2008).

Chapter 18

1   Geert Hofstede and Gert-Jan Hofstede, *Cultures and Organizations: Software of the Mind* (New York: McGraw-Hill, 2005).

2   Edwin M. Schur, *Crimes without Victims: Deviant Behavior and Public Policy* (Englewood Cliffs: Prentice-Hall, 1965); Edwin M. Schur and Hugo Bedau, *Victimless Crimes: Two Sides of a Controversy* (Englewood Cliffs: Prentice-Hall, 1974).

3   At a crucial moment a Christian Democrat changed the discourse style from criminal justice to public health when she declared that it was more Christian to help addicts than to punish them.

4   Or even the free distribution of heroin. A real life experiment among 430 addicts between 1998 and 2000 revealed that free distribution of heroin compared to the substitute methadone resulted in significantly less criminal behavior. M.G.W. Dijkgraaf et al., "Cost Utility Analysis of Co-Prescribed Heroin Compared with Methadone Maintenance Treatment in Heroin Addicts in Two Randomised Trials," *British Medical Journal* 330, no. 7503 (June 2005): 1297-1300.

5   C. Chatwin, "Drug Policy Developments within the EU: The Destabilizing Effects of Dutch and Swedish Drugs Policies," *British Journal of Criminology* 43, no. 3 (2003): 567-582. See also Boekhout van Solinge (2004).

6   Asked for advice on two proposed Acts (one from the government and one parliamentary initiative), the *Raad van State* (Council of State) found it almost impossible to formulate substantive grounds for euthanasia; it advised that more case law should first be awaited.

7   The number of voluntary reports of unnatural death decreases gradually: 2,216 in 1999, 2,123 in 2000, 2,054 in 2001, 1,882 in 2002, 1,815 in 2003, 1,886 in 2004, and 1933 in 2005. According to Griffiths et al. (2008) the number of voluntary reports reflects the actual number of euthanasia decisions.

8   The top of the prosecution services (*College van Procureurs-Generaal*) announced in 2005 that palliative sedation followed by death would not be prosecuted if the guidelines of the KNMG were followed. The number of this kind of physician-assisted death increased from 8,500 in 2001 to 9,700 in 2005.

9   Francis Fukuyama, *Trust: The Social Virtues and the Creation of Prosperity* (New York: Free Press, 1995). A down to earth explanation for the extraordinary economic revival is the increasing supply of female labor force and the economic expansion in labor-intensive commercial consultancy (Sociaal en Cultureel Rapport 2000).

10 In 1996 and 1997 the *poldermodel* was a worldwide hype: the press reported favorably about the economic successes and the reduction of the welfare state, the social partners (employers and employees) received a German prize, and Prime Minister Wim Kok was given the opportunity to address the G-7 in Denver.

11 Pikmeer I, 23/04/1996, and Pikmeer II, 06/01/1998.

12 A committee chaired by the former national ombudsman, M. Oosting, looked into the Enschede disaster, while a committee chaired by Queen's Commissioner J.G.M. Alders, investigated the Volendam disaster.

Chapter 19

1   This campaign website is only available in Dutch: www.nederlandleeftmetwater.nl. The Dutch text of the ad: "Hoe doen we dat toch? Zo'n klein land. Zoveel water en een klimaat dat verandert. En dan toch die balans houden. Knap lastig. Maar samen met u zorgen we voor droge voeten en schoon water. Duik daar maar 'ns in."

2   See: G.P. van de Ven, ed., *Man-made Lowlands: History of Water Management and Land Reclamation in the Netherlands* (Utrecht: Matrijs, 2004). This book was written from the perspective of historical geography. Another recent book, from a civil engineering perspective: Robert J. Hoeksema, *Designed for Dry Feet: Flood Protection and Land Reclamation in the Netherlands* (Reston: ASCE Press, 2006).

3   *A Different Approach to Water: Water Management Policy in the 21st Century* (The Hague: Ministry of Transport, Public Works and Water Management, 2000), www.waterland.net.

4   *Spatial Planning Key Decision "Room for the River": Investing in the Safety and Vitality of the Dutch River Basin Region* (The Hague: Ministry of Transport, Public Works and Water Management, 2006), www.ruimtevoorderivier.nl.

5   Deltacommissie, *Working Together with Water. A Living Land Builds for its Future; Findings of the Deltacommissie* 2008 (Deltacommissie, 2008), www.deltacommissie.nl.

6   The so-called "Water Vision" of the Dutch government has a separate chapter about water consciousness. The report suggests a policy mix of communication, participation, and education in order to raise awareness of water issues among the Dutch population. *Water Vision: Safeguarding our Future: The Government's Vision of National Water Policy* (The Hague: Ministry of Transport, Public Works and Water Management, 2007), www.verkeerenwaterstaat.nl.

7   J. de Boer, H. Goossen and D. Huitema, *Bewust Werken aan Waterbewustzijn: Studie naar de Rol en Relevantie van het Begrip Waterbewustzijn voor het Waterbeleid* (Amsterdam: Instituut voor Milieuvraagstukken, 2003).

8   T. Lohan, ed., *Water Consciousness: How We All Have to Change to Protect our Most Critical Resource* (San Francisco: AlterNet Books, 2008).

9   TNS-NIPO, *Nederlanders Zijn Niet Goed op de Hoogte van Waterproblematiek* (Amsterdam: TNS-NIPO, 2005), www.waterland.net.

10 Landelijke Werkgroep Evaluatie Watertoets, *Watertoetsproces op Weg Naar Bestemming. Landelijke Evaluatie Watertoets 2006* (The Hague: Ministerie van Verkeer en Waterstaat, 2006).

11 Transition in Dutch water management is the central theme in R. van der Brugge, J. Rotmans and D. Loorbach, "The Transition in Dutch Water Management," *Regional Environmental Change* 5, No. 1 (May 2005): 164-176.

Chapter 20

1   For foreign descriptions of the Netherlands see Robert Fruin, "De Nederlanders der zeventiende eeuw door Engelschen geschetst [1861]" in *Robert Fruin's Verspreide Geschriften*, ed. P.J. Blok and P.L. Muller (The Hague: Martinus Nijhoff, 1901); J.S. Bartstra, "Onze voorouders door vreemden beoordeeld (Voornl. 18e Eeuw)," *Onze eeuw: maandschrift voor staatkunde, letteren, wetenschap en kunst* 12, no. 2 (1912); Johan Huizinga, "Engelschen en Nederlanders in Shakespeare's tijd," *De Gids* 88 (1924); G. Brugmans, *Onder de loupe van het buitenland* (Baarn: Hollandia, 1929); Pieter Jan van Winter, *De Chinezen van Europa* (Groningen: J. B. Wolters, 1965); J.M. Fuchs and W.J. Simons, *Het zal je maar gezegd wezen: Buitenlanders over Nederland* (The Hague: Kruseman, 1977); Frans Naeff, "58 Miljoen Nederlanders in andermans ogen," in *58 Miljoen Nederlanders*, ed. A.F. Manning and M. de Vroede (Amsterdam: Amsterdam Boek, 1977); Margarete van Ackeren, *Das Niederlandebild im Strudel der deutschen romantischen Literatur: Das Eigene und die Eigenheiten der Fremde* (Amsterdam: Rodopi, 1992); Rob van Ginkel, *Notities over Nederlanders: Antropologische reflecties* (Amsterdam: Boom, 1997).

2   Samuel Butler, *The Poetical Works of Samuel Butler*, 2 vols. (London: William Pickering, 1835), II, 290-91.

3   Lisa Jardine, *Going Dutch: How England Plundered Holland's Glory* (London: HarperPress, 2008).

4   René Descartes, letter to Guez de Balzac, 5 May 1631, in René Descartes, *Oeuvres de Descartes* (Paris: F.G. Levrault, 1824), XVI, 200-01 [my translation].

5   See Chapter 74, "Fondation de la République des Provinces-Unies" and Chapter 187 "De la Holland au XVIIe Siècle" in Voltaire, *Essai sur les moeurs et l'espris des nations et sur les principaux faits de l'histoire depuis Charlemegne jusqu'à Louis XIII* [Essay on General History and on the Customs and the Character of Nations] Vol. 2 (1756).

6   John Lothrop Motley, *The Rise of the Dutch Republic. A History*, 3 vols. (New York: Harper & Brothers, 1856); Mary Mapes Dodge, *Hans Brinker or the Silver Skates: A Story of Life in*

Holland (New York: Scribners, 1865); Annette Stott, *Holland Mania: The Unknown Dutch Period in American Art and Culture* (Woodstock: Overlook Press, 1998).

7   James Murray, *A Hand-Book for Travellers on the Continent: Being a Guide through Holland, Belgium, Prussia and Northern Germany and Along the Rhine, from Holland to Switzerland* (London: John Murray & Son, 1836).

8   Frederick Painton, "Holland: Drawing the Line; Has Permissiveness Gone Too Far?" *Time*, 10 August 1987.

9   Sarah Lambert, "Dutch Protest to Vatican Envoy Over 'Nazi' Charge," *The Independent*, 24 February 1993.

10 Bruce Bawer, *While Europe Slept: How Radical Islam Is Destroying the West from Within* (New York: Doubleday, 2006); Ian Buruma, *Murder in Amsterdam. The Death of Theo Van Gogh and the Limits of Tolerance* (London: Atlantic Books, 2006); Paul Scheffer, *Het land van aankomst* (Amsterdam: De Bezige Bij, 2007); Jaap Verheul, "The Dutch 9/11: A Transatlantic Debate About Diversity and National Identity," in *Four Centuries of Dutch-American Relations, 1609-2009*, eds. Hans Krabbendam, Kees van Minnen and Giles Scott Smith (Albany: State University of New York, 2009), 1106-1116.

11 J. Rentes de Carvalho, *Waar die andere God woont* (Amsterdam: Meulenhof, 1972); Derek Phillips, *De naakte Nederlander* (Amsterdam: Bert Bakker, 1985); M. Nasr, *Minder over meer: De Nederlandse samenleving door een Marokkaanse loep* (Hilversum: Nasr Mohammed, 1986); Christian Chartier, *Het verdriet van Nederland: Een Fransman stoeit met de Hollandse ziel* (Amsterdam: Prometheus, 1992); Sylvain Ephimenco, *Het land van Theo van Gogh* (Antwerpen: Houtekiet, 2004).

12 Erich Wiedemann, "Frau Antje in den Wecheljahren," *Der Spiegel*, 28 February 1994; Sophie Elpers, *Hollandser dan kaas: De geschiedenis van Frau Antje* (Amsterdam: Amsterdam University Press, 2009).

About the Authors

Wiljan van den Akker

is Professor of Modern Dutch Literature and Dean of the Faculty of Humanities at Utrecht University. Previously, he served as Director of Institutes at the Royal Netherlands Academy for Arts and Sciences (KNAW) and Chair of the Board of Humanities at the Netherlands Organisation for Scientific Research (NWO). He wrote a PhD thesis on the Dutch poet Martinus Nijhoff and has lectured in Berlin, Paris, and Berkeley. His special field of interest is modernist poetry in an international context. His first volume of poetry, *De Afstand* (De Arbeiderspers, 2008), was awarded the C. Buddingh' Prize for new Dutch poetry.

Emmeline N. Besamusca

is Assistant Professor of Dutch Culture and Society at Utrecht University and Lecturer in History and Culture of the Low Countries at the University of Vienna. She is frequently invited as a guest lecturer at various universities around Europe, and teaches at the Utrecht University Summer School. She has designed numerous courses related to Dutch culture, and authored applied course readings, such as her recent monograph *Kennismaken met Nederland* (*Getting Acquainted with the Netherlands*; University of Vienna, 2008).

David J. Bos

is Assistant Professor in History of Christianity at Utrecht University and Lecturer in Sociology at the International School for Humanities and Social Sciences of the University of Amsterdam. Previously, he worked as the editor of *Maandblad Geestelijke volksgezondheid* (published by the Netherlands Institute of Mental Health and Addiction). Among his publications in English are *Out in the Netherlands. Acceptance of Homosexuality in the Netherlands* (SCP, 2007), and *Servants of the Kingdom: Professionalization among Ministers of the Nineteenth-Century Netherlands Reformed Church* (Brill, forthcoming).

Freek J. Bruinsma

is Professor Emeritus of Law and Society at Utrecht University. His research interests are the judiciary and the legal professions in a comparative perspective. Among his publications in English that are relevant for foreign readers are *Dutch Law in Action* (Ars Aequi Libri, 2003 – a new edition is forthcoming) and (with David Nelken) *Explorations in Legal Cultures* (Reed Business, 2007), a collection of cross-cultural case studies.

Rosemarie L. Buikema

is Professor of Art, Culture and Diversity at Utrecht University. She is Head of the Department of Media and Culture Studies and chairs the Graduate Gender Program. She has published widely in the field of feminist theory, post-colonial theory and memory studies. She currently works in the field of transitional justice. Her latest book (co-edited with Iris van der Tuin) is *Doing Gender in Media, Art and Culture* (Routledge, 2009). See also www.genderstudies.nl.

Rob Dettingmeijer

is Assistant Professor of History and Theory of Architecture and Urban Planning at Utrecht University. He is Vice President of the European Architectural History Network. His PhD thesis is entitled *Open City, City Planning, Housing and Architecture between the Two World Wars in Rotterdam* (1988). He has lectured at numerous universities and participated in numerous international meetings including *Transfer and Metamorphosis: Architectural Modernity between Europe and the Americas 1870-1970* (Zurich 2008). Among his recent publications is an article about the *"Werkbund"* in *Archis/Volume* (2009). He has organized exhibitions at the Museum Boymans-van-Beuningen (Rotterdam) and the Dutch Architectural Institute (NAi, Rotterdam) and is currently preparing an exhibit on Rietveld for 2010.

Han B. Entzinger

is Professor of Migration and Integration Studies at Erasmus University Rotterdam. He is a board member of the Research Committee on Migration of the International Sociological Association and a member of advisory boards to several research institutes in a number of countries. He regularly acts as a consultant to the European Commission, the Council of Europe and various governments. His research interests include international migration, integration, multiculturalism and the welfare state. Among his recent publications are *Migration between States and Markets* (Ashgate Publishing, 2004) and "Changing the Rules While the Game is On: From Multiculturalism to Assimilation in the Netherlands," in *Migration, Citizenship, Ethnos* (Palgrave MacMillan, 2006).

Ido de Haan

is Professor of Political History at Utrecht University. His fields of interest are the political history of Western Europe in the nineteenth and twentieth century, the history of the Holocaust and other genocides, as well as regime changes and political transition since the early modern period. Among his recent publications in English are "Paths of Normalization after the Persecution of the Jews: The Netherlands, France, and West-Germany in the 1950s," in *Life after Death: Approaches to a Cultural and Social History of Europe during the 1940s and 1950s* (Cambridge University Press, 2003) *and* "The Paradoxes of Dutch History: Historiography of the Holocaust in the Netherlands," in *Holocaust Historiography in Context: Emergence, Challenges, Polemics and Achievements* (Yad Vashem, 2008).

Lex Heerma van Voss

is a Research Fellow at the International Institute of Social History in Amsterdam and Professor of History of Labor and Labor Relations at Utrecht University. He studied history in Utrecht and Paris and wrote a PhD thesis on the introduction of the eight-hour work day in the Netherlands. He has published on the comparative history of dockworkers and textile workers, and on the history of capitalism around the North Sea in the Dutch Golden Age.

Duco A. Hellema

is Professor of History of International Relations at Utrecht University. He studied political science at Leiden University and wrote a PhD thesis on the position adopted by the Netherlands at the time of the Hungarian Revolution and the Suez Crisis in 1956. He has published widely on Dutch foreign relations, the Cold War and the history of international relations in general. His most recent publication is *Foreign Policy of the Netherlands: The Dutch Role in World Politics* (Republic of Letters, 2009).

Ghislain J.P. Kieft

is Assistant Professor of Art History and Iconology at Utrecht University. His research interests involve paintings and artists of the Northern Netherlands in the seventeenth and eighteenth century, the production of art and the use of perspective. He co-authored *De Schilderkunst der Lage Landen*, a comprehensive three-volume overview of painting in the Low Countries throughout the ages up to the present day (Amsterdam University Press, 2007).

Christ P.M. Klep

is Assistant Professor of History of International Relations at Utrecht University. His research interests are the Second World War and international peace operations. He co-authored *De Bevrijding van Nederland 1944-1945 (The Liberation of the Netherlands, 1944-1945*; Sdu, 1995) and (with Richard van Gils) *Van Korea tot Kosovo*, a history of Dutch peace operations since the Second World War (now in its completely revised third edition).

Wijnand W. Mijnhardt

is Professor of Comparative History of the Sciences and the Humanities, and Director of the Descartes Centre for the History and Philosophy of the Sciences at Utrecht University. From 2001-2004 he was a visiting professor for Dutch History and Culture at UCLA. He has been affiliated with the Institute for Advanced Studies in Princeton and the Getty Research Institute in Los Angeles. He has published widely on Dutch intellectual history, on the Dutch Republic in the eighteenth century and on the Enlightenment. He co-authored (with Joost Kloek) *1800: Blueprints for a National Community* (Palgrave MacMillan, 2005) and (with Lynn Hunt and Margaret Jacob) *The Book that Enlightened Europe: Picart and Bernard's Religious Ceremonies of the World* (Harvard University Press, 2010).

Marco Mostert

is Professor of Medieval Written Culture at Utrecht University. In addition to many publications on the social history of literacy and communication, he has also written on the (early) medieval history of the Low Countries. Both interests are evident in "The Early History of Written Culture in the Northern Netherlands," in *Along the Oral-Written Continuum: Types of Text, Relations and Their Implications* (*Utrecht Studies in Medieval Literacy* 20, forthcoming). An English edition of his recent survey of "Dutch" history in the first millennium, *In de Marge van de Beschaving* (Bert Bakker, 2009) is in preparation.

Ben C. de Pater

is Associate Professor of Human Geography and Urban and Regional Planning at Utrecht University. He is Senior Lecturer in the Theory and History of Human Geography. He was editor-in-chief of the journals *Geografie* and *Geografie-Educatief*, published by the Royal Dutch Geographical Society (KNAG), and is co-author and co-editor of a number of Dutch books. Recently, he published (with B. Schoenmaker et al) *Grote Atlas van Nederland/Comprehensive Atlas of the Netherlands 1930-1950* (Asia Maior/Atlas Maior, 2005), co-authored (with Otto Verkoren) *Noord-Amerika. Een geografie van de Verenigde Staten en Canada* (Van Gorcum, 2007) and published *West-Europa. Hoofdlijnen van geografie en ruimtelijke planning* (2009).

Maarten R. Prak

is Professor of Economic and Social History at Utrecht University, where he is also Director of the Research Institute for History and Culture. He is currently working on projects concerning citizenship in Europe before the French Revolution, and cultural industries. Among his recent publications is *The Dutch Republic in the Seventeenth Century: The Golden Age* (Cambridge

University Press, 2005), which was also translated into Hungarian and Chinese. He co-edited (with S.R. Epstein) *Guilds, Innovation, and the European Economy, 1400-1800* (Cambridge University Press, 2008).

Frans Ruiter

is Managing Director of the Research Institute for History and Culture of Utrecht University. He wrote about the reception of North-American Postmodernism in Germany and the Netherlands in *International Postmodernism: Theory and Literary Practice*, edited by H. Bertens and D. Fokkema (John Benjamins, 1997), and about Dutch literary life in *Dutch Culture in a European Perspective, volume 4. 1950: Prosperity and Welfare,* edited by K. Schuyt and E. Taverne (Van Gorcum, 2004). He co-authored (with Wilbert Smulders) *Literatuur en Moderniteit in Nederland, 1840-1990* (De Arbeiderspers, 1996), a context-oriented literary history of modern Dutch literature. Since autumn 2009 he is the co-director (with Wilbert Smulders) of an NWO postgraduate research program which focuses on the moral dimension of autonomous literature.

Wilbert Smulders

is Assistant Professor of Modern Dutch Literature at Utrecht University. He wrote a PhD thesis on the narrative technique in *The Dark Room of Damokles* by Willem Frederik Hermans and has (co-)edited four volumes about the work and authorship of this Dutch writer. He co-authored (with Frans Ruiter) *Literatuur en Moderniteit in Nederland, 1840-1990* (De Arbeiderspers, 1996), a context-oriented literary history of modern Dutch literature. Since autumn 2009 he is the co-director (again with Frans Ruiter) of an NWO post-graduate research program which focuses on the moral dimension of autonomous literature.

Quirine L. van der Steen

is Curriculum Coordinator of the Department of History and Art History at Utrecht University. She worked at Christie's in London and graduated in Art History from Utrecht University with a thesis in Iconology. Previously she was Assistant Professor at Utrecht University, offering courses on Dutch History of Culture for international students, and lecturing on a broad range of themes related to Dutch art and artists. She regularly taught at the Utrecht University Summer School.

Jeroen L. Torenbeek

is Director of the Utrecht University Summer School, a collaboration between Utrecht University, Utrecht University of Applied Sciences and Utrecht School of the Arts (HKU). He is also Director of the James Boswell Institute at Utrecht University, the institute providing language training and other courses to university staff and students. He previously served as Director of International Relations at Utrecht University, and initiated the European Utrecht Network, which facilitates student mobility between the participating institutions. Between 2002 and 2004 he was president of the European Association for International Education (EAIE).

Iris van der Tuin

is Assistant Professor of Gender Studies at Utrecht University. She has published on feminist theory and the philosophy of science in *Australian Feminist Studies* and the *European Journal of Women's Studies*. Her main field of interest is the new materialism. She has edited *Doing Gender in Media, Art and Culture* (Routledge, 2009) with Rosemarie Buikema and is currently working on *The Engaged Humanities: Situating the Humanities within the Philosophy of Science* with Rick Dolphijn.

Rob van der Vaart

is Professor of Social Geography and Dean of University College, the honors college of Utrecht University. From 2000 to 2004, he held a chair in Geography and Geographical Education at Utrecht University. He represents Utrecht University in the Oxford Network, in which leading universities such as Cornell, Stanford and Princeton work together to strengthen learning and teaching in a research-intensive setting. He served on the Committee for the Development of the Dutch Canon. In addition to specific attention to the application of geography, particularly in secondary education, his research also focuses on the nature and effects of mental images of the world.

Jan G.F. Veldhuis

chairs the Board of Quality Assurance Netherlands Universities and the NUFFIC and is a board member of the Roosevelt Study Centre. He published numerous articles related to issues in education, mostly in Dutch. He studied history, economics and law at Utrecht University and was a Fulbright scholar at the University of Minnesota. He worked at the Ministry of Foreign Affairs and at Leiden University. From 1974 he was (successively) deputy permanent secretary and director- and inspector-general at the Ministry of Education and Science. He served as president of Utrecht University between 1986 and 2003, during which period he was awarded an honorary doctorate by the University of Florida. He chaired the Board of the Fulbright Centre, two national committees on secondary education and participated internationally in evaluation committees of institutions of higher education.

Jaap Verheul

is Associate Professor of History and Director of the American Studies Program at Utrecht University. He was a Fulbright scholar at the University of Pennsylvania, and has taught at UCLA and other American universities. His current research interest is in American perceptions of Europe and transatlantic cultural relations. He has published on Dutch and American cultural history, and on business history. He edited *Dreams of Paradise, Visions of Apocalypse: Utopia and Dystopia in American Culture* (VU University Press, 2004) and co-edited *American Multiculturalism after 9/11: Transatlantic Perspectives* (Amsterdam University Press, 2009).

Jan Luiten van Zanden

is Professor of Economic History at Utrecht University and President of the International Economic History Association. He has published widely on the economic history of the Low Countries and Indonesia, and is now working in the field of global economic history. His recent publications include *The Road to the Industrial Revolution: The European Economy in Global Perspective, 1000-1800* (Brill, 2009) and (with Tine de Moor) "Girlpower. The European Marriage Pattern (EMP) and Labour Markets in the North Sea Region in the Late Medieval and Early Modern Period," *Economic History Review* (forthcoming).

Illustrations

Index

Name Index

Subject Index